This book presents a theoretical treatm
(i.e., uncompensated interdependencies)
club goods. Aimed at well-prepared undergraduate
graduate students making their first serious foray into this
branch of economics, this book should also be of interest to
professional economists wishing to survey the recent advances
in public economics. As such, *The theory of externalities, public
goods, and club goods* brings together the most recent contributions in public economics; no other single source for this
material is currently available. The topics covered include
Nash equilibria, Lindahl equilibria, club theory, preference-
revelation mechanisms, the commons, Coase theorem, and
game theory.

Richard Cornes is Senior Lecturer of economics at the
Australian National University. Todd Sandler is Professor of
economics at the University of South Carolina.

The theory of externalities, public goods, and club goods

The theory of externalities, public goods, and club goods

RICHARD CORNES
Australian National University

TODD SANDLER
University of South Carolina and University of Wyoming

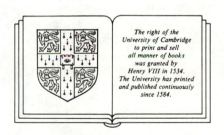

The right of the
University of Cambridge
to print and sell
all manner of books
was granted by
Henry VIII in 1534.
The University has printed
and published continuously
since 1584.

CAMBRIDGE UNIVERSITY PRESS

Cambridge
London   New York   New Rochelle
Melbourne   Sydney

Published by the Press Syndicate of the University of Cambridge
The Pitt Building, Trumpington Street, Cambridge CB2 1RP
32 East 57th Street, New York, NY 10022, USA
10 Stamford Road, Oakleigh, Melbourne 3166, Australia

First Published 1986

Printed in the United States of America

Library of Congress Cataloging-in-Publication Data

Cornes, Richard, 1946–
   The theory of externalities, public goods, and club
goods.
   Bibliography: p.
   Includes index.
   1. Externalities (Economics)   2. Public goods.
I. Sandler, Todd.   II. Title.
HB846.3.C67   1986   330′.01   85–19014

British Library Cataloguing in Publication Data

Cornes, Richard
   The theory of externalities, public goods and
   club goods.
   1. Externalities (Economics)
   I. Title   II. Sandler, Todd
   330   HB199
   ISBN 0 521 30184 X hard covers
   ISBN 0 521 31774 6 paperback

To
OUR PARENTS

Contents

vii

Contents

x   **Contents**

Preface

Concern with various potential sources of market failure, of which the topics treated in this book are important examples, has a long history, dating back at least to the writings of Adam Smith and David Hume in the eighteenth century. Recent years have witnessed a tremendous growth in this literature and, one hopes, a significant advance in our understanding of the principal issues. Much of this material is scattered throughout the economic journals, and some of it is technically demanding. At the same time, textbooks in micro-economics and public economics are able, by their very nature, to provide only a tantalizingly brief treatment of the nature and implications of externalities.

This book aims to provide a more extended discussion of the theory and policy implications of externalities, with particular emphasis on those special cases represented by public goods and club goods. We have attempted to discuss the main conceptual issues and have used mathematical techniques only as much as is necessary to pursue the economic argument. In particular, our exposition in Part III is, we believe, greatly clarified by the exploitation of a simple diagram capable of demonstrating many features of public goods that economists have found interesting.

The result, we hope, is a book that should be accessible to well-prepared undergraduates and should also be of interest both to graduate students making their first serious foray into this branch of economics and to professional economists wanting to find out what some of their colleagues in public economics have been up to in recent years.

We would like to thank a number of individuals for their help along the way. Parts of the initial draft were written by Cornes during a brief but productive stay at the Graduate Institute of International Studies in Geneva. He would like to thank Hans Genberg and Henryk Kierzkowski for providing this opportunity, and also Max Corden, who arranged a further short stay in the Research School of Pacific Studies at the Australian National University. Thanks, too, are owed to Ted Bergstrom for stimulating collaborative work on aspects of public goods theory, the influence of which is particularly evident in Chapter 6. We also thank John Tschirhart, whose joint work with Todd Sandler contributed significantly to the material in Chapters 10–14 on club goods. Finally, we acknowledge helpful comments provided by Fred Sterbenz and John McMillan.

We could not have wished for more cheerful, cooperative, and competent wordprocessing services than those supplied by Coralie Cullen and Gillian Scott in Canberra, and by Cindi Williams in Wyoming. We appreciate the excellent graphic arts, supplied by Allory Deiss at the University of Wyoming. To all these people we offer our gratitude. Finally, it is a pleasure to thank Colin Day of Cambridge University Press, whose enthusiastic encouragement, constructive advice, and, indeed, hospitality have been much appreciated during the writing of this book.

PART I

Introduction to the theory of externalities, public goods, and club goods

CHAPTER 1

Views on market intervention

Even Adam Smith, a champion of laissez-faire, *recognized* the need for government intervention and provision in a number of select areas, including the establishment of a justice system, the enactment and enforcement of laws, protection against invasion, and the provision of schools and other public goods. Thus, the interest in public goods, whose benefits simultaneously affect a group of individuals, can be traced back to classical economics. With the publication of Samuelson's (1954, 1955) seminal pieces, research interest in public goods and in their relationship with other types of goods grew rapidly among English-speaking economists. Samuelson's contributions gave a formal foundation to ideas mentioned earlier by European economists, such as Lindahl, Sax, and Wicksell (see Musgrave and Peacock 1958). At first, economists focused on the two poles of a spectrum of goods, the poles consisting of pure public goods and pure private goods. Private goods could be parceled out among individuals and efficiently allocated by markets, whereas public goods could not be divided among individuals owing to nonrivalry of benefits and nonexcludability problems. Collective provision was first thought essential for these public goods.

With the publication of Mancur Olson's (1965) *Logic of Collective Action* and James M. Buchanan's (1965) "An Economic Theory of Clubs," economists began rigorous explorations of the spectrum of goods to analyze what are called impure public goods, a catchall term for any good not purely public or private. Though its definition was later broadened (see Sandler and Tschirhart 1980), a club was viewed as a group sharing a particular type of impure public good, characterized by *excludable benefits*. Buchanan (1965) and others argued that goods whose benefits were simultaneously received by more than one individual (e.g., swimming pools, golf courses, highways) could be allocated privately by a sharing group (or club), provided that an exclusion mechanism could be installed at a reasonable cost. Costs of an exclusion mechanism are reasonable whenever the gains in allocative efficiency, achieved through the use of the mechanism, are greater than the associated costs. Exclusion costs include the value

3

of the resources expended to erect and to man barriers that force preference revelation. The exclusion mechanisms might consist of a toll booth, a guard, a fence, or a ticket office; only those individuals who pay a user fee or toll can pass through the exclusion device and use the good. Hence, the scope of government provision was duly reduced, since public goods admitting exclusion could be provided by firms or private collectives.

Once economists understood that few public goods at the local, state, national, or international level possess the nonexcludability and strict indivisibility of benefits properties required for pure publicness, the allocative principles of club theory as they applied to impure public goods took on added importance. Even defense, once thought to be the perfect example of a pure public good, was seen to permit excludability and partial divisibility, especially for tactical nuclear and conventional weapons, weapons that the North Atlantic Treaty Organization (NATO) and the Warsaw Pact have increased in importance since 1970 (see Olson and Zeckhauser 1966; Sandler 1977; Sandler and Forbes 1980; Murdoch and Sandler 1982, 1984, 1985). Gradually, the list of impure public goods expanded to include, among others, recreation areas, schools, highways, communication systems, information networks, national parks, waterways, and the electromagnetic spectrum. Thus, any theory that could analyze the allocative and distributive aspects of such a wide range of goods would indeed make an important contribution to the theory of public finance. Club theory was put forward for this purpose.

More than a century and a half after Smith's *Wealth of Nations*, Pigou (1946) introduced another rationale for government intervention into the marketplace that, at first, appeared not to involve public goods per se. The Pigouvian correction concerned externalities, in which the action of one economic agent influences the utility or production function of another and no mechanism for compensation exists. Governments were viewed as outside agents who, through the imposition of taxes (or subsidies), could induce the externality-generator to limit (or increase) his or her activity so as to achieve efficiency. In subsequent contributions, the notion of externality encompassed an ever-increasing variety of economic situations until it was equated by some with market failure (see, especially, Bator 1958). As such, externality included public goods as a special case. Thus, the list of market failures requiring government intervention was broadened way beyond those instances given by Adam Smith.

With the publication of Coase's (1960) "The Problem of Social Cost," economists realized that the mere existence of an externality was not a sufficient reason for government intervention. When, for example, few individuals were involved, participants could bargain with one another, thereby eliminating the potential inefficiency associated with the externality. Furthermore, Coase argued that any *liability assignment* for the uncompensated costs, whether imposed on the externality-generator or the recipient, would achieve efficiency. Hence, much as in the case of clubs, bargaining or liability assignments provided nongovernmental means for correcting externalities.

Since these early contributions, a vast literature has been written on externalities, public goods, and club goods. Many of these articles have examined the relationships among these three concepts, while others have investigated the best methods for correcting the associated inefficiencies. Corrective means include both governmental and nongovernmental (private) action. With the development of public choice, economists saw that governments, like markets, also could fail owing to incentive incompatibility, nonconvexities, (political) constraints, and imperfect information. Thus, nongovernmental corrections to market failures continued to grow in importance. The growth of public choice also renewed interest in governmental corrections that took account of potential pitfalls and that designed incentive schemes to elicit more efficient results. For example, more sophisticated preference-revelation mechanisms were proposed, including Clarke–Groves taxes, which provided individuals, in the absence of income effects, with the proper incentives to reveal honestly their preferences for pure public goods. In the instance of local public goods, the Tiebout Hypothesis suggested that the mix of public goods–tax packages offered by various local jurisdictions would induce an optimal partition of population through a process of voting-with-one's-feet. This process would lead to efficiency, provided that there were no impediments to mobility and that there were a sufficient number of jurisdictions to choose from.

Like the preceding studies mentioned above, this book concerns market failures and what can be done about them. Using modern tools of microeconomics, we reexamine the relationship between externalities, public goods, and club goods. Both allocative and distributive issues for these three types of market failures are discussed. The Tiebout Hypothesis, the Coase Theorem, preference-revelation mechanisms, Pigouvian corrections, the spectrum of public goods, institutional arrangements, and club theory are among the many topics examined. This volume provides both a survey of existing contributions and extensions to this body of knowledge. Many new principles of collective action are presented.

1.1   Some basic terms and definitions

Up to now, we have used such terms as indivisibility of benefits and nonexcludability rather loosely. Before proceeding, we should clearly define these and other terms. Throughout this book, the expressions *nonrivalry of consumption* and *indivisibility of benefits* are used interchangeably. A good is nonrival or indivisible when a *unit* of the good can be consumed by one individual without detracting, in the slightest, from the consumption opportunities still available to others from that *same* unit. Sunsets are nonrival or indivisible when views are unobstructed. Deterrence, as provided by a fleet of Trident submarines, does not diminish as more allies join an alliance and share in their threat-based protection; thus, strategic nuclear weapons yield nonrival benefits. Nonrivalry also characterizes benefits derived from pollution-control devices, weather-monitoring stations, disease-eradication programs, crisis-warning monitors, and information-dissemination networks.

If, however, an agent's consumption of a unit of a good fully eliminates any benefits that others can obtain from that unit, rivalry in consumption or perfect divisibility is present. Everyday goods such as food, clothing, and fuel are rival in their benefits; once a piece of pie is eaten, no further benefits remain whenever the consumer has been diligent in his or her consumption activity. Each unit of heat consumed from a fuel by one individual eliminates all others from using those same heat units; entropy sees to that.

Another distinguishing characteristic of goods is *excludability of benefits*. Goods whose benefits can be withheld costlessly by the owner or provider display excludable benefits. Benefits that are available to all once the good is provided are termed nonexcludable. Firework displays, strategic weapons, pollution-control devices, and street lighting yield nonexcludable benefits, since once provided it is difficult, if not impossible, to exclude individuals from their benefits. (In later chapters, we will argue that nonexcludability is the crucial factor in determining which goods must be publicly provided.) In contrast, homes, automobiles, and clothing yield excludable benefits whenever property rights are protected by law enforcement authorities or by private actions (e.g., locks, guard dogs). With these characteristics defined, the so-called spectrum of goods can now be distinguished. The benefits of private goods are fully rival and excludable, whereas the benefits of pure public goods are nonrival and nonexcludable. From the above examples, we see that food and fuel are private, whereas strategic weapons and pollution control are purely public goods.

In-between points along this spectrum refer to impure public goods whose benefits are partially rival *and/or* partially excludable. If, therefore, a good does not display both excludability (nonexcludability) and rivalry (nonrivalry) in their pure forms, the good is called impurely public. An important subclass of such goods are those whose benefits *are excludable* but partially nonrival; these goods are *club goods* and are analyzed extensively in Part IV. This spectrum is best viewed as a pedagogical device that provides a way of visualizing the diverse kinds of goods. Strictly speaking, however, there is no single spectrum or continuum, much as there is no single spectrum between perfect competition and monopoly, since impure public goods differ from one another along more than one dimension. Clearly, both nonrivalry and excludability properties can differ between classes of public goods. In some instances, an activity may give rise to multiple outputs, some of which are private, purely public, and impurely public. Such an activity yields *joint products*; these joint products are examined extensively in Part III and are shown to include the phenomenon of congestion, that is, the situation in which one individual's consumption reduces the quality of service available to others.

Other important definitions are gathered together in Chapter 2, where equilibrium concepts are presented. These concepts include Nash equilibrium, Lindahl equilibrium, and Pareto optimum.

1.2   Importance of externalities, public goods, and club goods

When one examines what governments do, a variety of activities appears at all fiscal levels. Governments allocate resources for those goods and services for which the private sector fails to assign sufficient resources. Defense, education, and highways were mentioned previously as examples. Governments also redistribute income for equity reasons; thus, progressive income taxation, social security, and socialized medicine are seen in many modern nations. Promotion of growth and stabilization of income and employment (i.e., fiscal policy) are other important governmental activities.

A study of externalities, public goods, and clubs, as attempted here, gives insight into the government's role in allocating resources. For instance, the theory can distinguish those cases in which government action is essential from those in which it is not. For the former cases, the theory of externalities, public goods, and club goods can help determine corrective taxes, provision levels, tolls or user fees, and financing decisions. This theory can also shed light on aspects of redistribution, especially when income distribution is itself viewed as a public good (see, e.g., Hochman and Rodgers 1969). The theory of public goods and clubs also applies to growth considerations to the extent that public investment, an important stimulant to growth, is analyzed; however, the theory has little to say about stabilization policy. The theory of this volume is important because it applies to many expenditure and revenue decisions required of governments.

The theory of clubs, in particular, provides the theoretical foundation for the study of allocative efficiency for an important class of impure public goods. Club theory can be used in determining the need for exclusionary zoning, the efficacy of busing, and the optimal sizes for alliances, communities, and cities. Even aspects of public utilities can be analyzed with club theory (Wiseman 1957). Since recreation areas, national parks, and wilderness areas are subject to crowding and depreciation owing to use and since both of these phenomena reflect partial divisibility of benefits, club theory can form the foundation for the management of these resources. In addition, an important linkage between welfare economics, public finance, and game theory is provided by club theory. Finally, aspects of two-part tariffs, peak-load pricing, and cost allocation problems can be better understood with club theory.

In the case of externalities, the underlying theory forms the foundation of environmental economics, in which economic activities are understood to produce environmental side-effects often ignored by the generator. Even some kinds of regulatory practices derive their justification from "curing" or internalizing externalities. Many tax issues are also founded on externality-related arguments. For example, tax exportation, as practiced by some western states in the United States, has been supported by the existence of externalities. Thus, Wyoming places a severance tax on minerals leaving its borders. Revenues collected are then used to rectify externalities associated with mineral extraction. That is, land is reclaimed following strip mining, and education is funded in impact areas. A careful analysis of externalities can therefore augment our understanding of regulation, environmental economics, and public finance.

1.3   Purposes of the book

The primary purposes of this book are (1) to evaluate critically the theoretical contributions of the literature on externalities and public goods, (2) to provide an analysis of the theory of clubs, (3) to break new ground with respect to this theory, (4) to provide a self-contained text on public expenditures analysis, (5) to indicate the far-ranging applications of the theory contained within, and (6) to apply modern tools of microeconomics to streamline the presentation. In pursuing these goals, we survey major contributions while emphasizing, extending, and illuminating their contents.

In particular, we hope to present a clearer analysis of externalities and their relationships to public goods and other forms of market failures. The overall goal of our investigation of public goods is to refine the theory of collective action by examining the influence of group size on suboptimality; the impact of income and substitution effects on equilibrium stability; the effect of Nash behavior on allocative efficiency; and the importance of group homogeneity on the equilibrium outcome. Furthermore, by including expectations in the study of public goods and externalities, we are able to extend the theory beyond the traditional Nash formulation, which assumes that individuals react passively to the optimizing actions of others. Pigouvian-type corrections for externalities are also studied for the case of nonzero conjectures.

Much of our analysis of public goods is illustrated with a graphic device capable of depicting both allocative and distributive considerations. This device makes the analysis of public goods, the commons, and joint products much simpler, while giving new insight. Because the graph allows us to compare Nash, Lindahl, and Pareto equilibria on the same diagram, it enables us to derive a measure of easy or free riding displaying suboptimality in terms of provision levels. The graph is sufficiently flexible to handle two-person asymmetric and n-person symmetric models.

For the theory of clubs, the analysis is extended to the effects of uncertainties on the membership, provision, financing, and toll decisions. Both demand-side and supply-side uncertainties are studied. In addition, intertemporal aspects of club decisions are examined for clubs having multiple generations of overlapping members. An expanded analysis of institutional considerations for clubs is also presented. A final extension includes an enlarged analysis of mixed clubs containing members whose tastes or resource endowments differ.

1.4   Plan of the book

The book is divided into five parts. Part I is concerned with definitions and preliminaries. Part II deals with externalities, beginning in Chapter 3 with alternative definitions and the underlying characteristics of externalities. Policy responses to externalities are discussed in Chapter 4, which looks at Pigouvian taxes and subsidies along with Coasian bargaining. Chapter 4 is primarily about tinkering with the competitive market allocation process to correct for noncompensated interactions.

Part III is devoted to the study of public goods. It opens in Chapter 5 with a discussion of pure public goods and an in-depth examination of Nash and Pareto equilibria. The issues discussed include suboptimality, stability of equilibrium, the influence of group size, immiserizing growth, and the effects of lump-sum redistribution. Chapter 5 also introduces our graphic device. Chapter 6, which presents alternative mechanisms for public good provision, compares Lindahl and Pareto equilibria, and demonstrates how the Lindahl thought experiment solves the problem of inefficiency for public goods. A careful analysis of preference-revelation mechanisms completes the chapter. Chapter 7 deals with public goods in general. It is here that impure public goods and joint products are examined. These concepts are then associated with the notion of congestion. The chapter concludes with a discussion of the commons. Game theory and public goods are taken up in Chapter 8, which looks at the Prisoner's Dilemma and the game of chicken in relation to the voluntary provision of public goods. Unlike club goods, noncooperative games are shown to be most appropriate for modeling public good problems. Chapter 9 concludes Part III with a discussion of non-Nash behavior, in which the effects of nonzero conjectures are related to externalities, public goods, and the commons.

Part IV takes up the theory of clubs. Chapter 10 contains a taxonomy for clubs based on the composition of membership (i.e., homogeneous or mixed), the type of utilization allowed (i.e., fixed or variable), and the division of the population among the set of clubs. Much of the chapter is concerned with clubs with homogeneous memberships in which utilization rates are fixed. In addition, the optimal number of clubs is analyzed and related to issues involving jurisdictional size and local public goods. A more general treatment of clubs and club goods follows in Chapter 11, which compares fixed and variable utilization rates. This chapter also distinguishes between homogeneous and heterogeneous clubs, and notes the required differences in their provision levels, memberships, financing, and tolls. Club discrimination, exclusion costs, two-part tariffs, and other issues are also taken up in Chapter 11. The institutional forms of clubs and their effect on optimality are investigated in Chapter 12. The inclusion of institutional considerations highlights the importance of transaction costs, which are expenditures associated with a mode of allocation. In certain well-defined situations, clubs can be operated by either the members or a firm without allocative implications. Cooperative game theory is applied to the analysis of clubs in Chapter 13. Issues having to do with the optimal number of clubs and their stability are included here.

Uncertainty is introduced into club theory in Chapter 14. For example, members may be uncertain as to whether they will be admitted on those occasions when they attempt to use the club; thus, a capacity constraint limits entry and makes admittance uncertain. The effects of members' attitudes toward risk are then related to the club's choice of provision and capacity. Furthermore, the uncertainty model is compared with standard certainty models. The final chapter of Part IV extends the analysis of clubs to intergenerational clubs. After deriving optimal membership size, membership span (i.e., a member's duration in the club), provision, tolls, and financing conditions, Chapter 15 examines the effects of institutional form in achieving these farsighted conditions. The analysis focuses on the issue of myopia and the presence of nonmyopic incentives.

In Part V, applications are presented for externalities, public goods, and club goods. Chapter 16 examines empirical procedures for estimating the demand for public goods and myriad applications drawn from club and public good theory. Chapter 17 looks at future directions and closes the discussion with some general conclusions.

CHAPTER 2

Equilibrium concepts in public finance

This chapter presents further preliminaries including methodological considerations, normative underpinning, equilibrium concepts, and important definitions. Since many of these concepts and definitions are dealt with extensively elsewhere in the book, the analysis here is brief. A much-used graphic device for depicting Nash–Cournot equilibrium is presented so that the reader will be able to better appreciate the diagrammatic device introduced in Chapter 5 and used throughout much of Part III.

This chapter is divided into five main sections. Methodological considerations are presented in Section 2.1. The normative under-pinnings of this study follow in Section 2.2, where Pareto optimality and related concepts are defined. Section 2.3 contains an analysis of equilibrium concepts such as Nash–Cournot and Lindahl equilibria. Fiscal equivalence, spillovers, and local public goods are defined in Section 2.4. The final section concerns clubs and club goods.

2.1   Methodological considerations

This book is designed to serve the needs of both students and researchers with an interest in a modern treatment of market failures. The discussion is aimed at advanced undergraduates and graduate students who are familiar with both microeconomic theory and the standard techniques of optimization.[1] Whenever possible, theoretical concepts are illustrated diagrammatically in the belief that geometric representations facilitate learning by providing intuition. Although other sources have examined aspects of the topics analyzed here, no systematic, current, and widely accessible study of this subject exists. This book is meant to fill this void.

Much of the volume's analysis is theoretical. In particular, resource allocative efficiency requirements are presented for externalities, public goods, and club goods. In examining these requirements, we take into account both first-order necessary and second-order conditions. Essentially, the second-order conditions include information on the shape or convexity of the objective function and the constraints so as to ascertain whether a peak or a trough or neither characterizes the point(s) satisfying the first-order conditions.

A second mathematical tool used throughout is the theory of games, whereby agents choose strategies to maximize payoffs while accounting for the expected strategies of their opponents.[2] Games may be cooperative or noncooperative. The former refers to the formation of coalitions in which participants must work together to maximize a payoff, which is later divided among members. Coalition participants who can gain more by defecting will leave and will either go it alone or form a new coalition. Cooperative game theory is especially germane to clubs that represent voluntarily formed coalitions, since members always have the option to leave the club.

Noncooperative game theory is more relevant to externalities and public goods in which individuals seeking to maximize their own utility often ignore both beneficial and detrimental side-effects that their optimizing behavior has upon others. A classic case is the so-called Prisoner's Dilemma, in which two (or more) prisoners are made to turn state's evidence by confessing to a crime that they did not commit. To elicit this noncooperative response from the prisoners, the district attorney promises each of them less than the maximum sentence if they both confess. If, however, only one confesses, then the confessor receives a light sentence and the nonconfessor gets the maximum penalty. When neither confesses, they both receive a moderate penalty, greater than the light sentence offered to a lone confessor. Each of the prisoners is interrogated separately, and is thus denied the opportunity to communicate or to cooperate with the other. This same pattern of payoffs often characterizes the game matrix associated with the private provision of public goods. In this case, defecting means either not contributing or undercontributing to the provision of a public good, and the cooperative strategy means contributing honestly toward the provision of a public good. As in the case of the prisoners, the dominant strategy has the individuals defecting and thus implies no provision or a suboptimal provision. Nonexcludability is responsible for making defection the best strategy. This dominant noncooperative strategy becomes more prevalent when group size increases. Repeated plays of the game might, however, elicit the cooperative strategy as players see that cooperation augments everyone's payoffs when compared with noncooperation. (A more complete analysis of the Prisoner's Dilemma is presented in Chapter 8.)

The theory of uncertainty is also used in select places in this volume. For example, this theory forms the basis for examining resource allocation in clubs in which some potential users might have to be turned away owing to capacity limits or breakdowns in the club good. When optimizing in the face of uncertainty, the *expected utility* is maximized subject to the relevant set of resource constraints. When uncertainty characterizes a decision, risk attitudes of the agents are usually crucial in determining the nature of the final equilibrium. Risk-averse agents are those who would turn down an actuarially fair bet. That is, a risk-averse agent would not pay 50 cents for the chance to win a dollar by correctly calling the toss of an unbiased coin.[3] To accept an actuarially fair bet, a risk-averse agent must be paid a premium or a side payment. Hence, in the coin toss problem, the risk-averse individual might accept the bet if he or she has to wager only 40 cents—here, the effective side payment is 10 cents. The greater the required side payment, the more risk-averse the individual. A risk-neutral individual might gamble on a "fair prospect," that is, one in which the expected value of the bet equals the cost of the bet. In contrast, a risk lover would gamble on lotteries that are not actuarially fair. In terms of insurance, a risk-averse agent is apt to insure against losses due to fire, theft, or accident. Such individuals prefer the certain loss associated with the insurance policy to the risky, greater loss involved with the contingency that they have insured against.

Although the emphasis is on theory throughout most of the book, some empirical illustrations are indicated in Chapter 16, where applications are presented. A rudimentary knowledge of the basic linear regression model is all that is needed as a prerequisite.

2.2   Normative aspects

An analysis is *normative* when it is based on value judgments involving a preestablished criterion. Statements about "what ought to be done" are normative. In contrast, a *positive* analysis presents facts about "what will happen" or "what has happened." When, for example, the behavior of policymakers is studied to determine how they are expected to act in response to resource and institutional constraints, a positive analysis is being undertaken. If, however, the researcher is more interested in establishing how the policymaker should behave, then a normative analysis is being conducted. When words such as *optimal* and *suboptimal* are employed, as they are throughout public finance and much of economics, an ethical or normative criterion is typically implied. This is especially germane to questions about resource allocative efficiency. When the underlying ethical criterion is fully satisfied, the resulting allocation is said to be optimal; when it is not fulfilled, the allocation is said to be suboptimal, and corrective measures such as subsidies or taxes are proposed.

The most-used normative criterion of modern economics is that of *Pareto optimality*. A position is said to be a Pareto optimum if it is impossible to improve the well-being of one individual without harming at least one other individual. To derive a Pareto-optimum position, one individual's utility is maximized, subject to the constancy of the utility levels of the other individuals and subject to the relevant resource constraints. A Pareto optimum is not necessarily unique, since changing the fixed utility levels for the rest of the community typically implies a different Pareto optimum. Deciding which of these Pareto optima is "best," when more than one exist, requires a *social welfare function* that weights the utility levels of individuals according to some normative rule.

The criterion of Pareto optimality is applied to the determination of exchange efficiency, production efficiency, and the welfare optimum. For private goods, exchange efficiency is achieved when the marginal rate of substitution (*MRS*) between each pair of goods is equal for all consumers who consume both goods. Hence, for goods x and y, we have

$$MRS_{xy}^i = MRS_{xy}^j \text{ for all } i \text{ and } j,$$

(EXCHANGE EFFICIENCY)

where the superscripts refer to the individuals and the subscripts indicate the two goods being exchanged. Production efficiency is achieved for any type of good where the marginal rate of technical substitution (*MRTS*) between each pair of inputs is equated across all industries using these inputs. That is,

$$MRTS_{KL}^p = MRTS_{KL}^q \text{ for all } p \text{ and } q,$$

(PRODUCTION EFFICIENCY)

where the superscripts now refer to the industry, and the subscripts K and L denote capital and labor. When production efficiency is reached, it is not possible to trade inputs among producers and still increase one producer's output while leaving the outputs of the other producers unchanged. For a two-industry, two-factor economy, Bator (1957) has shown that production efficiency is satisfied on the contract curve connecting the tangencies of the isoquants in an Edgeworth-Bowley production box. Points on this contract curve can be mapped in a one-to-one fashion into the production possibility frontier. For a two-person economy, exchange efficiency is satisfied on the contract curve joining the tangencies of the indifference curves in an Edgeworth-Bowley exchange box. This contract curve can be mapped into a utility possibility frontier.

In the case of private goods, a Pareto optimum is achieved when exchange efficiency, production efficiency, and a top-level condition are all satisfied. This top-level condition ties together the exchange and production sides and requires

$$MRS_{xy} = MRT_{xy}, \qquad \text{(TOP-LEVEL CONDITION)}$$

where the MRT_{xy} is the marginal rate of transformation between goods x and y and corresponds to the slope of the production possibility frontier. As such, the MRT_{xy} indicates how society can trade off the two goods in production, given inelastically supplied factors and production efficiency. The MRS_{xy} in the top-level condition is equal to each individual's common MRS and depicts how society desires to trade off the two goods.

For pure public goods, a different top-level condition must be satisfied. Since the pure public good simultaneously benefits all community members, each of these individual's marginal valuation must be accounted for when resource allocation is being decided. Samuelson (1954, 1955) has shown that Pareto optimality for a pure public good requires that the following first-order condition be satisfied:

$$\sum_{i=1}^{n} MRS_{zy}^{i} = MRT_{zy}, \qquad (1)$$

where n is the number of community members and z is the pure public good. This condition is derived by maximizing the utility of any individual, subject to the constancy of the utility levels of the rest of the community, the economy's transformation function, and the private good's production-distribution constraint. Equation (1) will be referred to as the *Samuelsonian condition* throughout this book. Pure public goods must always satisfy production efficiency if Pareto optimality is to be achieved; however, these goods do not have an exchange efficiency requirement, because nonexcludability precludes exchange.

To understand why Pareto optimality is the preferred normative criterion in economics, we must examine a perfectly competitive private goods economy. Under ideal conditions, such market econ-omies automatically end in a position of Pareto optimality, provided that individuals maximize their utility and firms maximize their profits. This result is one of the two fundamental theorems of welfare economics. These ideal conditions rule out the existence of externalities, public goods, wrongly shaped utility and production functions, and information failures (see Bator 1957; Arrow 1970). With perfect competition, consumers face the same prices; thus, equating their *MRS*s with the relevant price ratios must imply exchange efficiency, since price ratios are the same for everyone. To maximize profits, firms employ inputs so as to equate their *MRTS*s with the relevant input price ratios. Production efficiency is therefore achieved because everyone faces the same input price ratios. By a similar argument, top-level efficiency is also implied by individuals' pursuit of self-interest in a perfectly competitive market economy (Bator 1957).

The second fundamental theorem of welfare economics indicates that *any* Pareto optimum may be sustained by a perfectly competitive economy through a suitable lump-sum transfer of resources. Pareto optimality is the preferred normative criterion owing to its close relationship to results obtained by ideal market economies. If some other result, such as maximizing the least well-off individual's utility, had been implied by market economies, then this criterion would surely have been the normative standard for economics.

With Pareto optimality as our standard, economies that do not achieve Pareto optimality are said to result in *market failure;* a substantial portion of welfare economics and public finance is concerned with these market failures and what, if anything, can be done about them. Recent studies have shown that the cost of correction may on occasion outweigh the benefits associated with correction (i.e., the gains in efficiency derived from the correction). In such cases, the market failure should be maintained; otherwise it should be corrected.

In the case of pure public goods, the Pareto criterion requiring $\sum MRS = MRT$ will not necessarily be satisfied when individuals pursue utility maximization. The nonexcludability property of pure public goods induces individuals to undercontribute to provision in the belief that they can rely on the contributions of others. That is, individuals have no incentive to include the marginal valuation of the rest of the community (i.e., $\sum_{j \neq i} MRS^j$ for individual i) when deciding their own public good contribution. This reliance on others is known as free-riding behavior and is discussed in greater detail in the next section.

A term related to Pareto optimality is that of *Pareto improvement*. A resource reallocation results in a Pareto improvement if at least one individual achieves an improvement in well-being and no one else is harmed. Similarly, a position is said to Pareto-dominate another when the utility of at least one individual improves without a deterioration in the utility levels of anyone else.

Pareto optimality and its associated concepts gained popularity with the new welfare economics primarily because Pareto optimality eliminated the need to make interpersonal comparisons of utility. An older welfare criterion still in use today requires society's welfare to be measured as the weighted sum of the utilities of the community members. Such a welfare concept requires interpersonal comparisons. Making these interpersonal comparisons is a strong assumption that requires a cardinal welfare index in which each individual's utility can be calculated and added to those of others to derive a social welfare measure. Currently, economists employ this welfare sum concept, called a *Benthamite social welfare function*, when mathematical tractability necessitates a simple objective function for representing society's well-being. A Benthamite social welfare function may include equal or unequal weights, depending on how the individuals are viewed by the ethical observer in charge of aggregation. Such a social welfare function has the following form:

$$W = \sum_{i=1}^{n} w^i U^i(\cdot), \tag{2}$$

where W is social welfare, w^i are the welfare weights, and $U^i(\cdot)$ is the ith individual's utility function. A second social welfare function is the *Samuelson-Bergson* social welfare function:

$$W = W[U^1(\cdot), \ldots, U^n(\cdot)]. \tag{3}$$

Strictly speaking, this function is also based on cardinal interpersonal welfare comparisons (Mueller 1979, p. 181). When $\partial W/\partial U^i > 0$ for all i, then the social welfare function satisfies the Pareto criterion, since improving any individual's utility augments society's welfare. In order to choose among the many Pareto optima, some social welfare function is needed. This function introduces distributive considerations into allocative decisions.

2.3   Equilibrium concepts

Nash–Cournot or Nash equilibrium

The notion of Nash–Cournot or Nash equilibrium is crucial for an understanding of market failures. Consider an economy consisting of two persons, each of whom purchases a private and a pure public

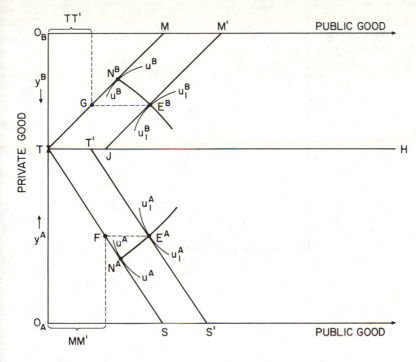

Figure 2.1

good. If the two individuals adjust their public good contributions independently, each holding zero conjectures about the effects of his optimizing choice on the choice of the other, the resulting solution, at which each is maximizing utility given the current level of the other's contribution, is the Nash–Cournot or *independent adjustment equilibrium*. A zero conjecture implies that one agent believes that his optimizing choice will not influence the choice of the other agent. Nash–Cournot equilibria are typically not Pareto optimal, since neither individual accounts for the well-being of the other (see Chapter 5); thus, each agent attempts to gain at the other's expense as in the Prisoner's Dilemma. In other words, a Nash–Cournot equilibrium is based on purely self-interested maximizing behavior subject to a quantity constraint reflecting the other agent's previous public good contribution. For more than two individuals, each person treats the total contributions to the public good of all others as constant when maximizing their utility in a Nash–Cournot manner.

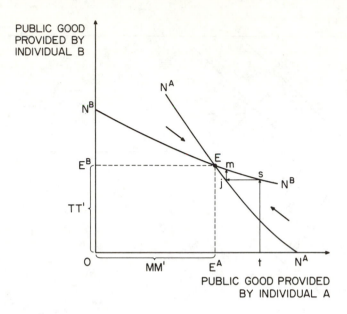

Figure 2.2

Nash–Cournot behavior often characterizes pure public goods and externalities and is an important factor in causing a market failure.

Figures 2.1 and 2.2 illustrate the Nash–Cournot equilibrium for a two-person economy. A modified Edgeworth-Bowley box is displayed in Figure 2.1, where the amounts of the public good are measured on the two horizontal axes. For individual A, consumption of the private good, y^A, is measured upward along the vertical axis; for individual B, consumption of the private good, y^B, is measured downward along the vertical axis. Distance $O_A O_B$ on the vertical axis denotes the entire quantity of the private good that can be purchased (produced) in this two-person economy; hence, line TH can be slid up and down to show resource redistribution. In the absence of any public good provision by the other individual, each agent chooses his or her own public good provision to maximize utility subject to a linear budget constraint—TS for individual A and TM for individual B. These "isolation" equilibria correspond to N^A and N^B for agents A and B, respectively. At these equilibria, an individual's indifference curve ($u^A u^A$ and $u^B u^B$) is tangent to the budget constraint. These tangencies indicate that a person's MRS is equated to the price ratio.

Pareto optimality, however, requires the *sum* of MRSs to equal this price ratio.

The agent's optimizing adjustments to nonzero levels of public good provision by others is easily shown in Figure 2.1. If, say, individual B provides TT' units of a public good, then these units are automatically received by individual A owing to nonexcludability. To find the new Nash solution for A, simply displace A's budget constraint TS everywhere by the horizontal distance TT' ($=SS'$), corresponding to agent B's provision. TT' is known as a *spillover*, since one person's provision amount spills over to another. The new solution for person A, associated with TT' spillovers, is E^A where $u_1^A u_1^A$ is tangent to the displaced budget constraint, $T'S'$. Analogously, E^B is the Nash solution for B when spillovers of TJ ($=MM'$) are generated by A. Each level of spillovers implies both a displaced budget constraint and a new point of tangency. The line connecting these tangencies is a "spillover expansion path," which indicates the Nash solutions for each individual as spillovers vary parametrically. Segments of these paths are labeled $N^A E^A$ and $N^B E^B$ in Figure 2.1.

The expansion paths in Figure 2.1 are used to derive the Nash reaction paths showing an agent's own public good provision levels in response to those of the other agent. To find a person's public good provision for each level of spillovers, one must relate an equilibrium such as E^A in Figure 2.1 back to the original budget constraint TS. In particular, the amount of spillovers must be deducted from consumption point E^A to determine the actual amount of the public good provided by agent A at point E^A. In Figure 2.1, this amount is MM'. By a similar exercise, point E^B implies that agent B gives TT' when A provides MM'. The figure is drawn so that E^A and E^B denote the final Nash equilibrium, in which no further adjustments to spillovers are needed.

This provision information is now translated over to Figure 2.2 to derive the two Nash reaction paths—$N^A N^A$ for agent A and $N^B N^B$ for agent B. Public good provision amounts are those associated with the nonshifted budget constraints—e.g., MM' for point E^A. In Figure 2.2, point E refers to E^A and E^B from the previous figure, and points N^A and N^B on the axes denote the isolation solutions. Adjustment path $tsjm$ . . . indicates that the Nash equilibrium is stable.

This exercise serves two purposes: (1) it illustrates Nash solutions and equilibrium, and (2) it demonstrates the cumbersomeness of traditional graphing procedures.[4] In this standard approach, everything is graphed in private good–public good space and is then translated to public good space. Not only is this two-step procedure cumbersome, but it also limits what can be shown. For example, nowhere in either figure can we locate the Pareto-optimal points for comparison purposes. Furthermore, a change in income requires us to shift *TH* and then redraw all of the budget constraints (see McGuire and Aaron 1969). What is needed is a one-step procedure that starts and finishes in public good space. Such a procedure is presented in Part III and is applied to public goods, the commons, and externalities.

The Nash equilibrium *E* in Figure 2.2 leads to the so-called *free-rider* problem, in which one individual relies on the public good supplied by another. The term *free rider*, which is used rather loosely in the literature, applies to at least three distinct phenomena (see, e.g., McMillan 1979, pp. 96–7). First, it refers to the suboptimality that typically characterizes Nash–Cournot behavior. In this case, free riding relates to the negative slope of the Nash reaction path and indicates one agent's reliance on the public good provision of another (Murdoch and Sandler 1984). Second, free riding relates to the failure of individuals to reveal their true preferences for the public good through their contributions. Third, it denotes the tendency for public contributions to decline as group size increases (Olson 1965).

We saw in Figure 2.2 that the Nash equilibrium implied positive provision levels for each agent—that is, OE^A for agent *A* and OE^B for agent *B*. Strictly speaking, free rider is a misleading term since agents seldom ride completely free. Returning to Figure 2.1, we find that agent *A* (or *B*) rides free at the point where his extended spillover expansion path intersects *TH*. Although this corner solution is theoretically feasible, it is unlikely unless the two agents' endowments differ significantly. The term *easy riding* is more appropriate for the suboptimality associated with pure public good provision since it does not imply zero provision (see Cornes and Sandler 1984a). Throughout this volume, easy riding will be used to denote the suboptimality of independent adjustment.

Lindahl equilibrium

A concept of considerable importance for public goods is the *Lindahl equilibrium* (Johansen 1963). Consider a two-person economy with a private good and a pure public good, each with exogenously given prices. To find a Lindahl equilibrium, an auctioneer calls out tax shares for the public good and the two individuals respond with their utility-maximizing public good quantities. That is, each maximizes utility taking his or her tax share for the public good as given. Unless both individuals call out the same public good quantity, the auctioneer proposes a new tax-share arrangement. This procedure continues until both agents' utility-maximizing response for the public good agrees. When both opt for the same public good provision level based on a set of tax shares, a Lindahl equilibrium has been reached. In essence, the Lindahl thought experiment mimics the tatonnement process for finding a general-equilibrium price vector capable of clearing private markets. Unlike the tatonnement process, the Lindahl experiment is subject to strategic misrepresentation of preferences as one agent tries to induce another to agree to larger tax shares.

When the process succeeds, the Lindahl equilibrium is a Pareto optimum. However, not all Pareto optima are Lindahl equilibria (as will be shown in Chapter 6).[5] A Lindahl equilibrium is a curious phenomenon representing a pseudo–market equilibrium for the pure public problem, in which a small number of individuals can through bargaining or arbitration on tax shares arrive at a Pareto-optimal position.

Non-Nash equilibria

When interactions are sporadic or take place among a large number of heterogeneous individuals, the Nash–Cournot zero conjectural variation is reasonable; however, another conjectural variation might be appropriate if the agents interact repeatedly, since anticipated responses of others to one's own actions may then be learned. In this latter case, an individual would presumably take these anticipations into account when choosing his or her own public good provision level. We term such behavior *non-Nash* (for a detailed analysis of this behavior, see Chapter 9). Quite simply, non-Nash behavior assumes that each agent anticipates that his or her own optimizing choice influences the decisions of the rest of the community; hence, the agent no longer treats the actions of the rest of the community as given. In the case of public goods, the relevant non-Nash conjecture is negative, implying that an agent expects increases in his or her provision to influence negatively the other agents' provision levels. In particular, non-Nash behavior may worsen or reduce easy riding, depending upon the nature of the conjecture formed. If the proper conjecture (i.e., one that reduces easy riding) can be induced, the need for corrective action may be fully or partly eliminated.

A non-Nash reaction path can be formed for each agent. This path accounts for tastes, constraints, and conjectures. In the two-agent case, the intersection of these non-Nash reaction paths denotes the non-Nash equilibrium. The shapes of these reaction paths determine both the stability of equilibrium and the number of equilibria.

2.4   Local public goods, spillovers, and fiscal equivalence

Chapter 1 defined two important characteristics of pure public goods: nonexcludability and nonrivalry of benefits. A third characteristic is the size of the group affected by the good's benefits. Public goods whose benefits involve only a small jurisdiction such as a municipality or town are called *local public goods* and are analyzed at various places in the book. Local public goods may be pure or impure and include, among others, city parks, roadways, museums, and tennis courts. State public goods, national public goods, and transnational public goods provide benefits to a state, a nation, and a multinational region, respectively. When a public good confers benefits outside the political jurisdiction that provides it and no compensation is paid by these outside recipients, spillovers of benefits exist. The concept of spillovers was previously illustrated for two individuals, but it applies to any type of agent, including counties or nations. If, for example, two countries border a polluted lake and only one expends resources to clean the lake, then the nonpaying country receives a benefit spillover from the other nation's action.

Once spillovers are introduced, political and economic jurisdictions can be distinguished. The former refers to the government deciding an action, and the latter denotes the region benefiting from the action. For public goods, the action consists of the provision of the good, and the economic jurisdiction includes all individuals receiving the good's benefits. When these jurisdictions exactly coincide, fiscal equivalence results (Olson 1969). Nonequivalence exists whenever the two jurisdictions do not match. If, for example, the political jurisdiction is smaller than the economic jurisdiction, as in the case of the polluted lake, then suboptimal provision is predicted since those who benefit from and those who decide provision differ. Suboptimality also results when the political jurisdiction exceeds the economic jurisdiction owing to tax spillovers as nonrecipients are taxed.

2.5   Clubs and club goods

A club is a voluntary group deriving mutual benefit from sharing one or more of the following: production costs, the members' characteristics (e.g., members' scholarly activities in learned societies), or a good characterized by excludable benefits. Much of Part IV deals with clubs that share a good characterized by excludable benefits. Such goods were previously called club goods. Our analysis of clubs allows us to examine a most important subclass of public goods—a subclass whose allocation can be achieved through private collectives. These collectives are able to set tolls or user fees so as to force honest preference revelation and thus escape the easy-riding problem. The essential difference between club goods and pure public goods depends on the existence of an exclusion mechanism, which establishes a pseudo–marketing device to overcome prefer-ence-revelation problems. With technological advances, exclusion may be invented for some pure public goods, thus transforming them into club goods. For example, scrambling devices for television transmissions by satellites represent technological advances, meant to exclude nonpayers.[6] New laser-coded access cards also represent a technologically sophisticated exclusion device.

Our definition broadens clubs to include more than collectives sharing excludable public goods. By this definition, a public utility that sells a private good is a club because production costs are shared. Since average costs of many public utilities decline owing to economies of scale as more consumers are served, a strong rationale for group provision exists.

We return to an analysis of clubs in Part IV. First, however, we examine externalities and public goods.

Externalities

Theory of externalities

There is a strong temptation to avoid an explicit definition of an externality, since even this first step has been a fertile source of controversy, and instead to approach the matter obliquely by putting to work various models in which an externality is evidently present. Whatever problems it raises, a brief definition provides a useful focus for further clarification of our ideas, and we begin by considering the following definition proposed by Meade (1973): "An external economy (diseconomy) is an event which confers an appreciable benefit (inflicts an appreciable damage) on some person or persons who were not fully consenting parties in reaching the decision or decisions which led directly or indirectly to the event in question."

Meade's definition has at least two notable features. First, it is not at all specific about the institutional framework within which social interactions take place. It simply suggests that, whatever that framework is, it places constraints on the ability of individuals to take steps to encourage (discourage) actions of others that confer benefits (costs) on them. It is very much a policy-oriented definition, leading one naturally to consider alternative means of providing such encouragement or discouragement. Pigou's suggested remedy of using taxes and subsidies, which we explore in Chapter 4, is one such alternative.

Second, Meade's definition casts the net extremely widely, labeling as externalities situations that other writers prefer to call by some other name. It includes, for example, what Meade calls a "distributional externality," produced when the action of a group of agents changes the prices at which others trade, thereby engineering a redistribution of income. There is no implication of inefficiency or market failure here, just a reflection of the fact that, even in the simplest competitive equilibrium system, prices are endogenously determined and will therefore generally respond to exogenous shocks. Meade's other category, which he calls a "real-income externality," involves a discrepancy between different agents' marginal valuations of commodities and implies that changes in outputs cause changes in total real income of the recipient. Meade himself provides a thoughtful discussion of cases that may be regarded as debatable.

For example, such matters as the employer's exercise of authority in firing an employee, Shakespeare's image of the child creeping like a snail unwillingly to school, and the determination of tax rates all raise questions about the degree of consent on the part of the affected agent, as do situations involving monopolistic markets and quantity rationing in the face of price rigidities.

In addition to Meade's treatment, further discussions of definitional issues may be found in Baumol and Oates (1975), Buchanan and Stubblebine (1962), and Heller and Starrett (1976). Rather than pursue these debates further, we now turn to an alternative formulation of the notion of an externality presented by Arrow (1970). Unlike Meade, Arrow places the definition of an externality within a very specific institutional framework—namely, that of competitive markets. In addition, although ultimately motivated by the research for optimal—or at least more efficient—allocations, Arrow relies on a definition that is in the first place more analytical, inviting one to consider why it is that externality recipients may be unable to consent fully to actions that affect them.

3.1   Externalities as absence of markets

Consider a two-person two-commodity exchange economy of the type commonly presented with the aid of the Edgeworth-Bowley box diagram. Assume that each individual is initially endowed with given quantities of the two commodities. One may imagine a model in which individuals A and B have preferences over both their own bundle and also that of their neighbor. Thus, in general, the utility functions may be written as

$$U^i(\cdot) = U^i(y_{i1}, y_{i2}, y_{j1}, y_{j2}) \qquad i, j = A, B; \; i \neq j, \tag{1}$$

where y_{ik} is individual i's consumption of commodity k. Arrow (1970) suggests that the quantity of a given commodity consumed by a given individual may be further distinguished according to whose utility function it appears in. Hence i's utility function may be written as

$$U^i(\cdot) = U^i(y_{i1}^i, y_{i2}^i, y_{j1}^i, y_{j2}^i) \qquad i, j = A, B; \; i \neq j. \tag{2}$$

Consumer A, for example, may be thought of as a producer with two production processes. One uses commodity 1 as an input and produces, as joint outputs, y_{A1}^A and y_{A1}^B. Similarly, the other converts commodity 2 into y_{A2}^A and y_{A2}^B. B's consumption activities may be viewed in the same way. The reason for such extreme disaggregation is that, as Arrow points out, any Pareto-optimal allocation may be sustained as a competitive equilibrium with an appropriate price, p^i_{jk}, associated with each and every commodity defined in the utility functions appearing in (2). If we interpret externalities as additional commodities in this way, the model may be accommodated within the framework of competitive equilibrium theory and we can appeal to such theorems as the first fundamental theorem of welfare economics, which states that if every commodity can be exchanged in a market, a competitive equilibrium is Pareto optimal. This is so even though the consumption of one enters the utility function of the other. The failure of equilibrium to result in Pareto optimality depends not only on such interdependence, but also on the absence of a sufficiently rich set of markets.

Arrow's formulation of externalities may be characterized as follows. Consider first a competitive equilibrium with a full set of markets. Every quantity that any individual cares about and that is determined by the actions of agents has a competitive price attached. The vector of all such prices is **P**. Then in equilibrium each consumer's utility may be described by his or her indirect utility function:

$$V^i = V^i(\mathbf{P}, \Omega^i), \tag{3}$$

where Ω^i is his exogenous endowment of commodities. Similarly, each firm's profit is described by the profit function:

$$\Pi^j = \Pi^j(\mathbf{P}, T^j), \tag{4}$$

where T^j summarizes the exogenous technology available. If, however, the set of markets is not complete, then the utility and profit functions cannot be reduced to this form, and instead will take the form

$$V^i = V^i(\mathbf{P}, \Omega^i, \mathbf{A}^i) \tag{5}$$

$$\Pi^j = \Pi^j(\mathbf{P}, T^j, \mathbf{A}^j) \tag{6}$$

where $\mathbf{A}^i$ and $\mathbf{A}^j$ are vectors of actions by others, for example the consumption behavior of other consumers, or production choices of other firms. Such actions are endogenous to the economic system, but are not controlled by the recipient in whose objective function they appear. Thus the natural next step is to ask why such markets may fail to exist. Three observations spring to mind. First, before trade in a commodity can be voluntary, it must be possible, and not too costly, to define and to enforce property rights over that commodity. Second, the costs of operating the market should not be too high. If the cost per unit transacted exceeds the difference between supply and demand price, voluntary transaction will not take place. A particular concern is often voiced about high setup costs associated with certain markets, since these violate the convexity requirement that plays an important role in establishing existence of equilibrium and the sustainability of a Pareto optimum by a decentralized competitive mechanism. Third, although the economist may be able to imagine the existence of a competitive market, such an institution cannot become a reality if there are small numbers of buyers and sellers. In Arrow's general formulation, each commodity has precisely one supplier and one demander.

3.2   Property rights and externalities

Consider briefly the more orthodox exchange model, in which each individual cares only about his or her own consumption. The textbook treatment pictures each as starting from an endowment point and optimizing, subject to whatever institutional rules govern the exchange of commodities, the simplest and most common of which is the competitive market process. This picture, of course, depends on a host of assumptions. In particular, it presupposes that there are no arguments about the initial endowments. Each individual has clearly defined rights concerning the use and disposal of his or her endowment—rights that are generally respected or (analytically equivalent) costlessly enforced. Any surrender of such rights is only done with the individual's full consent, as when he or she offers to give up quantitites of one good in exchange for another.

One can imagine an alternative scenario in which such rights are not automatically taken for granted. Bush and Mayer (1974) study a model in which, at the beginning of each period, every agent is endowed with a given pile of "manna." Rights to manna are not recognized in their anarchical society, and individuals choose between two activities: They may stay at home and guard their pile against theft by others, or they may go out and steal from others. The more time they spend in the latter activity, the more will be stolen from their own unguarded pile. Stealing represents a less preferred use of time, involving sacrifice of leisure. Bush and Mayer define and show the existence of an anarchical equilibrium. They also show that there are gains to be had by setting up an institutional framework within which one has well-defined rights on one's own endowment—

rights, moreover, that are enforced. To such gains may be attributed the origins of the state, and the complicated rules and restrictions that characterize societies of any complexity. It can pay each to accept constraints on his or her own behavior—to give up, for example, the right to take from the endowments of others—in return for having those same constraints imposed on others. The model of anarchy shows clearly the vital role of property rights as a precondition for voluntary exchange—in other words, for the evolution of markets.

In the present discussion, we are interested in those circumstances that may constitute obstacles to the establishment of private property rights. It is clear that, in order to set a price for a commodity, it must be possible to exclude those who do not pay the price. For some goods, exclusion is possible but costly. The metering of water supplies and the scrambling of radio and television broadcasts are examples of costly, and not universally adopted, exclusion devices. One can imagine exclusion being possible at a cost in a situation involving environmental pollution or congestion. There are, however, other goods for which exclusion is intrinsically impossible. If citizens are excluded from a public park, then it is, by definition, no longer a public park. National defense is another commonly cited example of a good from which exclusion is not possible. In any event, if exclusion is impossible or too costly to be privately profitable, an essential precondition for the establishment of effective property rights is absent. (Situations in which exclusion is costly but profitable to enforce are discussed in Chapter 11.)

The failure of property rights to be well-defined is, then, an important ingredient of many externality situations. However, such failure is not by itself reason enough to conclude that there is an inefficiency and, hence, scope for policy intervention. A celebrated example involves the conflict of interests between the farmer and the cattle rancher. The farmer can exclude cattle, thereby establishing and protecting his grazing rights, by building fences. However, if there are many small farmers scattered throughout an area of open rangeland, the costs of building the necessary fences may exceed the social benefits to be gained. In such a case, governmental provision of fencing, whether directly or through subsidies to farmers, will be socially undesirable. This raises the question: Under what circumstances may we expect to observe an equilibrium in which certain markets do not exist because there are no private incentives to do so, and yet from which there are feasible changes that are socially advantageous?

3.3   Nonconvexity and externalities

One well-known class of situations in which privately unprofitable courses of action may be socially profitable arises from the presence of nonconvexities in agents' feasible sets or preferences. Figure 3.1 depicts a single-input, single-output economy in which, before any positive production is possible, a substantial quantity of input is required to set up the process. The production possibilities set is the hatched area together with the line segment OS. The figure also depicts the preferences of this single-consumer economy by an indifference map with the usual properties. As drawn, the point P is a Pareto optimum. It is also not sustainable as a decentralized competitive equilibrium, since at the implied equilibrium price vector the production activity generates a loss of OB measured in terms of output. Faced with this price, firms would do better by closing down. Malinvaud (1972, pp. 219–29) provides a good discussion of the problems involved in attaining efficient allocation through decentralized mechanisms in the presence of fixed costs.

It has been argued that transactions technologies tend to involve substantial setup costs and hence give rise to nonconvexity and consequent problems in attaining efficient decentralized allocations. Indeed, the impression is sometimes given that if property rights are well defined, such nonconvexity is necessary if there is to be a genuine externality since, by analogy with the literature on fixed costs, it is in this situation that transactions fail to take place that, in some social sense, ought to take place. Nonconvexities then become an important ingredient of externalities models. The significance of this observation, which we believe is often developed in a misleading way, is discussed in the next section.

There are two further quite distinct ways in which nonconvexity may become an important feature of externalities models. Baumol and Bradford (1972) give the example of a power station that inflicts a detrimental externality on a laundry through its generation of smoke. The two marketed commodities are electricity and laundry services. Their example shows that if the negative externality is sufficiently strong, the transformation frontier will exhibit nonconvexity. The labor requirements in the two industries are

$$l_0 = y_0^2/2 + \alpha y_1 y_0$$

and

$$l_1 = y_1^2/2,$$

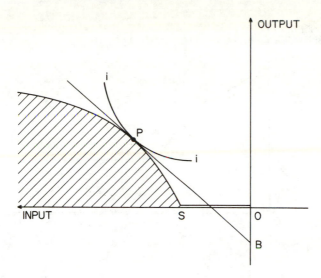

Figure 3.1

where l_0 and y_0, are the input and output levels of the laundry industry, and l_1 and y_1 are their counterparts in the electricity industry. The parameter α represents the intensity of pollution suffered by the latter as a result of the smoke generated in the production of electricity. The formulation assumes a monotonic increasing relation between power generation and the production of smoke. For simplicity, we assume that one unit of electricity produces one unit of smoke. Clearly a positive value of α implies that a given level of laundry services requires more input, the higher the level of electricity, and hence smoke, generation. Substitution readily yields the transformation frontier between the marketed outputs:

$$y_0^2/2 + \alpha y_0 y_1 + y_1^2/2 = l_0 + l_1 = L,$$

where L is the exogenous total labor supply. The relationship between the marginal rate of transformation and the pattern of output is, by differentiation,

$$\frac{dy_0}{dy_1} = -\frac{y_1 + \alpha y_0}{y_0 + \alpha y_1}. \tag{7}$$

Suppose α is raised parametrically. If $\alpha = 1$, the marginal rate of transformation is constant. Sufficiently strong interdependence, cor-

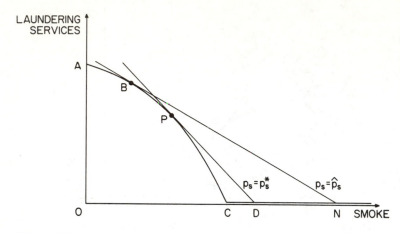

Figure 3.2

responding to $\alpha > 1$, leads to nonconvexity in the production possibilities set.

Why should such nonconvexity concern us? In one sense, it is not such a serious problem as it might seem, since although the aggregate production set may be nonconvex, the individual feasible sets over which competitive electricity generators and launderers optimize are convex. It is therefore possible to sustain an optimum, through appropriate taxes and subsidies, by a decentralized process. The problem is rather one of information. Even if we have complete knowledge of the technologies of the interacting industries, we cannot infer anything from current equilibrium prices about whether an observed allocation is Pareto optimal. The reader is referred to Baumol and Bradford (1972) or Baumol and Oates (1975, pp. 117–23) for further discussion.

Starrett (1972) identifies a quite distinct phenomenon, which he calls a "fundamental nonconvexity" associated with externalities (see also Laffont 1976). If a firm is the recipient of a detrimental externality, it always has the option, which sooner or later will be the preferred course of action as the intensity of the externality increases, of going out of business. Thereafter, by definition, further increases in the level of the pollutant will have no adverse effect, since the potential victim has ceased to exist. Thus, if the commodity space is defined to include the externality "smoke," there is an inherent nonconvexity, as Figure 3.2 shows. Let the level of input into the laundry industry be fixed. Even if that portion of the transformation frontier AC exhibits convexity, generation of further smoke at the point C cannot further reduce the output of the laundry. Points along the horizontal axis to the right of C are therefore on the frontier.

In contrast to Baumol and Bradford's example, this fundamental nonconvexity does not depend on the externality being sufficiently strong. This nonconvexity is inherent in situations where the recipient of a detrimental externality can avoid it by going out of business. It is also defined with respect to the commodity space augmented to include the externality as a commodity, whereas the previous example exhibited nonconvexity with respect to the space of marketed commodities alone. Finally, the implications of this nonconvexity are different, as can be seen if we push Arrow's thought experiment to its logical conclusion and imagine the operation of a market dealing with the commodity smoke.

Suppose that the rights to enjoy clean air—or, conversely, to pollute that air—can be costlessly defined and enforced. The laundry owner, for example, may initially possess the right to enjoy clean air in the neighborhood of his laundry. He may, however, choose to sell some of this right. In effect, he can sell tickets, or permits, each of which allows its buyer to inflict a "unit" of pollution—for example, a specified concentration of particulates over a specified time period—on the laundry. Let s be the number of units of pollution, or smoke, and p_s be the price per unit charged by the laundry. Then the profits of the laundry owner and the electricity generator are, respectively,

$$\Pi_0 = (p_0 y_0 - w l_0) + p_s s \qquad (8)$$

and

$$\Pi_1 = (p_1 y_1 - w l_1) - p_s s, \qquad (9)$$

where y_j and l_j are the output and input levels of the two activities, and p_0, p_1, and w are the market prices of laundering services, electricity, and labor input. Note that the laundry owner has two sources of profit: the provision of laundry services, and the sale of his clean air rights. For simplicity, we suppose that l_0, the laundry owner's input level, is already determined. We can also choose units so that one unit of laundry services corresponds to one unit of profit from laundering. Suppose that in Figure 3.2 the allocation P is the optimum. It would seem at first that to sustain P as an equilibrium the laundry owner should receive the price p_s^* per unit of pollution. However, a less myopic examination of the figure shows that at this price the laundry will not operate at P, but can do better by producing no laundry services and selling rights to pollute in excess of OD. Even if an arbitrary finite limit to the number of rights is imposed, a problem remains. If the limit ON exceeds OD, the laundry owner can maximize profits by selling the maximum number of permits.

The initial allocation of rights to clean air to the laundry is, of course, somewhat arbitrary. However, the analysis is similar if instead it is the electricity generator who possesses salable rights to pollute. Suppose that initially the electricity generator has the right to produce $\bar{s}$ units of smoke. The launderer may pay a price p_s to obtain a reduction of one unit in smoke production. The profits of the two sectors are now

$$\Pi_0 = (p_0 y_0 - w l_0) - p_s(\bar{s} - s) \tag{10}$$

and

$$\Pi_1 = (p_1 y_1 - w l_1) + p_s(\bar{s} - s). \tag{11}$$

For a given value of p_s, these expressions differ from (8) and (9) only by virtue of an exogenous redistribution of profits. The producers' choices will be unaffected by this.

This example raises two issues. First, it shows that a competitive equilibrium may fail to exist in the space of commodities that includes externalities. Retain the assumption that ON is the maximum number of permits, so that the transformation frontier is $APCN$. Then if $p_s = 0$, the laundry owner will prefer to be at A and sell no pollution permits. As p_s rises, the profit-maximizing allocation moves along the frontier towards B. But at $p_s = \hat{p}_s$, it suddenly becomes profitable to jump from B to N. Thereafter, the laundry will sell as many rights as it can, and produce no laundry. Figure 3.3 shows the implied discontinuity in the launderer's supply schedule, and the consequent possibility that the supply and demand schedules may not intersect.

It is tempting to suggest that the problem can be overcome by choosing ON "appropriately." If it is made small enough, an intersection can be generated. However, this raises an informational problem. In general the optimum is not known. We simply assumed P was optimal to make one particular point. In general, for all we know, the optimal allocation should involve the laundry closing down. In this case, while making ON sufficiently small may guarantee an interior equilibrium, it does so by ruling out the optimum. This is hardly a satisfactory outcome!

There are circumstances, then, in which Arrow's thought experiment of imagining markets in externalities cannot be carried right

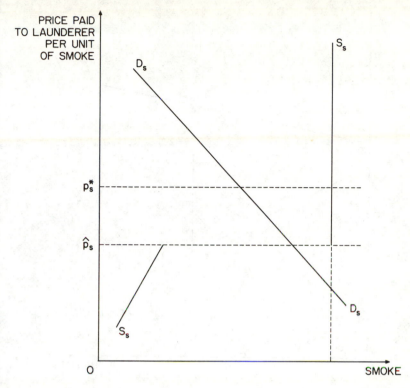

Figure 3.3

through. There may exist no competitive equilibrium relative to the full set of markets, and attempts to force existence by essentially ad hoc restrictions on the endowments of polluting rights may produce equilibria with no particularly attractive normative properties.

3.4 More on transactions costs

Suppose that property rights are well defined, but that the costs of coordination and marketing necessary for certain commodities to be traded voluntarily are very high, so that markets for those commodities are not active. Is nonconvexity in the transactions technology necessary in order to conclude that the equilibrium outcome is inefficient? A reading of Heller and Starrett (1976, p. 11) suggests that the answer is yes. They appeal to a model developed by Foley (1970b) in which it is shown that if transactions costs exhibit convexity,

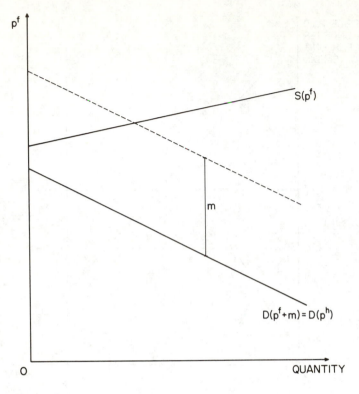

Figure 3.4

the resulting equilibrium is Pareto optimal even though certain potential markets are not operative.

It is not clear, however, that Foley's model is relevant in the context of externalities. If high transactions costs imply the absence of a particular market in Foley's model, each agent is voluntarily choosing a zero level of exchange in the relevant commodity. Each optimizes subject to a single constraint—the budget constraint for the consumer, and the production, or transformation, function for the producer. Figure 3.4 provides a partial equilibrium demonstration of the situation envisaged by Foley. Let p^f and p^h be, respectively, the price received by the firm and that paid by the household for a unit of a given commodity. They differ by the amount m, which represents the cost of marketing a unit of the commodity—in effect, of transforming it from a unit of output at the factory gate, via a voluntary act of exchange, into a generator of consumption services in the home. It is conceivable that if m were zero, there might be a positive quantity transacted, the demand function being the dashed line in the figure. However, if m is sufficiently large, the demand and supply curves will not intersect in the positive quadrant, and equilibrium involves no transactions in the commodity. If m is constant, the transactions technology is convex and the corner solution is consistent with optimality.

In the externality model, the situation is somewhat different. In the absence of a market, the commodity in question—smoke, or perhaps a beneficial externality such as bees' pollinating services—continues to be produced in positive quantities as a joint product, and the recipient consumes an amount that he or she cannot control but that is endogenous to the economic system. He or she cannot choose to receive no smoke. Formally, this implies that the recipient's feasible set is defined by multiple constraints, and this gives rise to the possibility of suboptimality. In the case of a detrimental externality, suboptimality depends crucially on the failure of "free disposal" to hold. If the recipient could, without cost, avoid the adverse effects of smoke, then he or she would in effect face only a single budget constraint. Conversely, beneficial externalities are ones that the recipient would prefer to see increased. The free disposal assumption, or its failure, plays no role there. In either event, the presence of quantity constraints in addition to the conventional budget and technological constraints plays a crucial role in externality models, whereas they are absent in Foley's model. It is these multiple constraints, regardless of whether or not the market transactions technology is convex, that create the possibility of an inefficient externality-ridden equilibrium.

3.5 Special types of externalities

Our argument to this point suggests that it is useful to distinguish sharply between two types of commodity. There are those, called marketed commodities, that individual consumers or producers may freely choose subject only to the single constraint imposed by their budgets or production functions. In addition there are nonmarketed or environmental commodities, the quantities of which are exogenous to particular agents or groups of agents. Hence a typical consumer's direct and indirect utility functions may be written

$$U^h = U^h(y_1^h, \ldots, y_m^h; e_1^h, \ldots, e_n^h)$$

$$= V^h(p_1, \ldots, p_m; e_1^h, \ldots, e_n^h, I^h).$$

The environmental commodities e_j^h are, in the simplest model, taken as exogenously given by the recipient. However, they are endogenous to the general system, depending on the choices made by others. Formally, the resulting model is one of quantity-constrained behavior, for which a well-developed theory exists. Neary and Roberts (1980) provide a modern treatment, and Cornes (1980) explicitly models externalities within such a framework. Indeed, there are striking parallels with the literature on fix-price macroeconomic models and with rationing discussed by Malinvaud, the main difference being that the actual price of e_j^h is zero in the externality model, there being no market at all in the relevant commodity.

It is valuable to have this insight but, as is so often the case, the most general formulation does not allow us to reach very specific conclusions. Chapter 4 deals with policy analysis in the context of simple models of general externalities, and Parts III and IV concentrate on special cases that have sufficient extra structure to enable us to make stronger statements about the characteristics of equilibrium and optimal allocations, the relationship between them, and the problems involved in devising policies to sustain optimal allocations. The rest of this section is devoted to a brief description of the most important special cases. First, we restate the general externality model using a notation that facilitates comparison with the subsequent variants.

General externality

The recipient's maximization problem is

$$\text{Maximize}_{\{y^h, z^h\}} \quad U^h(y^h, z^h; z^1, z^2, \ldots z^{h-1}, z^{h+1}, \ldots z^H) \qquad (12)$$

$$\text{subject to} \quad p_y y^h \; p_z z^h = I^h.$$

The individual consumer chooses quantities of two marketed commodities, y^h and z^h, each of which may be a vector, subject to a budget constraint. From the consumer's point of view, the consumption levels of commodity z by other individuals, $z^1, \ldots z^{h-1}, z^{h+1}, \ldots z^H$, are environmental commodities, which he or she takes as given. This "general" case may be written even more generally, by letting the other agents' consumption of y also enter his or her utility function. A particular example of this, which we do not explore in this book, is that of nonmeddlesome altruism or envy. Here the quantities of consumption by others enter through their utility functions. Individual h cares about the utility levels of others, but does not presume to any view about how they should allocate their income. The analysis of models in which environmental commodities appear in the form given in (12) is typically very aggregated, with two representative agents.

Pure public good

The consumer's problem is

Maximize $U^h(y^h, z^1 + z^2 + \ldots + z^h + \ldots + z^H)$
$\{y^h, z^h\}$

or

Maximize $U^h(y^h, z^h + \tilde{Z}^h)$
$\{y^h, z^h\}$

subject to $p_y y^h + p_z z^h = I^h,$

where

$$\tilde{Z}^h \equiv \sum_{i=1}^{H} z^i - z^h,$$

the sum of the rest of the community's expenditure on commodity z. The significant characteristics of this model are that the z^i's all enter additively to define an aggregate quantity, $Z \equiv \sum_{i=1}^{H} z^i = z^h + \tilde{Z}^h$, which appears in each consumer's utility functions. In particular, z^h is included in the summation, indicating that z^h is a perfect substitute for z^i, $i \neq h$. The usual interpretation of this structure views z^i as the ith agent's contribution toward a single good—a pure public good—the total quantity of which is then made available to all. Not only can it be made available to all, but the emphasis in this book is on that class of situation in which it is impossible, or prohibitively costly, to deny access to individuals who do not contribute. Part III discusses this model at length.

Impure public good or bad

This represents an extension of the pure public good model. There is an individual commodity that appears twice in the consumer's utility function, once on its own as a private commodity, and once in combination with the quantities consumed by others, thereby forming a public good or bad. The consumer's problem is

Maximize $U^h(y^h, z^h, z^h + \tilde{Z}^h)$
$\{y^h, z^h\}$

subject to $p_y y^h + p_z z^h = M^h.$

The authors have elsewhere modeled this situation using the house-hold production theory approach (see Cornes and Sandler 1984a). The consumer is thought of as purchasing two goods, say y^h and q^h. Each unit of y^h produces one unit of a final commodity, also called y^h, while each unit of q^h produces α units of a characteristic x^h and also β units of a public characteristic z^h. The problem of the consumer is then

$$\text{Maximize} \quad U^h(y^h, x^h, z^h + \tilde{Z}^h)$$
$$\{y^h, q^h\}$$

$$\text{subject to} \quad x^h = \alpha q^h$$

$$z^h = \beta q^h$$

and

$$p_y y^h + p_q q^h = I^h,$$

where

$$\tilde{Z}^h \equiv \sum_{i \neq h} z^i = \sum_{i \neq h} \beta q^i.$$

This formulation, which many economists regard as more empirically important than that of the pure public good, is very versatile. The quantity $Z \equiv z^h + \tilde{Z}^h$ may be interpreted as either a good or a bad. An example of the former is the case of the individual who, by being inoculated against an infectious disease, incidentally confers a public benefit by reducing the risk of spreading the disease through the community. The latter encompasses a wide range of models of congestion and pollution. x^h, for example, may represent the amount of driving done by consumer h, which is a private good. However, the total quantity of driving by members of the community produces a bad in the form of road congestion or air pollution, this being captured by the variable Z, for which $\partial U/\partial Z < 0$. (The properties of this model are developed in some detail in Chapter 7.)

Impure public bad with public amelioration

The impure public bad model may be extended in a natural way to accommodate the possibility of using resources to ameliorate, or mitigate the effects of, the public bad. The congestion generated by a given amount of driving depends also on the amount of highway provided, and the public sector may be faced with deciding the optimal amount of highway. It is convenient to handle this issue by defining a congestion function, $C(z^h + \tilde{Z}^h, H)$ where H is the quantity of, say, highway. It is assumed that $\partial C/\partial Z > 0$ and $\partial C/\partial H < 0$. The consumer's problem is then

Maximize $\quad U^h(y^h, x^h, C(z^h + \tilde{Z}^h), H)$
$\{y^h, q^h\}$

subject to $\quad x^h = \alpha q^h$

$\qquad\qquad z^h = \beta q^h$

$\qquad\qquad y^h + (p+t^h)q^h = I^h - T^h.$

The appearance of a tax, t^h, on consumption of q and of a lump-sum tax T^h is explained by the need to finance highway provision. As we shall see in Chapter 7, t^h can play a dual role in this model. It raises revenue to finance H, while helping to discourage the activity that generates congestion. Under certain special assumptions, clear-cut results can be obtained concerning the optimal value of t^h.

Impure public bad with private amelioration

For completeness, one should note that amelioration of a public bad may be undertaken by individuals in the private sector. Inhabitants of smog-ridden cities may wear masks over their mouths, or plant trees and erect fences to keep out noise or visual pollution. Denote the private good by r and its price by ψ. Then the consumer's problem is

Maximize $\quad U^h(y^h, x^h, C(z^h + \tilde{Z}^h, r^h))$
$\{y^h, q^h, r^h\}$

$\qquad\qquad x^h = \alpha q^h$

$\qquad\qquad z^h = \beta q^h$

$\qquad\qquad y^h + pq^h + \psi r^h = I^h.$

Models of this sort, which we do not pursue further in the present book, are discussed by Shibata and Winrich (1983) and by Oates (1983).

Club goods

In all the models presented above, the size of the community consuming the public good is exogenously fixed. Consequently this characteristic does not appear explicitly in the analysis. Club goods and local public goods generalize the public good concept to situations in which the community size is endogenous. The facilities of a swimming pool are available to those who join a swimming club. Similarly, individuals may vote with their feet and thereby choose the local community, or country, in which to contribute to and consume public goods. These can no longer be pure public goods, since there would be no finite limit to the equilibrium or optimal size of the community. Each entrant generates benefits to fellow members by reducing the per capita cost of a given quantity of public good. Club goods models therefore share the common feature of some form of congestion phenomenon that places bounds on the desirable size of the club. A simple model (see Chapter 10) involves the following problem for each member:

$$\text{Maximize} \quad U^h(y^h, X, s)$$
$$\{y^h, X, s\}$$

$$\text{subject to} \quad F^h(y^h, X, s) = 0,$$

where X is the club good, and is essentially a public good from the viewpoint of each member of the community; s is the membership size; and $F^h(\cdot)$ is a technological or budget constraint. The assumptions on first derivatives are that $\partial U^h/\partial y^h > 0$, $\partial U^h/\partial X > 0$ and $\partial U^h/\partial s < 0$. This last one represents the congestion effect, familiar to any user of a swimming pool. Concerning $F(\cdot)$, we assume $\partial F^h/\partial y^h > 0$, $\partial F^h/\partial X > 0$, and $\partial F^h/\partial s < 0$. Whereas increases in y^h and X increase the cost per member, an increase in the size of the club spreads a given total cost over more individuals, thereby reducing the cost per member. Models of club goods have proliferated and display a daunting variety. However, as we show in Chapter 10, there is an underlying unity in these models, inasmuch as they all contain the elements present in this formulation.

3.6   Concluding remarks

This chapter has developed the view that an externality arises when the private economy lacks incentives to set up a potential market in some commodity and when the nonexistence of this market results in a Pareto-suboptimal allocation. The absence of a potential market certainly denies individuals one avenue by which they can exercise some choice in situations where the decisions of others may confer appreciable benefit or inflict appreciable damage on them, and confronts them with multiple constraints. Such a view clearly has common ground with Meade's definition. Most of the controversy that continues to surround the theory of externalities concerns the evaluation of the outcome. In what sense can the outcome be termed Pareto suboptimal? How can one distinguish between outcomes that are, and those that are not, capable of being improved upon by some form of intervention? Economists have been criticized, with some justification, for a tendency to forget that institutions other than markets exist and play important roles in allocating resources. Perhaps the absence of a market reflects the availability of some other institutional device that, in the light of all the frictions and costs of coordination and information-gathering, does a good job. Consider the humble traffic light. It does a remarkable job of coordinating motorists' behavior at busy intersections. True, there are times when a motorist who is not in a great hurry is allowed to pass straight through while another, in danger of missing a vital meeting, and hence with a higher marginal cost associated with waiting, fumes and frets at the red light. However, given the current state of technology, it is difficult to imagine how a more efficient method of coordination can be achieved through more market-oriented devices.

In the next chapter, we discuss some of the policy responses to externalities that have been suggested. The emphasis is on those approaches that involve extending or tinkering with an essentially competitive market allocation process. But, again, we will find lurking in the background difficult and unresolved issues involved in the comparison of alternative institutional structures for coping with social interactions.

CHAPTER 4

Externalities, equilibrium, and optimality

Our discussion in Chapter 3 of the definition and pathology of externalities has laid the groundwork that enables us now to consider some of their policy implications. Our starting point is again the competitive equilibrium model. The absence of a complete set of markets raises the possibility that a competitive equilibrium will not be Pareto optimal, and it is the search for ways of sustaining Pareto optima that has motivated much of the literature on policy intervention to deal with externalities. In discussing this literature, we draw attention to the distinction between, on the one hand, characterizing and sustaining a Pareto optimum and, on the other hand, achieving a Pareto improvement with respect to a given initial allocation. This distinction is familiar to students of other branches of tax theory, which distinguish between de novo tax design and the reform of an existing system (see, e.g., Atkinson and Stiglitz 1980, pp. 382–6). However, the relationship between the number of policy instruments and the possibility of Pareto improvement has not been so clearly recognized in the externalities literature.

The most celebrated form of intervention—suggested by Pigou (1946) and clarified, extended, and criticized by countless others— consists of a system of taxes and subsidies designed to distort individuals' choices toward an optimal outcome. An alternative to such manipulation of the price system involves the enforcement of quantitative constraints such as a set of environmental standards that must be maintained. Examples are automobile emission control standards, nighttime restrictions on the landing and taking off of aircraft near residential areas, and the insistence on rehabilitation of natural environments in the wake of open-cut mining. In very simple models, the two approaches are equivalent. However, departures from competitive behavior or the introduction of uncertainty or information problems breaks down this equivalence and raises the issue of whether, and under what conditions, one approach may be better than the other. Even where there is an equivalence between a tax and a quantity constraint policy, it is sometimes easier to work with one rather than the other. In this context, various writers have noted the possibility of anomalous results in the following sense: If a set of activities creates detrimental externalities, it is possible to show that taxes on these activities are appropriate policies for achieving optimality. However, it does not necessarily follow that, in the move from the suboptimal pretax equilibrium to the optimum, the level of each of these activities should fall. The following sections elaborate on the various points raised in this introduction.

4.1 Competitive equilibrium, externalities, and inefficiency

In the theory of competitive equilibrium, there are two particularly important assumptions, violations of which are central to the missing markets approach to the theory of externalities. The first is that of convexity. Applied to consumers, this means that given any two commodity bundles between which they are indifferent, then convex combinations of those bundles are at least as attractive to them. Put differently, the set of all bundles that are at least as attractive to them as some arbitrary given reference bundle is a convex set. Applied to producers, it means that if there are two input-output combinations that the current technology renders feasible, then it should also be possible to achieve any convex combination of them. This implies, for example, that production activities must not exhibit increasing returns to scale.

The second assumption is that of the universality of markets. This means, as we have already seen, that if we disaggregate sufficiently to distinguish between every object that appears in the objective functions of the agents in the economy, there should be a market allowing voluntary transactions in every commodity. The importance of these two assumptions, both of which may frequently be factually invalid, stems from their role in establishing the two fundamental theorems of welfare economics. Of course, a number of other assumptions are also required, and useful discussions may be found in Bator (1957), Arrow (1970), and Koopmans (1957). For our present purposes, we ignore the additional requirements and simply assert that, under certain conditions, the following two theorems hold:

Theorem I: If markets are universal, a competitive equilibrium is Pareto optimal.

Theorem II: If households' preferences and firms' production possibility sets are convex, and if markets are universal, any Pareto optimum can be sustained as a competitive equilibrium.

The assumption that markets are universal, or complete, is required for both theorems. For the moment, we focus our attention on Theorem I, since the situations that we are analyzing are competitive equilibria with a less than universal set of markets. The first step is to demonstrate the suboptimality resulting from competitive behavior when externalities cannot be competitively traded.

Consider a simple model involving two consumers and two marketed commodities: y_j^h is individual h's consumption of commodity j. Each has a given money income, I^h, and can trade with the rest of the world at fixed prices, p_1 and p_2. An alternative interpretation is that I^h represents an exogenous endowment of, say, labor services, which can be used to produce the goods at constant costs, in which case p_j is the unit input requirement of commodity j. The final ingredient is a unilateral externality, since the quantity of commodity 2 chosen by individual b also appears in the utility function of individual a. We assume that, in the absence of any opportunity to trade in the externality, individual a takes its value as given in determining his or her own choices. The individuals' problems are

Individual a: $\underset{\{y_1^a, y_2^a\}}{\text{Max}}$ $\{U^a(y_1^a, y_2^a, e^a) \,|\, p_1 y_1^a + p_2 y_2^a = I^a, e^a = y_2^b\}$

Individual b: $\underset{\{y_1^b, y_2^b\}}{\text{Max}}$ $\{U^b(y_1^b, y_2^b) \,|\, p_1 y_1^b + p_2 y_2^b = I^b\}.$

The equilibrium allocation is characterized in the usual way by the equalities

$$\frac{\partial U^a / \partial y_1^a}{\partial U^a / \partial y_2^a} = \frac{\partial U^b / \partial y_1^b}{\partial U^b / \partial y_2^b} = \frac{p_1}{p_2}, \tag{1}$$

together with the requirement that the quantity e^a equals the equilibrium level of y_2^b. Now suppose an infinitesimal tax is imposed on individual b's consumption of commodity 2, and the revenue is returned in a lump-sum manner, so that there is no redistribution of income between consumers. Such a policy is precisely identical to a quantity constraint applied to y_2^b. Denoting the price that b faces in the market for commodity 2 by $p_2^b = p_2 + t_2$, and assuming that the initial value of the tax is zero, the indirect utility function yields the result that

$$dV^b = (\partial V^b / \partial p_2^b) dp_2^b + (\partial V^b / \partial I^b) y_2^b dp_2^b,$$

where the second term captures the effect of the lump-sum return of the revenue, $y_2^b dp_2^b$. Roy's identity tells us that at the initial

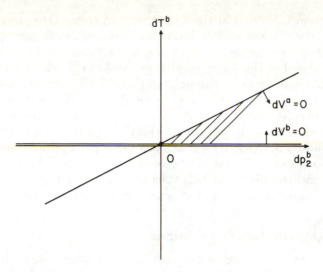

Figure 4.1

equilibrium $\partial V^b/\partial p_2^b = -y_2^b(\partial V^b/\partial I^b)$. Substitution confirms that $dV^b = 0$. More generally, now suppose that there is simultaneously a net transfer of income from individual a to individual b, $dT^b = -dI^a$. Then we obtain

$$dV^b = (\partial V^b/\partial T^b)dT^b. \tag{2}$$

Now consider individual a, whose utility is affected by two changes, de^a and dT^b. In the present simple economy this individual faces unchanged prices. His or her indirect utility function may be written $V^a(p_1, p_2, e^a, I^a)$, from which, recalling that $dI^a = -dT^b$, we obtain

$$dV^a = (\partial V^a/\partial e^a)de^a - (\partial V^a/\partial I^a)dT^b.$$

Since $e^a = y_2^b$, we can eliminate de^a by using individual b's demand function for y_2. Rather than give the expression for dV^a, it is more convenient to consider what combinations of dp_2^b and dT^b leave V^a unchanged. It may be shown that, in order that $dV^a = 0$,

$$\frac{dT^b}{dp_2^b} = \frac{(\partial V^a/\partial e^a)\sigma_{22}^b}{(\partial V^a/\partial I^a) - (\partial V^a/\partial e^a)(\partial y_2^b/\partial I^b)}, \tag{3}$$

where σ_{22}^b is the compensated response in individual b's demand for commodity 2 to a change in p_2^b. Figure 4.1 summarizes the outcome. The horizontal axis depicts the change in price p_2^b faced by individual b, and the vertical axis measures the net transfer from a to b. The initial situation is located at the origin, and in considering any shift away from 0 we assume that individual a faces unchanged prices throughout. Hence $dp_2^b > 0$ reflects the introduction of a tax. Equation (2) shows that the locus of changes (dp_2^b, dT^b), which leave b's utility unchanged, must, in the neighborhood of 0, coincide with the horizontal axis. Equation (3) shows that if the externality is detrimental, so that $(\partial V^a / \partial e^a) < 0$, and if the compensated response σ_{22}^b is strictly negative, the locus associated with $dV^a = 0$ must have nonzero slope. Certainly, if $\partial y_2^b / \partial I^b > 0$, this locus will have a positive slope in the neighborhood of 0, and values of dp_2^b and dT^b may be found to make both individuals better off. Starting at the origin in Figure 4.1 movements into the hatched area represent Pareto improvements.

4.2   Pigouvian taxes and subsidies

We have shown that the imposition of a quantity constraint or, equivalently, a tax on the generator of a unilateral detrimental externality can, if combined with an appropriate redistribution of income, lead all agents to more preferred allocations than those implied by competitive equilibrium, thereby demonstrating that such an equilibrium is not optimal. If the externality is positive, or beneficial, the same argument holds, except that the tax is a subsidy, and the equivalent quantity constraint would force the externality-generator to consume more of y_2^b than he or she would wish to if acting as a price-taker. It is natural to go one step further and attempt to characterize allocations that cannot be improved upon in Pareto's sense, and in particular to characterize the sets of prices that, if confronted by the various agents, would sustain such allocations. This is precisely what the Pigouvian tax/subsidy scheme attempts to do. Consider the first-order necessary conditions associated with a Pareto-optimal allocation in the present model given freedom to choose the distribution of initial endowment $I \equiv I^a + I^b$ without restriction or resort to distortionary instruments. Such an allocation satisfies the first-order conditions associated with maximization of the weighted sum of utilities for some arbitrary set of nonnegative weights, α^a and α^b. The implied Lagrangean is

$$L = \alpha^a U^a(y_1^a, y_2^a, e^a) + \alpha^b U^b(y_1^b, y_2^b) - \lambda[p_1(y_1^a + y_1^b)$$
$$+ p_2(y_2^a + y_2^b) - I^a - I^b]$$

We should remind the reader that the p_i's may be interpreted as technical coefficients associated with constant cost production of the consumption goods from the single primary factor I. Since we are not directly interested in the α^i's, it is convenient to eliminate them as well as λ in the statement of the first-order conditions. For our purposes, the important conditions are that

$$\frac{p_2}{p_1} = \frac{\partial U^a/\partial y_2^a}{\partial U^a/\partial y_1^a} = \frac{\partial U^b/\partial y_2^b}{\partial U^b/\partial y_1^b} + \frac{\partial U^a/\partial e^a}{\partial U^a/\partial y_1^a} \tag{4}$$

or, in the language of marginal rates of substitution and transformation,

$$MRT = MRS_{21}^a = MRS_{21}^b + MRS_{e1}^a. \tag{5}$$

These conditions, it should be emphasized, fall a long way short of providing "the solution" to the social optimizing problem. For one thing, we have already noted that there will be an infinite number of Pareto optima. For another, the conditions simply state a feature that must necessarily characterize an interior optimum. It is analogous to saying that a necessary feature of a hilltop is that the slope should be locally zero in all directions. To generate a solution one must still (i) specify a distributional rule, so as to pick out one particular optimum, (ii) confirm that second-order conditions are also met, and (iii) have information about the precise form of the agent's constraints and objective functions—more precisely, about the MRS functions appearing in (5). Once these considerations are taken care of, it is possible to solve, at least in principle, for the implied consumption and production choices of every agent. Denote by $(\hat{y}_1^a, \hat{y}_2^a, \hat{e}^a)$ and $(\hat{y}_1^b, \hat{y}_2^b)$ the arguments of the utility functions of consumers a and b, respectively, at an optimum. Given convex preferences, one may define a set of shadow, or virtual, prices for each individual, these being the prices that would lead the individual, acting as a price-taker over all the arguments in his or her objective function, to choose the implied bundle. For example, if commodity 1 is chosen as the numeraire, there is a pair of prices, π_2^a and π_e^a, that would touch a's indifference surface at the point $(\hat{y}_1^a, \hat{y}_2^a, \hat{e}^a)$. These virtual prices, which Neary and Roberts (1980) discuss in the general context of quantity-constrained choice, are, of course, simply the individual's marginal rates of substitution, or marginal valuations of the commodities in question in terms of the numeraire. For b, there is a single relative virtual price, which we denote by π_2^b. Each virtual price is a function of the commodity bundle. Indeed, they are simply inverse demand functions. The conditions (4) or (5) may then be written as

$$p_2 = \pi_2^a(\hat{y}_1^a, \hat{y}_2^a, \hat{e}^a) = \pi_2^b(\hat{y}_1^b, \hat{y}_2^b) + \pi_e^a(\hat{y}_1^a, \hat{y}_2^a, \hat{e}^a). \tag{6}$$

If the optimal allocation is to be sustained with price-taking behavior but with no market in the externality, then (6) shows that the consumers must be faced with the following prices:

$$\pi_2^a(\cdot) = p_2 \tag{7}$$

and

$$\pi_2^b(\cdot) = p_2 - \pi_e^a(\hat{y}_1^a, \hat{y}_2^a, \hat{e}^a). \tag{8}$$

If the externality is detrimental, $\pi_e^a(\cdot)$ must be negative for a positive value of $\hat{e}^a$. In order to persuade an individual voluntarily to absorb a bad, it will be necessary to compensate that individual. In short, the price that he or she would pay must be negative. Conversely, a beneficial externality implies a positive valuation, or virtual price. Equation (7) shows that the recipient of the externality who does not impose externalities on others should face relative prices that reflect the marginal rate of transformation. He or she should not face any distortionary taxes or subsidies. Consumer b, by contrast, should face a price that includes a's marginal valuation of the externality. If he or she faces a specific tax of $t^b = -\pi_e^a$, this will induce him or her to choose the bundle $(\hat{y}_1^b, \hat{y}_2^b)$. The tax will be positive or negative according to whether the externality is detrimental or beneficial.

The argument carries over to situations involving producers, whether they are generators or recipients of externalities, and also to reciprocal externalities, in which each individual is both a recipient and a generator of an externality. Whatever the circumstance, the Pigouvian prescription is to see taxes and subsidies such that when an individual chooses a consumption or production quantity, he or she equates his or her marginal valuation to the total social marginal cost associated with his or her action. This is precisely what equation (8) requires.

A good deal of effort has been devoted to extending the tax/subsidy remedy to situations in which it is not possible to impose the "first-best" tax solution proposed by Pigou. His solution recognizes the distortions introduced by externalities and attempts to nullify them by imposing precisely equal and opposite tax distortions, thereby effectively internalizing the externality. But such policy instruments may not always be available. To begin with, it may be infeasible to have such finely discriminatory taxes. Consider again the example of the laundry and the pollution created by electricity generation. Suppose there are two power stations, one of which, for reasons of location, is a far more intensive polluter of the laundry's environment than the other. The Pigouvian solution will involve the two plants being taxed at different rates. What if we are constrained to use a single tax rate? To analyze this question, consider a simple extension of the earlier model. The output of electricity at plant j, denoted by y_{1j}, is a function of the labor input at that plant:

$$y_{1j} = g_{1j}(l_{1j}) \qquad j = 1, 2.$$

The laundry's output, y_0, depends on its own labor input, l_0, and on that of each electricity plant:

$$y_0 = f(l_0; l_{11}, l_{12}).$$

All firms act as price-takers, and the prices of outputs and of the labor input, exclusive of any tax, are p_0, p_1, and w. Since there is a one-to-one relationship between y_{1j} and l_{1j}, it does not matter whether the output or the input of a generating plant is taxed. We will suppose that the input use is taxed. Denote the specific tax on plant j by t_{1j}. The jth plant, acting as a competitive profit-maximizer, then equates its marginal product to $(w + t_{1j})/p_1$. First, we derive the ideal discriminatory Pigouvian tax. The objective is to maximize the value of output net of input costs, valued at the prices (p_0, p_1, w). This is necessary for Pareto optimality in the system of which this little industrial complex is a part, if there are no other externalities. The objective function, then, which is maximized without any side constraints, is

$$p_0 y_0 + p_1(y_{11} + y_{12}) - w(l_0 + l_{11} + l_{12})$$

or

$$p_0 f(l_0, l_{11}, l_{12}) + p_1[g_{11}(l_{11}) + g_{12}(l_{12})] - w(l_0 + l_{11} + l_{12}),$$

for which the first-order conditions are

$$p_0(\partial f/\partial l_0) = w$$

and

$$p_0(\partial f/\partial l_{1j}) + p_1(\partial g_{1j}/\partial l_{1j}) = w \qquad j = 1, 2$$

or

$$MVP_0 = w$$

and

$$MVP_j = w - p_0(\partial f/\partial l_{1j}) \qquad j = 1, 2, \tag{9}$$

where MVP_0 is the marginal value product of the recipient, and MVP_j is the private marginal value product of the jth externality-generating plant. Since the competitive electricity generators equate MVP_j with the price of labor, the ideal Pigouvian tax should involve the specific tax rate $t_{1j} = -p_0(\partial f/\partial l_{1j})$, reflecting the marginal valuation by the externality recipient of the labor input in the jth plant. If we are now constrained to tax both plants at the same rate, an additional complication arises. This is most easily seen if one of the plants is downwind of the laundry, so that $\partial f/\partial l_{11}$, say, is zero. An increase in the common tax t reduces output of the polluting plant, but at the same time has the undesirable effect of discouraging output at the plant that generates no pollution. The formula for the optimal common tax will involve a tradeoff, and the terms $\partial l_{1j}/\partial t_1$ will appear. In carrying out the optimization, observe that, since p_1 and w are exogenously given in the current context, we can write labor demand functions at the generating plants as $l_{1j}(t_1)$. The problem can be solved using t_1 as the endogenous variable:

$$\text{Maximize} \quad p_0 \, f(l_0, l_{11}(t_1), l_{12}(t_1)) + p_1[g_{11}(l_{11}(t_1))$$
$$\{t_1\} \qquad\qquad + g_{12}(l_{12}(t_1))] - w(l_0 + l_{11} + l_{12}),$$

from which we can derive the first-order necessary condition,

$$p_1\left(\frac{\partial g_{11}}{\partial l_{11}}\frac{\partial l_{11}}{\partial t_1} + \frac{\partial g_{12}}{\partial l_{12}}\frac{\partial l_{12}}{\partial t_1}\right)$$

$$= \left(w - p_0\frac{\partial f}{\partial l_{11}}\right)\frac{\partial l_{11}}{\partial t_1} + \left(w - p_0\frac{\partial f}{\partial l_{12}}\right)\frac{\partial l_{12}}{\partial t_1},$$

or

$$\sum_j \gamma_j \, MVP_j = \sum_j \gamma_j \, [w - p_0(\partial f/\partial l_{1j})], \tag{10}$$

where the γ_j's are weights reflecting the responsiveness of the various plants' labor inputs to a change in the tax rate t_1. A special case of (10) is instructive. Suppose that the electricity plants have identical technologies, so that $g_1(\cdot) = g_2(\cdot) = g(\cdot)$. If they face the same relative prices, their behavior will be identical. Consequently $\gamma_1 = \gamma_2 = \gamma$, and $MVP_1 = MVP_2 = MVP$. Then (10) becomes

$$MVP = w - (p_0/2)(\partial f/\partial l_{11} + \partial f/\partial l_{12}). \tag{11}$$

Suppose further that the laundry's production function is such that $\partial f/\partial l_{11}$ is independent of l_{12}, and $\partial f/\partial l_{12}$ is independent of l_{11}. For example, it may take the form

$$f(l_0, l_{11}, l_{12}) = \phi_1(l_0, l_{11}) + \phi_2(l_0, l_{12}).$$

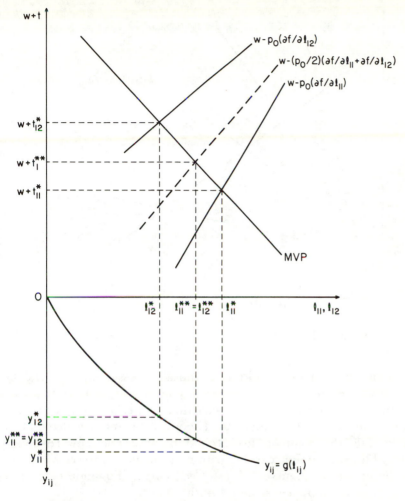

Figure 4.2

Finally, assume that the laundry's own input, l_0, is already deter-mined. Given all these assumptions, a graphic comparison is possible between the optimal tax policy with and without the constraint that each power plant faces the same tax. In Figure 4.2, the horizontal axis measures each plant's labor input. For each plant, the vertical axis can be used to measure the quantity $w - p_0(\partial f/\partial l_{1j})$ which, under our assumptions, is a function of l_{1j} alone. It also measures the marginal value product of the individual plant, $p_1 \partial g/\partial l_{1j}$, which is

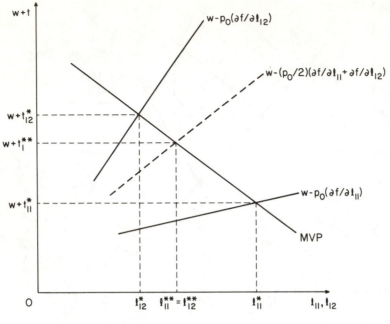

Figure 4.3

again a function of l_{1j} and is identical across plants. If the tax authority can discriminate between plants, the optimal taxes are t_{11}^* and t_{12}^*, since these are the taxes that lead each plant, acting as a price-taker, to fulfil equation (9). If both plants must be taxed at the same rate, the common tax should be t_1^{**}. The upward-sloping dashed line in the figure is the arithmetic mean, in the vertical plane, of the individual plants' $w - p_0(\partial f/\partial l_{ij})$ curves. Equation (11) shows that t_1^{**} leads to the constrained optimum.

The bottom half of the figure depicts the power plant's production functions and enables us to read off not only the aggregate labor input, but also aggregate output of electricity. The diagram is drawn so that aggregate input and output levels are both higher under the uniform than under the discriminatory tax system. However, this is not necessarily the case. In Figure 4.3, the optimal uniform tax is much closer to the higher of the two optimal discriminatory taxes, and the implied level of input into electricity generation is lower in the uniform tax regime. If the marginal returns to labor in electricity generation are not too sharply diminishing, the same is true of the implied output level.

Analysis along the lines of this section may be helpful in understanding externality policies in situations involving risk. Suppose, for example, the two plants are really at one physical location, but that at the time of determining the tax rate it is not known which way the wind will blow at the time of production. There are, in effect, two state-contingent plants, or at least two sets of technological relationships. In general, the optimal tax structure will involve a vector of state-contingent tax or subsidy rates. Indeed, a noncontingent quantitative restriction is equivalent to a particular—possibly far from optimal—vector of contingent tax rates. Under certain circumstances, a uniform or noncontingent tax may be optimal. It should also be possible to identify circumstances under which a uniform quantitative restriction is the superior of the two policies.

4.3 Criticisms and modifications of the Pigouvian approach

Pigou's tax/subsidy solution to the externality problem is not without its critics. A well-known paper by Coase (1960) argues that the reliance on market mechanisms gives a rather narrow view of the problem. Suppose it is possible for the recipient and generator of an externality to bargain costlessly. Then it is natural to suppose that the outcome of such a process would be Pareto optimal. A real income externality represents a "free lunch," and would surely not persist. In the laundry-electricity example, consider the inefficient allocation from which the Pigouvian analysis starts. There is an amount that the laundry would be prepared to pay as compensation, or bribe, in return for a reduction in smoke, and that it would pay the electricity generator to accept. This is true of any allocation that fails to satisfy the conditions for Pareto optimality. Hence, without any formal market in the externality, or taxes, the equilibrium of such a costless bargaining process will be optimal. Pigouvian taxes, however well-intentioned, can only do harm. Coase goes on to point out that the particular outcome will depend upon the initial assignment of property rights, and indeed that economists take an asymmetric view of the situation, labeling one agent as the damager or culprit and the other as the victim, in a way that presupposes a certain initial assignment of such rights. If the electricity generator is recognized by the law as having the right to pollute, it is natural to think of the laundry as being damaged by its exercise of this right. However, if the law recognizes the laundry's right to clean air, it is equally natural to think of the electricity generator as being harmed by the laundry's exercise of its right.

A further, more specific, criticism may be raised concerning the logic of the Pigouvian tax/subsidy scheme. If agents regard the tax rate as exogenously given, then they should logically recognize that the tax revenue itself is affected by the level of the externality-generating activity. Therefore the disbursement of this revenue, whether by lump sum or other means, should be regarded as endogenous.

Both these criticisms can be answered by emphasizing that the Pigouvian analysis must be interpreted as taking place within a competitive framework. To ignore alternative institutional arrangements is not a major weakness as long as we are aware that we are doing so. Further, the competitive framework is one that envisages many agents, both on the generating and on the receiving end of an externality. In such an environment, the process of bargaining may use up substantial resources, in which case the thought experiment involving costless bargaining will be of limited relevance. In addition, the presence of many generators makes it more reasonable to assume that each takes his or her income as exogenous when deciding how much of the relevant commodity to consume or produce. In a large economy, Pigou's analysis is logically coherent.

Having said this, we must admit that the Pigouvian approach, by remaining within one specific institutional context, cannot address issues concerning the optimal design of institutions in the presence of interdependence. These are, however, difficult issues, and it is not clear that economists have reached anything remotely resembling a definitive analysis. The extreme positions can be characterized—perhaps caricatured—as follows. The "vulgar Pigouvians," on the one hand, see the problem entirely in terms of adjusting certain parameters within the context of an imperfectly functioning market system, whereas the "vulgar Coasians" cannot envisage persistent inefficiencies and come close to arguing that what is, is best. Neither extreme view does justice to the economist whose name appears in the label.

The step from an analytical statement of necessary conditions to the implementation of an optimal allocation through taxes and subsidies raises severe informational problems. The virtual price, or marginal valuation, function $\pi_e^a(\cdot)$ that appears in (6) and (8) is not directly observable. Moreover, as (6) and (8) make clear, the relevant value is that which obtains at an optimal allocation. We can have all the information we like about marginal valuations in the neighborhood of the initial inefficient equilibrium without being any the wiser concerning $\pi_e^a(\hat{y}_1^a, \hat{y}_2^a, \hat{e}^a)$.

The problem of obtaining quantitative estimates of magnitudes not directly observable arises regardless of the particular remedy sought, and is hardly a criticism of Pigou's approach. However, it may be worthwhile to consider alternative schemes that are less ambitious and that have less exacting information requirements. One such approach rests on the observation that the social optimization problem consists of two parts. Suppose in our example of the laundry and the two power plants that the level of pollution can be defined as the function $\phi(l_{11}, l_{12})$. We may regard $\phi(\cdot)$ as arbitrarily given, and note that social welfare is maximized, or Pareto optimality attained, subject to this given level of pollution. The second stage involves choice of the optimal value for $\phi(\cdot)$. To undertake the second stage, we require information concerning the relationship between the output of the recipient and the level of the externality. In the literature on detrimental externalities, this is commonly termed the damage function. It is widely agreed that this is the most problematic relationship from an informational viewpoint, and a less ambitious approach is to set a given target value for $\phi(\cdot)$—that is, to set a given environmental standard—and at least choose taxes to ensure an efficient allocation subject to $\phi(\cdot) = \bar{\phi}$. The social optimizing problem is then

$$\underset{\{l_0, l_{11}, l_{12}\}}{\text{Maximize}} \quad p_0 f(l_0, \bar{\phi}) + p_1(g_1(l_{11}) + g_2(l_{12})) - w(l_0 + l_{11} + l_{12}).$$

Notice that, having set $\phi(\cdot) = \bar{\phi}$ at the outset, this maximization problem does not involve consideration of the marginal damage function, $\partial f/\partial\phi$. The set of taxes that support the resulting allocation will be a function of the exogenously set standard, $\bar{\phi}$, and the information required to obtain them involves the externality-generating function $\phi(l_{11}, l_{12})$, which presents fewer estimation problems. The reader will find further discussion of the informational requirements of alternative policies in Mäler (1974).

4.4 Equilibrium and optimum quantities compared

The Pigouvian tax/subsidy solution implies that an activity that causes costs to others should attract a tax, and one that generates benefits to others should be subsidized. It seems but a short step from there to the statement that activities that impose external costs should be discouraged, and those conferring external benefits should be encouraged. There are, however, good reasons for being cautious in

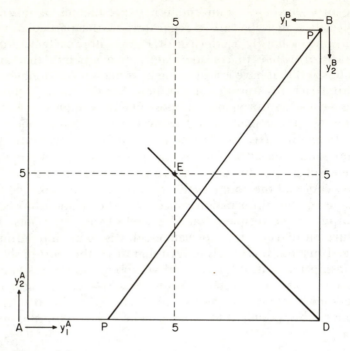

Figure 4.4

nferring conclusions about optimal quantities from statements about optimal taxes and subsidies.

To begin with, as we have already noted, there are generally an infinite number of optimal allocations, each consistent with a particular distribution of income. A simple example, slightly amended from Feldman (1980), is sufficient to clarify the point. Consider a two-consumer exchange economy, in which the agents' utility functions are

$$u^A(\cdot) = y_1^A y_2^A + e^A = y_1^A y_2^A + y_2^B$$
$$u^B(\cdot) = y_1^B y_2^B.$$

A's and B's endowments of commodities 1 and 2 are, respectively, $\Omega^A = (10, 0)$ and $\Omega^B = (0, 10)$. B's activity of consuming commodity 2 confers an external benefit on A. It is easy to show that if A takes the current value of y_2^B as given, the competitive equilibrium involves a symmetric allocation in which each individual consumes five units of each marketed commodity. This is the point E in Figure 4.4. The equilibrium price line is the line DE. There is also a locus of Pareto optima, the line PP. For any point on PP to be sustained as an equilibrium, the appropriate Pigouvian policy would involve a subsidy on B's consumption of commodity 2. An equivalent policy in this model would be to tax B's consumption of commodity 1, since it is relative prices that matter. Indeed, since there is no production in this example, the appropriate differential between the prices faced by A and B can be obtained by taxing A's consumption of commodity 2. However, if there were production in the model, such a policy would introduce additional gratuitous distortions. The important point is that the direct Pigouvian policy is certainly a subsidy on y_2^B. It is also true that if lump-sum transfers are arranged to maintain the two consumers on the budget line implied by competitive equilibrium DE, the optimal allocation thereby attained involves an increase in y_2^B. However, as Figure 4.4 shows, there are many points on the optimal locus at which y_2^B is less than its equilibrium value.

Even in the absence of such income effects, caution is required in making statements about quantity responses in moving from equilibrium to optimum. Buchanan and Kafoglis (1963) provide examples, two of which we discuss below, in which pure substitution effects imply a reduction in the level of an activity in moving to an optimum, even though it generates a beneficial externality. The first example involves a unilateral externality. Let the two consumers' utility functions be

$$u^A(\cdot) = u^A(y_1^A, y_2^A, e^A)$$
$$u^B(\cdot) = u^B(y_1^B, y_2^B),$$

where $e^A = y_2^B$. From A's viewpoint, e^A is an environmental commodity whose current value he or she takes as given. In addition to this constraint, each chooses values of the marketed commodities to maximize utility subject to a standard budget constraint. Letting the first commodity be the numeraire, denote the price of commodity 2 faced by individual h by p_2^h, $h = A,B$. One can imagine a given producer price, p_2, and a tax imposed on h such that $p_2^h = p_2 + t_2^h$. Then compensated demand functions for commodity 2 may be defined for both consumers:

$$c_2^A(\cdot) = c_2^A(p_2^A, e^A, u^A)$$

$$c_2^B(\cdot) = c_2^B(p_2^B, u^B).$$

Of course, the level of utility achieved by each is endogenous, and may be expressed in the form of the indirect utility function.

However, we follow other authors in ignoring the effect of real income changes, in effect putting $du^A = du^B = 0$. Consider then the effect of changes in p_2^A and p_2^B on aggregate consumption of commodity 2, which we denote by C_2:

$$C_2 = c_2^A(p_2^A, e^A, u^A) + c_2^B(p_2^B, u^B).$$

Holding utility constant while prices change,

$$dC_2 = (\partial c_2^A/\partial p_2^A)\, dp_2^A + (\partial c_2^B/\partial p_2^B)\, (1 + \partial c_2^A/\partial e^A)\, dp_2^B. \qquad (12)$$

Our formulation allows us to consider different tax rates for each individual. Consider a simple case in which $dp_2^A = dp_2^B < 0$, corresponding to the introduction of a uniform subsidy on the consumption of y_2 across consumers. Inspection of (12) shows that $\partial c_2^h/\partial p_2^h < 0$, from standard economic theory. However, the term $\partial c_2^A/\partial e^A$ cannot be signed on a priori grounds. We follow other authors in interpreting y_2 as the acquisition of immunization against an infectious disease. B's private purchase of immunization incidentally reduces A's risk of infection. In this event, it is quite possible that $\partial c_2^A/\partial e^A < 0$, since immunity purchased by A directly is a very close substitute for immunity that he or she enjoys as a by-product of B's actions.

If this effect is sufficiently strong, it can make the right-hand side of (12) positive, so that C_2 may fall as a result of the introduction of a subsidy on commodity 2. This result is most easily understood by noting that B's purchase of y_2 has risen. The move from equilibrium to optimum involves an increase in the consumption of commodity 2 by the individual who is the more efficient producer of immunity. In suitable circumstances, the resulting increase in the efficiency with which immunity is generated can allow the aggregate resources devoted to its production to fall.

Most of the subsequent discussion of such "anomalous" quantity responses have been based on a model of reciprocal externalities. Diamond and Mirrlees (1973) and Sandmo (1980) suppress real income effects by assuming a quasi-linear form of utility function, so that $\partial c_2^h/\partial u^h$ is zero for all h, whereas Cornes (1980), and also Cornes and Homma (1979), adopt no particular functional form. Instead, they use compensated functions and impose the restriction that $du^A = du^B = 0$. The utility functions are, in the reciprocal externalities model,

$$u^h(\cdot) = u^h(y_1^h, y_2^h, e^h), \qquad h = A, B,$$

where $e^A = y_2^B$ and $e^B = y_2^A$. If the consumers face a common price for commodity 2 both before and after the introduction of a subsidy, the aggregate response is given by

$$dC_2/dp_2 = \frac{(\partial c_2^A/\partial p_2)(1 + \partial c_2^B/\partial e^B) + (\partial c_2^B/\partial p_2)(1 + \partial c_2^A/\partial e^A)}{1 - (\partial c_2^A/\partial e^A)(\partial c_2^B/\partial e^B)}. \tag{13}$$

The two-way interdependence raises stability issues, which are reflected in the denominator of (13). However, given a simple adjustment mechanism, local stability implies that this term is positive. This means that at least one of the responses $\partial c_2^h/\partial e^h$ must lie between -1 and $+1$, but the other may be numerically large and negative. In such a case, the numerator of (13) may again be positive, indicating a reduction in C_2 in response to subsidy on its consumption. This requires a certain asymmetry, since one of the responses $\partial c_2^h/\partial e^h$ must lie within the closed interval $[-1, +1]$, and the other outside it. Such asymmetry again suggests the interpretation that the optimal policy encourages the activity level of the more efficient generator of a beneficial externality, so that the aggregate resources devoted to its generation may, in certain circumstances, fall.

4.5   Concluding remarks

The policies discussed in this chapter flow from the following observation. In a competitive equilibrium with an incomplete set of markets, a quantity ration that pushes a generator of externalities infinitesimally away from his or her equilibrium allocation has only a second-order effect on his or her welfare. Such a ration may always be found, which, by raising (reducing) the level of a beneficial (detrimental) externality, has a first-order beneficial effect on the externality recipient. Appropriate combinations of quantity constraints and lump-sum income redistributions exist that generate Pareto improvements and sustain Pareto-optimal allocations. If preferences and technology exhibit convexity in the space of marketed commodities, suitably chosen taxes or subsidies may be found that precisely simulate quantity constraints. The Pigouvian tax/subsidy remedy is precisely such a policy.

We have seen that there is a sense in which, though taxes are an indirect means of achieving a certain allocation, they may be easier to characterize qualitatively than the corresponding quantities.

Our treatment has referred to, but not treated in any detail, the important informational problems that have to be tackled as part of any policy intervention. Chapter 6 considers theoretical issues that arise in the design of allocation mechanisms so as to elicit honest revelation of agents' preferences in a particularly simple model of interdependence, that of the single, or pure, public good, and Chapter 16 surveys attempts to estimate demands for such goods empirically. Clearly, any detailed policy application requires more careful attention to such matters than we are able to provide in this volume.

PART III

Public goods

CHAPTER 5

Pure public goods: Nash–Cournot equilibria and Pareto optimality

The purpose of this chapter is to present and analyze a model of the simplest and perhaps best-known special case of an externality, that of the pure, or single, public good. Developed long before Samuelson (1954, 1955) brought it to the attention of a wider audience in the mid-1950s, it remains a natural and useful starting point for the elaboration of more general and complex models of public goods. Our exposition begins with a simple but versatile graphic representation and concentrates on two important features. First, we characterize and explore the comparative static properties of a simple and widely used concept of equilibrium, variously described in the literature as Nash–Cournot, Nash, noncooperative, zero conjecture, or subscription equilibrium. Then we compare such equilibria, hereafter called Nash–Cournot, with the set of Pareto-optimal allocations. The comparison, which the diagram depicts very simply, reveals the tendency for equilibrium to result in the provision of an amount of the public good that falls short of its Pareto-optimal level.

5.1 A simple representation of Nash–Cournot behavior

Consider a consumer whose preferences are defined over two commodities. The first, quantities of which are denoted by y, is an ordinary private good, and will be used as the numeraire in subsequent discussion. The second is a pure public good, of which the consumer is able to consume the total available quantity, Q. His utility function, $U(y, Q)$ is continuous, strictly increasing, strictly quasiconcave and everywhere twice differentiable with respect to its two arguments. The consumer receives an exogenous money income, I, which can be put to either of two uses. The consumer may purchase units of the private good or may acquire additional units of the public good. The number of units of the public good acquired by the individual is denoted by q. The quantity appearing in his or her utility function, Q, differs from his or her contribution q by virtue of the fact that the individual can enjoy the contributions of others. If there are n individuals in the community, $Q = \sum_{i=1}^{n} q^i$, where q^i

is the quantity contributed by individual i. From the point of view of the utility function, the individual's own contribution and that of the rest of the community are perfect substitutes. However, the individual is likely to be keenly aware of the distinction, since the former involves an opportunity cost in terms of the private good foregone in acquiring q, whereas the latter involves no such cost. Like the individual, we find the distinction important and find it useful to refer to the rest of the community's contribution separately. This we denote by $\bar{Q} = Q - q$.

Maximization of utility is subject to constraints. The simplest formulation assumes a linear tradeoff between y and q:

$$y + pq = I. \tag{1}$$

Our terminology and notation invite one to interpret this as a budget constraint, with p being the given money price of a unit of acquisition of the public good. It may equally well be thought of as reflecting any constant cost technology that converts the given quantity I of primary resource (e.g., labor services) into either of two final goods, in which case p is the marginal rate of transformation between the public and private good. Indeed, the diagram is consistent with an increasing cost technology. The total contribution, Q, may be thought of as producing the final public good, Z, with decreasing returns to scale:

$$Z = Z(Q), \quad Z'(Q) > 0, \quad Z''(Q) < 0. \tag{2}$$

If the individual's utility function is $U(y, Z(Q))$, the diagram and all subsequent analysis remain valid.

The pure public good is often contrasted with its extreme opposite, the pure private good, by reference to the nonrivalry and nonexcludability of its benefits. Nonrivalry is reflected in the fact that the total available quantity, Q, can be made available to each consumer. In the present model, this potential is actually fulfilled, so that each consumer, whatever his or her contribution q, is not denied consumption of the units provided by other members of the community. This is the nonexcludability assumption.

These two characteristics are clearly important ingredients of the notion of the pure public good. However, the classification of goods along a spectrum bounded by the two extremes, pure private goods and pure public goods, can be misleading. It suggests that applications to the real world will typically have to cope with situations somewhere on the murky line between the extremes, in which the special properties implied by the purity of the public good are no longer relevant and can therefore not help the analysis. As later chapters show, the present model is indeed especially simple, not because of the purity of the public good, but rather because there is in effect only one such good. Models involving so-called impure public goods are in reality models in which there are many pure public goods. Purity, it transpires, is a more robust and relevant quality than is commonly acknowledged.

The graphic representation of the single public good model rests on the observation that, since the budget constraint holds with equality, it can be used to eliminate the private good from the utility function, making it possible for the individual's utility to be defined as a function of the two quantities, q and $\tilde{Q}$:

$$U(y, Q) = U(I - pq, q + \tilde{Q}) = V(q, \tilde{Q}; p, I). \tag{3}$$

The variables p and I, while affecting utility, are regarded as exogenously fixed in developing the exposition. It turns out that exogenous changes in income can readily be handled, as we shall see. This is true also of the nonlinear formulation (2).

As a first step in exploiting the function $V(q, \tilde{Q})$ we generate the family of indifference curves in $(q, \tilde{Q})$ space implied by the individual's preferences. Clearly, higher values of $\tilde{Q}$ imply more preferred allocations. Further, the set of points weakly preferred to any given reference allocation must be convex, since it is itself the intersection of two convex sets. One is the set of all allocations preferred to the reference point, the other is the set of feasible consumption vectors defined by the linear budget constraint, (1). Thus in Figure 5.1 the points in the shaded area bounded by the indifference curve ii form a convex set. The indifference map is truncated by the vertical line BB, which corresponds to the value of q that would, by itself, completely exhaust the consumer's budget.

The individual's choice of q cannot be determined without reference to the value of $\tilde{Q}$. The simplest and most common assumption is that of Nash–Cournot, or independent adjustment, behavior. This envisages the individual as choosing the most preferred level of q consistent with his or her budget constraint, given the current value of the rest of the community's contribution. Starting at any allocation in $(q, \tilde{Q})$ space, the individual expects that any adjustment in his or her own contribution will provoke no perceptible response in that of the community. For each value of $\tilde{Q}$, we can imagine a horizontal line—the dashed lines in Figure 5.1—along which the individual perceives alternative feasible allocations as lying. The point of tangency between such a line and an indifference curve represents the

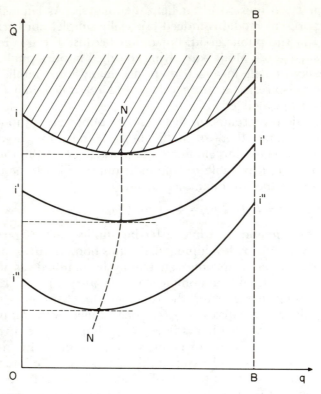

Figure 5.1

individual's optimal choice given the prevailing level of $\tilde{Q}$. Parametric variation of $\tilde{Q}$ generates a locus of such tangencies, which is the individual's Nash–Cournot reaction curve. This is the curve NN in Figure 5.1. It is worth characterizing points on NN algebraically. We know that movements along any given indifference curve imply, by definition, unchanged utility. Utility can be expressed in terms of either $V(q, \tilde{Q})$ or $U(I - pq, q + \tilde{Q})$. Therefore, along any indifference curve,

$$V_q dq + V_{\tilde{Q}} d\tilde{Q} = -pU_y dq + U_Q dq + U_Q d\tilde{Q} = 0.$$

The slope of an indifference curve is therefore

$$\left.\frac{d\tilde{Q}}{dq}\right|_{U=\bar{U}} = -\frac{V_q}{V_{\tilde{Q}}} = p\frac{U_y}{U_Q} - 1. \tag{4}$$

Recall that Nash–Cournot behavior implies allocation for which this expression is zero. The intuition is straightforward. An increment of q yields a marginal benefit to the individual of $U_Q dq$. The marginal cost is the quantity of numeraire good that has to be sacrificed. The utility cost of this sacrifice is $pU_y dq$. The optimum entails equality of marginal cost and marginal benefit, or $pU_y = U_Q$, which equates the right-hand side of (4) to zero, as stated.

A common concern in the literature on public goods is that the individual will tend to take a free—in our terminology, an easy—ride by relying on the rest of the community to supply quantities of the public good that he or she can then enjoy. More precisely, many analyses are based on a presumption that individual Nash–Cournot reaction curves are downward sloping, reflecting the idea that the higher the expected contribution by the rest of the community the lower will be the individual's own contribution. Figure 5.1 does not commit itself on this matter, which is easily explored with the help of some simple duality theory. The consumer's optimal choice can be thought of as minimizing the level of y, given the equilibrium values for Q and U. This defines the restricted expenditure function:

$$y(Q, U) = \underset{y}{\mathrm{Min}}\{y \mid U(y, Q) = \overline{U}\}, \tag{5}$$

where Q and U take their equilibrium values. We assume that $y(\cdot)$ is everywhere twice continuously differentiable. Figure 5.2 depicts this problem, and makes it clear that as Q is varied, the response $\partial y/\partial Q$ is simply the slope of the indifference curve at the equilibrium—in other words, it is minus the marginal rate of substitution, expressed as a function of Q and U:

$$\partial y/\partial Q = -MRS_{Qy} = -\pi_Q(Q, U), \tag{6}$$

where $\pi_Q(\cdot)$ is the marginal rate of substitution, or marginal valuation, function appearing in (6). Points on the Nash–Cournot reaction curve are characterized by

$$p = \pi_Q(Q, U) = \pi_Q(q + \tilde{Q}, U). \tag{7}$$

Letting $\tilde{Q}$ vary, while holding p constant, yields

$$0 = \pi_{QQ}(dq + d\tilde{Q}) + \pi_{QU}dU,$$

from which the individual's response to a change in $\tilde{Q}$ is easily derived:

$$\frac{dq}{d\tilde{Q}} = -1 - \frac{\pi_{QU}}{\pi_{QQ}}\left(\frac{dU}{d\tilde{Q}}\right). \tag{8}$$

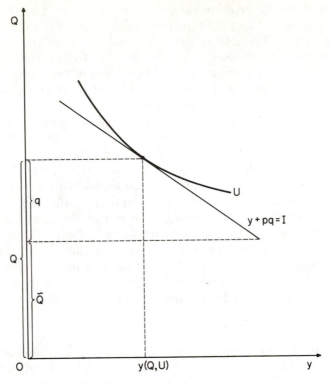

Figure 5.2

Equation (8) decomposes the total response of an individual's contribution to a change in the community's provision into two parts. The pure compensated substitution response is captured by the term (-1) in equation (8), which by itself precisely offsets the change in $\bar{Q}$. This accords with intuition, since $\bar{Q}$ and q are perfect substitutes. If a reduction of $\bar{Q}$ is accompanied by an increase in money income, $dI = -pd\bar{Q}$, the consumer's real situation is unchanged. Figure 5.2 indicates that the consumer will choose the same (y, Q) bundle, substituting q for $\bar{Q}$ at a one-to-one rate. The second term in (8) captures the real income effect. The term π_{QQ} will be negative, since an increase in Q will, at constant utility, reduce the consumer's marginal valuation of Q by comparison with y. Also, since Q is a good, $dU/d\bar{Q}$ is positive. Hence, the income effect will tend to encourage a positive or negative response according to whether π_{QU} is positive or negative. A positive value indicates that Q is a normal good. Equation (8) thus demonstrates the possibility that if the public good is a normal good and the income effect is sufficiently strong, the Nash–Cournot reaction curve may have a positive slope.

Taking a closer look at the slope of the reaction curve, we find that the individual's total consumption of the public good can itself be regarded as a function of the exogenous variables, p, I, and $\tilde{Q}$. It is, indeed, composed of two parts: $Q(p, I, \tilde{Q}) = \tilde{Q} + q(p, I, \tilde{Q})$. We have already argued that an increase in money income has exactly the same effect on the individual's real situation as does an increase in $\tilde{Q}$ of the same value—indeed, an increase in the latter is simply an increase in income paid in kind. An alternative way of confirming this is to use the budget constraint to eliminate q from the utility function, which then becomes $U(Y, \tilde{Q} + I/p - y/p)$. Clearly any change in $\tilde{Q}$ and I that leaves $(\tilde{Q} + I/p)$ unaffected has no real effect. Relative prices are unchanged, the individual faces the same constraint set, and his or her optimal values for y and Q remain unchanged. Consequently, we can write

$$\partial Q/\partial \tilde{Q} = p\partial Q/\partial I.$$

But we know that $Q = \tilde{Q} + q(p, I, \tilde{Q})$, which implies

$$1 + \partial q/\partial \tilde{Q} = p\partial q/\partial I$$

or

$$\partial q/\partial \tilde{Q} = p\partial q/\partial I - 1. \tag{9}$$

Consequently, if both the private and the public goods are normal, so that $0 < p\partial q/\partial I < 1$, then the slope of the individual Nash–Cournot reaction curve lies between -1 and $-\infty$. Most economists would accept the presumption that both goods are normal. This assumption, the validity of which is an empirical matter, has interesting implications for the model, since it ensures uniqueness of the Nash equilibrium and its stability under simple adjustment rules. Bergstrom, Blume, and Varian (1984) provide a more rigorous treatment of these issues than is possible in the present book.

Students of the literature on oligopoly will find Figure 5.1 strongly reminiscent of the reaction curve diagram often encountered in that branch of economics. This is hardly surprising since any situation involving interdependence between two agents can, if it is sufficiently simple, be cast in a form in which the welfare level of each depends partly on the value of one's choice variable and partly on the value of the opposite number's choice variable. As we shall argue below, the pure public goods model has a special structure that leads to particular and convenient properties unique to that model. One useful property should be mentioned here. Because of the convexity of preferences in $(q, \tilde{Q})$, inherited from the quasi-concavity of $U(y, Q)$, the Nash–Cournot reaction curve is continuous. This has agreeable implications for the existence of a Nash–Cournot equilibrium, to which we now turn our attention.

5.2   Nash–Cournot equilibrium

Consider an economy consisting of two consumers, each of whom behaves like the individual modeled in the last section. Their preferences and income levels may differ, but they face the same price p. Each has the problem:

$$\text{Maximize} \atop \{y^i, q^i\} \quad \{U^i(y^i, q^i + q^j)| \, y^i + pq^i = I^i\} \qquad i, j = 1, 2; \, i \neq j. \quad (10)$$

The two implied utility functions, $V^i(q^i, q^j; p, I^i)$, are represented by indifference curves in Figure 5.3. In this two-agent example, the rest of the community's contribution is simply the other individual's provision. Measuring individual 2's contribution along the vertical axis, we obtain an indifference map and reaction curve in the same way as for individual 1. At the intersection of their reaction curves— the point E in Figure 5.3—each is choosing his or her optimal q given the other's current contribution. Such an allocation, the existence of which is guaranteed by convexity of preferences, is called a Nash–Cournot, or simply a Nash, equilibrium. The aggregate provision of the public good implied at E may be read off by drawing a line through E of slope -1 and measuring the distance between its intersection with either axis and the origin—for example, OT.

The Nash–Cournot equilibrium has several noteworthy features. First, it is typically not Pareto optimal. The shaded area of Figure 5.3 constitutes a region of mutual advantage with respect to E, consisting as it does of allocations that Pareto dominate the Nash–Cournot equilibrium. The suboptimality of Nash–Cournot equilibrium will receive a good deal more attention below. A second feature is that, even in an economy of identical individuals, there is no guarantee that the equilibrium is unique. The prospect of multiple equilibria suggests that one should examine conditions for local stability, both to rule out some equilibria and also to shed light on the comparative static properties of those that remain. Sandmo (1980)

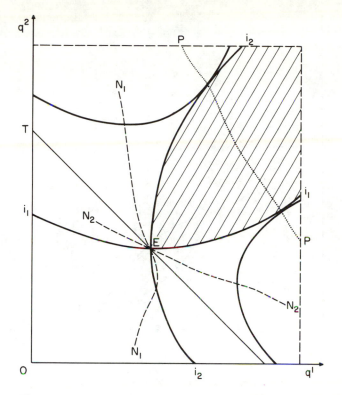

Figure 5.3

and Cornes (1980) have done this for a more general externalities model. Their analyses indicate that, under a simple adjustment process, local stability of an equilibrium requires that, in its neighborhood, the absolute value of the product of each individual's response to a change in the other's contribution should be less than one.

If there are multiple Nash equilibria in a public goods economy with a finite number of consumers, it is possible for a stable equilibrium to involve identical consumers choosing different allocations. Indeed, there is no guarantee that the symmetric equilibrium, in which consumers with identical tastes and income choose identical allocations, is itself stable. Figure 5.4 depicts equilibria of an economy consisting of two identical consumers. The two reaction curves are reflections of one another about the 45° ray through the origin,

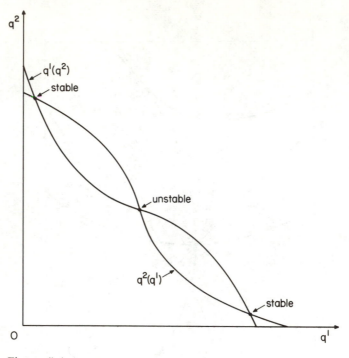

Figure 5.4

implying identical consumers. There exists a symmetric equilibrium but it is unstable. On the other hand, there are two locally stable equilibria. At each, one individual perceives his or her companion, making a small contribution and is consequently encouraged to contribute more substantially, whereas the companion, perceiving generous social provision, is led to take a relatively easy ride. Hence, the asymmetric behavior regarding public good contributions noted by Olson (1965, pp. 35–6) does not require income differences among the participants. This asymmetric possibility for public goods contrasts sharply with the "equal treatment of equals" flavor of equilibrium concepts in private goods economies.

Positively sloped reaction curves give rise to the possibility of multiple stable symmetric equilibria. In this case, such equilibria can be ranked using Pareto's criterion. This is not surprising when it is recalled that the Nash equilibrium is a second-best allocation. One may argue that multiple equilibria are not likely to be a problem since, as we have already argued, the assumption that both goods are normal is enough to rule them out. Although this is indeed the case, it is interesting to note that in Chapter 6 we encounter a model of an impure public good in which multiple equilibria may arise even though all commodities are everywhere normal goods.

Returning to Figure 5.3, we see that the locus *PP*, which passes through the points of tangency between the two individuals' sets of indifference curves, represents the set of Pareto-optimal allocations given the values of p, I^1, and I^2 that underlie the diagram. We later argue that it represents the set of Pareto-optimal points consistent with alternative distributions of income, a characteristic that greatly enhances its usefulness. For the moment, we focus on the first-order conditions associated with a Pareto-optimal allocation in order to emphasize the suboptimality of the Nash equilibrium. Geometrically, a Pareto optimum is characterized by equality of the slopes of the individuals' indifference curves. Equation (4) enables us to convert this into an algebraic expression:

$$pU_y^1/U_Q^1 - 1 = \frac{1}{[pU_y^2/U_Q^2 - 1]},$$

which may be simplified into the statement

$$p = \frac{U_Q^1}{U_y^1} + \frac{U_Q^2}{U_y^2},$$

or, expressed in terms of marginal rates of substitution,

$$p = MRS_{Qy}^1 + MRS_{Qy}^2. \tag{11}$$

This is the familiar Samuelson condition: The provision of a public good should be taken up to the point at which the marginal rate of transformation equals the sum over the individuals of the marginal rates of substitution between the public and the private goods. The intuition behind this cost-benefit calculus is straightforward. The price p measures the marginal cost in terms of the amount of private good foregone. On the other hand, since the benefits of the public good are not exclusive to any one individual, the marginal benefit is obtained by summing the marginal valuations over all individuals, hence the right-hand side of (11). Comparison with (7) clarifies the source of suboptimality in the Nash equilibrium. Individuals adjusting their own contributions independently of their neighbors will only add to the public good up to the point at which their private marginal rate of transformation, p, equals their private marginal rate of substitution. No account is taken of the external benefits flowing to others as a result of an increment of contribution to the public good.

The tendency for public goods to be provided at suboptimal levels is a celebrated result in public economics. It is also keenly debated. At issue are the relevance of the behavioral assumptions underlying the model of Nash equilibrium, the quantitative significance of the divergence between equilibrium and optimum, and the ability of economists to devise alternative practicable mechanisms that can be relied on to produce superior outcomes. For the moment we continue to work within the Nash framework and address the quantitative issue. The other problems will be taken up later.

5.3   An index of easy riding

By itself, a comparison of equilibrium with optimality conditions provides no direct information about output or consumption levels. However, the claim that Nash equilibrium will tend to imply under-provision of the public good is easily confirmed by looking at Figure 5.3. Both of the Nash–Cournot reaction curves, hence also their intersection, lie below and to the left of the locus of Pareto-optimal allocation, PP. The tendency for the equilibrium level of public good to fall short of its socially optimal level is one of several phenomena that have, at some time or another, been associated with the label of free riding. We prefer to use the term *easy riding*, since the problem is one of degree. It should perhaps be called systemic easy riding, to distinguish it from that of microlevel easy riding, or the tendency of an individual to contribute less in the face of higher perceived contributions by his fellows. As we saw in Section 5.1, microlevel easy riding depends upon the absence of strong income effects. However, systemic easy riding is an inherent feature of the present model, absent only in one somewhat extreme circumstance.

It is a surprising fact that, even though a good deal of literature is concerned with circumstances in which systemic easy riding may or may not be an empirically serious phenomenon, little attention has been paid to the construction of measures of easy riding. Figure 5.5 suggests such a measure. What is required is a scalar that provides a straightforward comparison between equilibrium and optimal levels of provision. In general, there is not a unique optimal level, and the measure shown in the figure deals with this problem by picking out the optimum that is consistent with the shares of individual contri-butions implied at the equilibrium E. The measure OE/OR expresses the Nash–Cournot equilibrium production of Q as a proportion of the associated optimal level, which lies at the intersection of the ray OE with the locus PP. Thus defined, the value of the index of easy riding will, in the case of a public good, lie between 0 and 1. A low

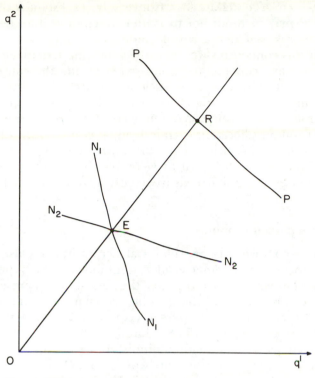

Figure 5.5

value reflects a substantial level of easy riding, while a value of 1 indicates its complete absence. Although it should not be interpreted as a welfare index, it gives precision to a widely discussed aspect of the public goods model. One obvious determinant of the extent of easy riding springs to mind: Suppose the indifference curves of both individuals are drawn so that, in the neighborhood of E, they exhibit a high degree of curvature. Then the optimum R will be relatively close to E, and the index will be close to unity. In the extreme case, suppose that preferences are such that in (y, Q) space indifference curves are L-shaped. There is then no substitutability in consumption. In (q^1, q^2) space, individual 1's indifference curves will be V-shaped, and the equilibrium will lie on the locus PP. This is the extreme circumstance alluded to earlier.

We have stressed that the ratio OE/OR is in no sense a measure of the welfare loss arising from a suboptimal provision of the public good. The equilibrium may be very close to the optimum, yet be associated with a large welfare loss. Conversely, a substantial shortfall of E below R may turn out not to matter much in welfare terms. It is natural to ask whether a simple index of welfare loss may be defined. In this connection we offer the following tentative suggestion. Consider an economy at E, and experiencing the consequent deadweight loss by virtue of its inefficient mixture of outputs. If that same economy were operating efficiently, each consumer could have a certain fraction of income, ΔI, removed and thrown away, such that in the resulting allocation each individual is at the level of utility associated with the inefficient equilibrium, E. The amount ΔI is a measure of the loss in the spirit of Debreu's coefficient of resource utilization and other similar measures, recently discussed by Diewert (1981).

5.4   An n-person economy

If tastes and endowments are identical across individuals, and if attention is focused on symmetric allocations in which each consumer chooses the same value for y and q, then the idea of the "representative consumer" can be used and the graphic technique can still serve as a basis for exposition of the n-person economy. The analysis of the individual proceeds exactly as in Section 5.1.

Figure 5.6 depicts the individual's indifference curves in the usual way, with the rest of the community's provision, $\bar{Q}$, measured along the vertical axis. Consider the symmetric Nash–Cournot equilibrium in, say, the three-person economy. It must certainly lie on the individual's Nash reaction curve. In addition, any symmetric allocation must entail $q = Q/n = (\bar{Q} + q)/n$, or $q = \bar{Q}/(n - 1)$. Putting $n = 3$, draw the ray through the origin along which $q = \bar{Q}/2$. This is the ray marked $n = 3$ in Figure 5.6. The intersection of this ray with the Nash path–at E_3 in the diagram—is the Nash–Cournot equilibrium for $n = 3$. Varying n allows us to trace out the equilibria generated as the number of identical individuals is varied.

Figure 5.6 also depicts the symmetric Pareto-optimal allocations generated as n varies. For $n = 3$, for example, points on the appropriate ray pick out all those allocations consistent with equal treatment of equals. Given this restriction, the best that can be achieved by the individual is at the point P_3, where an indifference curve touches the ray. That such an allocation satisfies Samuelson's optimality condition is easily checked. Since $d\bar{Q}/dq = 0$, equation (4) allows us to write

$$ p = n\frac{U_Q}{U_y} = 3\frac{U_Q}{U_y}, $$

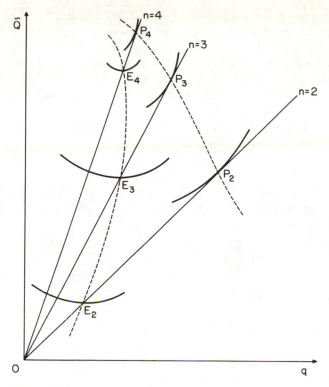

Figure 5.6

which is the equality between the marginal cost and the sum of marginal valuations of the public good. Figure 5.6 suggests that both the equilibrium and the optimal provision levels may behave in complex ways as n increases, so that the behavior of our index of easy riding, OE_i/OP_i, will not be straightforward.

Since the seminal work of Olson (1965), there has been much discussion of how the relationship between Nash equilibrium and Pareto optimum is affected by the size of the community. Olson himself suggested a presumption that, as n increases, the shortfall of equilibrium below optimum provision of a pure public good becomes, in some sense, a more severe problem. Such a result can certainly be obtained from a widely used special form of utility function, the so-called quasi-linear form,

$$U(y, Q) = y + f(Q). \tag{12}$$

This form implies that increments of income are entirely spent on the private good. In other words, the income elasticity of demand for the public good is zero. This has immediate implications for the slope of the Nash–Cournot reaction curve. In equation (8), π_{QU} is zero, reflecting the fact that the marginal rate of substitution is constant for given values of Q. Hence the slope of the Nash reaction curve is -1. This, in turn, implies that the aggregate provision of the public good in equilibrium is independent of n. On the other hand, the aggregate optimal provision can be shown to be an increasing function of n, since at an optimum

$$p = nMRS_{Qy} = n\pi_Q(Q, U). \tag{13}$$

As n changes, consequent changes in Q and U must maintain the equality (13) for given p. Hence, total differentiation of (13), suitably rearranged, implies that

$$dQ = -\frac{\pi_Q}{\pi_{QQ}}\left(\frac{dn}{n}\right) - \left(\frac{\pi_{QU}}{\pi_{QQ}}\right)dU. \tag{14}$$

But if $U = y + f(Q)$, then

$$\pi_Q = \frac{\partial U/\partial Q}{\partial U/\partial y} = f'(Q);$$

therefore

$$\pi_{QQ} = f''(Q) \text{ and } \pi_{QU} = 0.$$

Quasi-concavity of $U(\cdot)$ requires that $\pi_Q/\pi_{QQ} < 0$, so that Q increases with n. To sum up, the quasi-linear form implies that equilibrium provision is independent of n, while optimum provision rises with n. Hence, easy riding, as measured by OE_i/OP_i, becomes greater in larger communities.

The inclusion of income effects makes for ambiguity. Whatever one's judgment may be concerning the general presumption, Figure 5.6 demonstrates the possibility that easy riding may decrease with community size.

5.5   Some comparative statics

Up to now, we have explicitly assumed fixed values for p and for each individual's income. It is of interest to consider the consequences of changing these parameters. With regard to income, changes may be accommodated very simply without abandoning the diagram. Indeed, this is one of its major attractions. For convenience, initially set p equal to unity. Now consider the effect of increasing the representative consumer's income by ΔI—say, by one unit. Inspection of $U = U(I - q, q + \tilde{Q})$, the utility function underlying the indifference curves in Figure 5.1 and elsewhere, reveals that such an increase would be precisely nullified by a simultaneous increase in q of one unit combined with a decrease in $\tilde{Q}$ of one unit. This must be so, since these operations leave y and Q, and therefore $U(y, Q)$, unchanged. Hence, in Figure 5.1, the change in income has the effect of moving every point on every indifference curve one unit down and one unit to the right. The increase in income also shifts BB one unit to the right, since the maximum possible contribution, q, will now be one unit higher. Rather than shift every point in the preference map in the manner described, an equivalent and simpler procedure is to shift the origin upward, and also to the left, by ΔI (by $\Delta I/p$ if $p \neq 1$). This feature, the usefulness of which will shortly become apparent, distinguishes the pure public good model from more general externality situations, in which an income change generally shifts the indifference curves in complicated ways.

Slightly more generally, a change ΔI requires compensating changes in q and $\tilde{Q}$ of $\Delta I/p$, as can be seen from $U = U(I + \Delta I - pq, q + \tilde{Q})$. Figure 5.7, in which E is the Nash–Cournot equilibrium, demonstrates the effect of transferring an amount of income, ΔI, from individual 2 to individual 1. An important conclusion emerges. If attention is confined to allocations in which each individual is making a strictly positive contribution to the public good, the aggregate provision of the public good in the Nash–Cournot equilibrium is independent of the distribution of a given income among the consumers. This robust result, which appears to have been noticed first by Becker (1974), in no way depends on assuming identical tastes, but is rather a consequence of the purity of the public good. An income transfer of ΔI from individual 2 to individual 1 shifts the origin of Figure 5.7 upward and also to the left by $\Delta I/p$. The distance $O'T'$ equals the original distance OT, showing that the aggregate provision of Q is unchanged. The sole effect of the income transfer is to change the distribution of the public good contributions across individuals. An alternative way of understanding this invariance result, already exploited in our discussion of the slope of the Nash reaction curve in Section 5.1, involves substituting the budget constraint into, say, $U^i(\cdot)$ to remove q^i:

$$U^i(y^i, q^i + q^j) = U^i(y^i, I^i + q^j - y^i) \qquad i, j = 1, 2; i \neq j. \quad (15)$$

Observe that q^j and I^i appear only as a sum. Suppose we observe a Nash–Cournot equilibrium $(\hat{I}^1, \hat{I}^2, \hat{q}^1, \hat{q}^2, \hat{y}^1, \hat{y}^2)$. Inspection of (15)

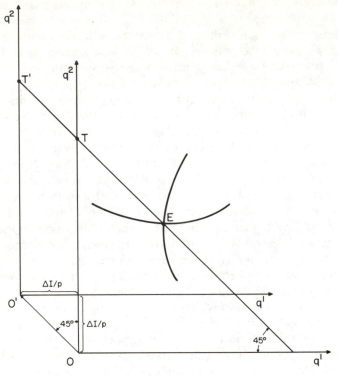

Figure 5.7

reveals that if income and contribution levels are changed in such a way that $dq^2 = -dI^1 = dI^2 = -dq^1$, then the resulting allocation is also an equilibrium. The marginal conditions for individual equilibrium are unaffected, and the values of Q, U^1, and U^2 are unchanged. In determining his or her equilibrium choice, individual i cares about the sum of $I^i + q^j$, not about I^i and q^j separately. The endogenous responses to an income transfer are such that the individual whose income has fallen experiences a spill-in—that is, an increase in the other's contribution—leaving the real situation unchanged. This property extends to the n-person economy since any redistribution can be decomposed into a series of simple bilateral transfers.

The invariance property is a consequence of the relationship between income responses and responses to community provision in the pure public good model, already given in equation (9). In addition to its role in the invariance property, this relationship is more generally useful in analyzing stability and further comparative statics, since it allows us to work with whichever set of responses is more convenient.

Since the effects of income transfers translate into a simple change of origin in diagrams such as Figure 5.3, it follows that the set of Pareto-optimal allocations represented by *PP* is unaffected. *PP* captures all allocations that are Pareto optimal, regardless of income distribution. Hence, our earlier assumption of fixed income shares, although convenient in the context of developing the diagram, is by no means an essential ingredient in exploiting it in the analysis of equilibrium and optimality.

What are the consequences of growth in the pure public goods economy? Recent years have witnessed many discussions of the disappointing fruits of economic growth, many of which base their analysis on an appeal to the role played by public goods in frustrating attempts to achieve the full potential for human welfare of advances in technical progress and accumulation of capital. Fred Hirsch (1976) provides a particularly provocative discussion of the "social limits to growth." To analyze such themes, we rewrite the individual's budget constraint and also use a different diagram. The question to be addressed, in an admittedly very simple model, is: Are there patterns of technical progress or resource accumulation that can lead to a reduction in welfare in a public goods economy?

The representative budget constraint is written

$$a_y y + a_q q = I. \tag{16}$$

The purpose of this modification is simply to allow technical progress to take place either in private goods production (a reduction in a_y) or in public goods production (a reduction in a_q). I is best thought of as a labor endowment. In an economy with a fixed population, an increase in I represents an increase in the effective labor force, brought about perhaps by an all-round increase in labor productivity. It is convenient to begin with this last case. We consider an economy of identical individuals, at a symmetric Nash–Cournot equilibrium. For illustrative purposes, the diagrammatic treatment considers the case where $n = 3$. Figure 5.8 depicts the representative individual's preferences in (y, Q) space. The line AA represents the set of allocations attainable by the individual if all three members behave in the same way. Since the total quantity of public good available for individual consumption is $Q = 3q$ for the three-person economy, along the line AA we have $a_y y + a_q Q/3 = I$. The symmetric Pareto optimum is the point P. However, each individual behaves independently and perceives each unit of Q as costing him, not $a_q/3a_y$, but

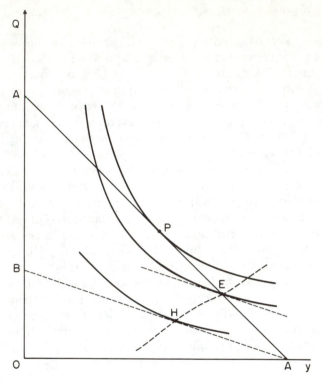

Figure 5.8

a_q/a_y units of y. For example, if the individual depicted in Figure 5.8 assumed $\bar{Q}$ to be zero, he or she would perceive his constraint to be AB, the slope of which is one-third that of AA, and would choose the point H. The equilibrium in this economy will be at the intersection of AA with the income expansion path passing through H. At E, each is equating his or her perceived marginal benefit and marginal cost, and each is contributing one-third of the total quantity, Q.

Now consider the effect on the equilibrium levels of y, Q, and U of an increase in I. Figure 5.9 shows an income expansion path, JJ, that allows for the possibility that the private good may be inferior. The initial feasible consumption frontier is AA. Two features immediately strike one about the diagram. First, there are three equilibria—E, F, and G. Second, it appears that an expansion of AA to $A'A'$, reflecting an increase in representative income I, might, if the original equilibrium is F, lead to welfare deterioration. The equilibrium F' represents a lower utility level than F. It turns out, however, that stability conditions rule out such a possibility. Consider first the response dq to a change dI, holding a_y and a_q constant. The demand function for q is

$$q = q(a_y, a_q, \tilde{Q}, I),$$

from which differentiation yields

$$dq = \frac{\partial q}{\partial \tilde{Q}} d\tilde{Q} + \frac{\partial q}{\partial I} dI.$$

But in symmetric equilibrium, $d\tilde{Q} = (n - 1)dq$; $d\tilde{Q}$ may therefore be eliminated, yielding

$$dq = \frac{\partial q/\partial I}{1 - (n - 1)(\partial q/\partial \tilde{Q})} dI.$$

From equation (9),

$$\frac{\partial q}{\partial \tilde{Q}} = a_q(\partial q/\partial I) - 1.$$

This may be used to substitute for $\partial q/\partial I$, yielding

$$\frac{dq}{dI} = \frac{1 + (\partial q/\partial \tilde{Q})}{a_q[1 - (n - 1)(\partial q/\partial \tilde{Q})]}. \tag{17}$$

Stability considerations (see Appendix) imply that, in the neighborhood of equilibrium,

$$-1 < (\partial q/\partial \tilde{Q}) < 1/(n - 1),$$

which implies that dq/dI is positive.

The implied utility change is given by

$$dU = U_y dy + U_Q dQ = U_y dy + nU_Q dq.$$

In equilibrium, $U_Q/U_y = a_q/a_y$; therefore

$$dU = U_y\left(dy + \frac{na_q}{a_y} dq\right).$$

Using the budget constraint to remove dy yields

$$dU = U_y\left(\frac{dI - a_q dq}{a_y}\right) + \frac{na_q dq}{a_y},$$

from which, by rearranging terms, we obtain

$$\frac{dU}{dI} = U_y \frac{1}{a_y} + (n - 1)\frac{a_q}{a_y}\frac{dq}{dI}.$$

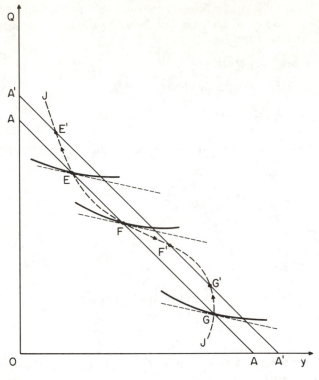

Figure 5.9

We have already shown that $dq/dI > 0$. Hence, dU/dI is positive. Essentially, the stability condition rules out the possibility of a welfare-reducing contraction in the level of public goods provision.

Technical progress in the public goods industry produces a similar effect. In addition to a real income effect, the relative price change generated by a reduction in a_q provides an additional stimulus to the production and consumption of Q, which is initially "too low." It is not surprising, then, that welfare must be enhanced by such technological change.

A reduction in a_y, reflecting technical progress in the production of the private good, is another story. Without pursuing the algebra, we show in Figure 5.10 the possibility that, as a_y falls, the level of welfare achieved in equilibrium may fall. The intuition is straightforward. Initially, Q is too low and y too high from the viewpoint of social optimality. A fall in the relative cost of producing y will, among other things, encourage further substitution out of Q into y. No

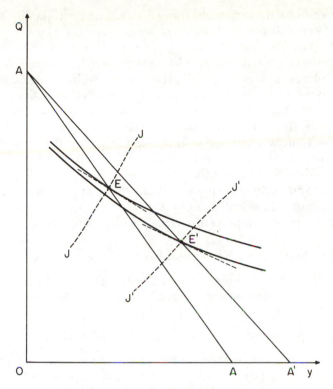

Figure 5.10

stability considerations protect the economy from the possibility that such substitution may dominate the welfare response. The greater the elasticity of substitution between Q and y and the smaller the initial value of y, the greater the possibility of immiserization. Such circumstances make the substitution effect large relative to the pure income effect flowing from the expansion in the feasible consumption set.

5.6   Concluding remarks

Of all situations involving reciprocal externalities, the example of the single nonexcludable public good is the simplest. This chapter has introduced a simple graphical exposition capable of showing the general inefficiency of the Nash equilibrium and also of displaying the comparative static properties of the model. Important questions remain. Given the inefficiency of equilibrium, it is important to consider whether there are alternative mechanisms capable of producing superior outcomes. This has motivated an enormous literature during the last 15 years, of which Chapter 6 reviews some of the more important contributions. The central problem confronted by this body of research is, arguably, the crucial problem encountered in any analysis of economic policy, namely, the fact that policy makers do not initially know the tastes of the individual consumers whose welfare levels are ingredients of any social welfare function. It is as if, in all the figures presented in this chapter, all indifference curves were omitted. It is easy to accept the claim that the design of a mechanism that simultaneously maximizes a function of individual preferences and elicits information about those preferences involves very significant additional complications. Viewed in this light, the material covered in the present chapter is but a small first step.

Appendix: Stability of Nash equilibria

First, we consider a two-person community. Following the analysis by Cornes (1980) of reciprocal externalities, we consider the following simple adjustment mechanism:

$$dq^i/dt = \mu^i\{q^i(q^j) - q^i[t]\} \qquad \text{for } i,j = 1,2 \text{ and } i \neq j, \qquad \text{(A-1)}$$

where μ^1, μ^2 are positive speeds of adjustment constants, $q^i[t]$ is the actual value of q^i at time t, and $q^i(q^j)$ is the uncompensated demand or Nash–Cournot reaction function for q^i, the statement of which suppresses the constants, p and I^i.

Linearizing the equation system in (A-1) in the neighborhood of the equilibrium $(\hat{q}^1, \hat{q}^2)$, we obtain

$$\begin{bmatrix} dq^1/dt \\ dq^2/dt \end{bmatrix} = \begin{bmatrix} -\mu^1 & \mu^1 \partial q^1/\partial q^2 \\ \mu^2 \partial q^2/\partial q^1 & -\mu^2 \end{bmatrix} \begin{bmatrix} q^1 - \hat{q}^1 \\ q^2 - \hat{q}^2 \end{bmatrix},$$

where $\partial q^1/\partial q^2$ and $\partial q^2/\partial q^1$ are the slopes of the first and second agents' Nash–Cournot reaction path, respectively.

Stability requires that the determinant associated with the 2 by 2 matrix be negative definite. Since the μ's are positive, stability requires that

$$\mu^1 \mu^2 \left(1 - \frac{\partial q^1}{\partial q^2} \cdot \frac{\partial q^2}{\partial q^1} \right) > 0$$

or

$$\left(\frac{\partial q^1}{\partial q^2} \cdot \frac{\partial q^2}{\partial q^1} \right) < 1.$$

If individuals are identical, then in the neighborhood of a symmetric equilibrium we can define $\omega \equiv \dfrac{\partial q^1}{\partial q^2} = \dfrac{\partial q^2}{\partial q^1}$. A necessary and sufficient condition for local stability is that

$$-1 < \omega < 1.$$

For the n-person community, we follow a similar procedure to establish local stability requirements. The assumed adjustment mechanism is

$$dq^i/dt = \mu^i\{q^i(\tilde{Q}^i) - q^i[t]\}, \qquad i = 1, 2, \ldots, n$$

where $\tilde{Q}^i = \sum_{j \neq i}^{n} q^j$ so as to include all but the ith individual's contribution to the public good provision.

As before, we assume identical individuals and linearize in the neighborhood of a symmetric equilibrium. Denoting the quantity responses $\partial q^i/\partial q^j$ by ω, the dynamic system can be written as

$$
\begin{bmatrix} dq^1/dt \\ dq^2/dt \\ \cdot \\ \cdot \\ \cdot \\ dq^n/dt \end{bmatrix} = \mu^1\mu^2 \ldots \mu^n
\begin{bmatrix} -1 & \omega & \ldots & & \omega \\ \omega & -1 & & & \cdot \\ \cdot & & \cdot & & \cdot \\ \cdot & & & \cdot & \cdot \\ \cdot & & & & \omega \\ \omega & & \ldots & \omega & -1 \end{bmatrix}
\begin{bmatrix} q^1 - \hat{q}^1 \\ q^2 - \hat{q}^2 \\ \cdot \\ \cdot \\ \cdot \\ q_n - \hat{q}_n \end{bmatrix}.
$$

A necessary and sufficient condition for local stability is that the matrix of coefficients be negative definite. To locate the implied bounds on the value of ω, it is helpful to apply elementary operations to the determinant of the matrix in order to make all terms below and to the left of the main diagonal equal to zero. If this is done, the value of the determinant, Δ, is seen to be

$$\Delta = |[(n-1)\omega - 1][-(\omega + 1)^{n-1}]|.$$

The determinants associated with the lower-order cofactors can be evaluated in the same way, and the requirement that they alternate in sign may be summed up by the condition that

$$\text{sign } \{[(i-1)\omega - 1][-(\omega + 1)^{i-1}]\}$$
$$= \text{sign } (-1)^i \qquad i = 1, 2, \ldots, n.$$

Let $A \equiv [(i-1)\omega - 1]$ and $B \equiv [-(\omega + 1)^{i-1}]$. Now consider an even value of i. The stability condition requires the product AB to be positive. If $\omega < -1$, then $A < 0$ and $B > 0$ and instability results.

Therefore, we must have $\omega > -1$. If this is satisfied, then $B < 0$, so that we must have $A < 0$. But this is equivalent to requiring that $\omega < 1/(i - 1)$.

A similar argument establishes the same bounds for ω when i is an odd integer. Clearly, also, if $\omega < 1/(i - 1)$, when i takes on the value n, the same inequality is satisfied for smaller values of i. Hence, the required stability condition is

$$- 1 < \omega < 1/(n - 1).$$

Since $dq^i/d\bar{Q} = (n - 1)\partial q^i/\partial q^j$, the local stability condition may be written as

$$(1 - n) < dq^i/d\bar{Q}^i < 1.$$

This shows that local stability is consistent with an upward-sloping reaction path, provided that the representative quantity response is not too large. In Figure 5.6, for example, an equilibrium is stable if, in its neighborhood, the locus of Nash equilibria has a slope greater than 1. If, however, quantity responses are negative, they can be quite large numerically without upsetting stability.

CHAPTER 6

Alternative mechanisms for the provision of public goods

The systematic tendency toward underprovision of a public good that seems to be implied by the model of Nash–Cournot equilibrium has encouraged extensive analysis of alternative allocative mechanisms and their evaluation against the yardstick provided by the set of Pareto-optimal allocations. The aim of this chapter, which is necessarily highly selective, is to review some of this large and varied literature. We begin with a closer look at the set of Pareto-optimal allocations.

6.1   Pareto-optimal provision of public goods

In the public goods economy, just as in its private goods counterpart, the optimality criterion typically identifies not one, but an infinite number of allocations—all the points on the utility possibility frontier between R and S in Figure 6.1. Any discussion of "the optimum" must presuppose either a very special structure, so that the segment RS collapses to a point, or the introduction of some kind of social welfare function that enables us to rank optima and pick out the optimum optimorum. Economists have, however, often expressed and relied upon the hope that certain allocation decisions can be made without reference to distributional considerations. In the present context, this is reflected in many treatments that refer to the optimal level of provision of a public good without any assumption concerning the distribution of private goods and hence of utility. Figure 5.3 makes it clear that such an attempt to divorce allocation from distributional considerations is generally not justified. Unless the locus PP had a slope of -1, the optimal aggregate level of Q will vary with the redistribution of private consumption, thereby requiring the distribution to be specified prior to the identification of the optimum level of Q. As drawn there, the optimal level of Q becomes higher as income, or utility, is redistributed in favor of individual 1, since the absolute value of the slope of PP is everywhere greater than 1. Returning to Figure 6.1, we find that the allocation X implies a higher level of public good than does Y.

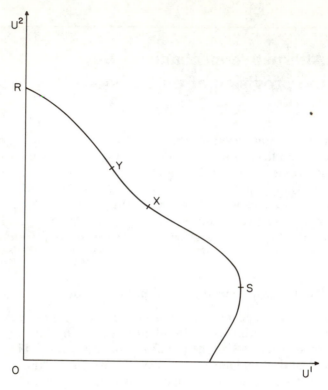

Figure 6.1

It is interesting to consider what restrictions must be placed on individual preferences in order to allow the optimal level of Q to be determined independently of distribution, so that allocations such as X and Y imply the same allocation of resources as between public and private goods production. It turns out that the answer to this question, which we provide below, is useful in dealing with a number of other aspects of public goods problems.

Consider the following experiment. Start from an allocation (y^1, y^2, Q^*) which is known to be optimal. Even if the aggregate tradeoff between Q and $Y \equiv y^1 + y^2$ reflects variable costs, there is a unique marginal rate of transformation associated with (Y^*, Q^*). Now suppose a quantity of the private good is transferred from one individual to the other. For the new allocation $(y^1 + \delta, y^2 - \delta, Q^*)$ to be optimal, it must be true that the sum of individual marginal rates of substitution, or marginal valuations of Q, be equal to the marginal rate of transformation at (Y^*, Q^*). If individual 1's marginal valuation falls by some increment when he or she receives δ, this must be precisely matched by the increase in individual 2's marginal valuation. This suggests that the marginal valuation functions of the individuals should take the form

$$v^i(y^i, Q) = \frac{\partial U^i(y^i, Q)/\partial Q}{\partial U^i(y^i, Q)/\partial y^i} = \alpha(Q)y^i + \gamma^i(Q), \qquad i = 1, 2, \quad (1)$$

where $\alpha(\cdot)$ and $\gamma^i(\cdot)$ are functions of Q. Notice that $\gamma^i(\cdot)$ can differ across individuals, whereas $\alpha(\cdot)$ is common to all. Differentiation of (1) with respect to y^i yields

$$\frac{\partial v^i}{\partial y^i} = \alpha(Q);$$

$\alpha(\cdot)$ is simply the response of each individual's marginal valuation to changes in consumption of the private good. Since Q is common to all, the formulation in (1) implies common response rates across individuals, so that transfers of income between them leave the sum of marginal rates of substitution, $\sum_i v^i(y^i, Q)$ unaffected.

The class of utility functions that give rise to (1) is easy to characterize. It has been shown by Bergstrom and Cornes (1981) that this class can be represented by the following functional form:

$$U^i(y^i, Q) = A(Q)y^i + B^i(Q). \tag{2}$$

$A(\cdot)$ and $B^i(\cdot)$ must, of course, satisfy certain restrictions if $U^i(\cdot)$ is to be quasi-concave, increasing in y^i and Q, and differentiable. The only further restriction is that $A(\cdot)$ be the same across individuals. It is this function that determines the responses $\partial v^i(\cdot)/\partial y^i$. A special case of (2) is that of quasi-linear utility, which assumes $A(Q) = k$, a constant. This implies that the marginal valuations $v^i(y^i, Q)$ are independent of y^i, which in turn implies zero income elasticities of demand for the public good. This is inconsistent with the findings of empirical studies, and is, as we have shown, more than sufficient to fix Q^* independently of distribution.

Equation (2) has an interesting parallel in the literature on aggregation of consumers in a private goods economy. Gorman (1953) shows that if the indirect utility function can be written in the form

$$V^i(\mathbf{P}, M^i) = F(\mathbf{P})M^i + G^i(\mathbf{P}), \tag{3}$$

where $\mathbf{P}$ is a vector of private goods prices and M^i is individual i's money income, then redistribution of income will not change aggregate demand at fixed prices. Equation (2) is of the same form, but is the direct utility function. It is not surprising that there should be such a close formal analogy. In a private goods competitive equilibrium, each individual faces the common price vector and chooses his or her own quantity. Individual quantities are then summed and equated with aggregate supply. In our model, prices and quantities change places. Each individual consumes the same quantity, Q, and his or her location in consumption space implies his or her own marginal valuation. Individual marginal valuations are then summed and their sum equated with the marginal rate of transformation at an optimum. Subject to certain technical qualifications, (2) characterizes the class of preferences that are necessary and sufficient for the optimal level of output of a public good to be independent of income distribution—in short, for the line segment PP in Figure 5.3 to have a slope of -1.

6.2   Lindahl's thought experiment

Consider now an alternative mechanism to the Nash–Cournot model presented in Chapter 5. Suppose we pick out the individual's most preferred contribution q, taking as given, not the rest of the community's provision $\bar{Q}$, but the rest of the community's share of the total provision, $\bar{Q}/(\bar{Q} + q)$. By varying this share parametrically, we can trace out the locus of optimal values of q. Such a locus might be termed a Lindahl reaction curve, after the economist who first explored the implications of such a thought experiment. Since the individual's own share is one minus the rest of the community's share, his or her contribution can be thought of as a function of his or her own share: $q^h = l^h(\Theta^h)$, where $\Theta^h \equiv q^h/Q$.

In Figure 6.2, the locus L_1L_1 is the Lindahl reaction curve for individual 1. A given share corresponds to a given ray through the origin, such as OR. Faced with this share, the individual's most preferred allocation is the point S. Parametric variation in the shares corresponds to rotation of the ray OR. The reaction curve is the locus of tangencies thereby generated. Individual 2's Lindahl reaction curve is constructed in a similar fashion. Convexity of preferences guarantees that both curves are continuous, like their counterparts, the offer curves, in the Edgeworth box diagram. This observation plays an important role in establishing the existence of a point of intersection of the two reaction curves. Consider L_1L_1 in Figure 6.2.

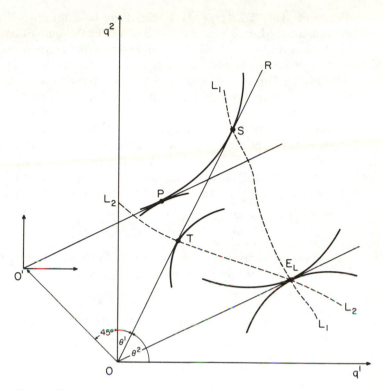

Figure 6.2

When $\Theta^1 = 1$, individual 1 will choose some finite contribution, implying a finite total output level Q. This is where L_1L_1 intersects the horizontal axis. As Θ^1 falls, and tends to zero, the individual will prefer larger and larger total contributions, Q, to which his or her contribution is small. In the limit when $\Theta^1 = 0$, his or her preferred allocation involves $\tilde{Q} = q^2 \to \infty$. This reaction curve asymptotes toward the vertical axis. Applying the same argument to L_2L_2 and appealing to continuity, we can establish the existence of at least one point of intersection.

Such a point—E_L in Figure 6.2—has an interesting interpretation. Denote the cost shares associated with E_L by Θ_L^1 and Θ_L^2. The diagram tells us that, given the vector of shares, (Θ_L^1, Θ_L^2), the two individuals agree on the most preferred level of aggregate public goods provision $\hat{Q}$. Since there is no incentive for either individual, acting as a cost-share taker, to depart from the unanimously preferred output level, the allocation $(\Theta_L^1, \Theta_L^2, \hat{Q})$ has a claim to be thought of as an equilibrium. Indeed, it is generally called a *Lindahl equilibrium*.

A Lindahl equilibrium has clear analogies with competitive equilibrium in a private goods economy as represented in the Edgeworth box diagram. In Figure 6.2, it is depicted as unique and as involving strictly positive contributions by both individuals. Neither of these properties is guaranteed to hold generally. One important property is, however, inherent in the concept of a Lindahl equilibrium. Since at E_L both indifference curves touch a common ray from the origin, the Lindahl equilibrium must be an optimum. Simple algebra, if desired, confirms that the necessary conditions for optimality are indeed fulfilled at E_L. The representative consumer's problem is:

$$\underset{\{y^h, q^h\}}{\text{Max}} \; \{U(y^h, q^h + \tilde{Q}^h) \mid y^h + pq^h = I^h, q^h/(q^h + \tilde{Q}^h) = \Theta^h\}.$$

The cost-share constraint can be substituted into the objective function, so that the Lagrangean becomes:

$$L = U^h(y^h, q^h/\Theta^h) - \lambda(y^h + pq^h - I^h).$$

Maximizing with respect to y^h and q^h yields the following first-order conditions:

$$U_y^h - \lambda = 0$$

$$U_Q^h \cdot (1/\Theta^h) - \lambda p = 0.$$

Rearrangement gives

$$U_Q^h/U_y^h = \Theta^h p.$$

Summing over all individuals, the familiar Samuelson condition emerges:

$$\sum_h U_Q^h/U_y^h = \sum_h \Theta^h p = p.$$

A Lindahl equilibrium, then, is optimal. The obvious parallels with the competitive equilibrium in a private goods economy raise the following question: Can any arbitrary optimum in the public goods economy be sustained as a Lindahl equilibrium? Consider an allocation such as P in Figure 6.2. It cannot be sustained by a ray through the origin O. However, suppose a lump-sum transfer is made from the second to the first individual. Such a transfer can move the origin to O', which lies on the common tangent at P. Starting from the origin O', there is now a vector of cost shares at which P can be sustained as a Lindahl equilibrium. We can summarize the analysis to this point in two fundamental welfare theorems of the public-goods economy:

Theorem I: A Lindahl equilibrium, if it exists, is optimal.

Theorem II: Any Pareto-optimal allocation may be sustained as a Lindahl equilibrium if preferences are convex.

Such a Lindahl equilibrium will generally be contingent upon a lump-sum transfer of income. In this respect, the model behaves precisely like its private goods counterpart. Mechanisms involving the combination of lump-sum transfers with sharing rules are commonly employed in negotiations involving institutional agents—for example, the block grants observed in negotiations between states and the federal authority may be seen as an attempt to deal with distributional concerns, while the system of matching grants helps to secure a more efficient allocation than would arise from the Nash–Cournot mechanism.

We finish this section with a brief discussion of the structure of the Lindahl equilibrium when preferences take the special form representable by (2). It turns out that in this case the tax schedules are particularly simple, with each individual's tax linearly related to his or her income. Recall that in a Lindahl equilibrium,

$$\Theta p^i = \frac{\partial U^i(y^i, \overline{Q})/\partial Q}{\partial U^i(y^i, \overline{Q})/\partial y^i} = MRS^i_{Qy}.$$

If preferences are of the form (2), then i's marginal rate of substitution is given by (1):

$$\Theta^i p = v^i(y^i, \overline{Q}) = \alpha(\overline{Q})y^i + \gamma^i(\overline{Q}).$$

But $y^i + \Theta^i pQ = I^i$. Therefore,

$$\Theta^i p = \alpha(\overline{Q})[I^i - \Theta^i p\overline{Q}] + \gamma^i(\overline{Q}),$$

which may be rearranged to yield

$$\Theta^i p = \frac{\alpha(\overline{Q})}{1 + \alpha(\overline{Q})\overline{Q}} I^i + \frac{\gamma^i(\overline{Q})}{1 + \alpha(\overline{Q})\overline{Q}}.$$

Given the optimal level $\overline{Q}$, individual i's tax bill has two components: a head tax, which depends on $\gamma^i(\overline{Q})$ and which could conceivably be negative, and a proportional income tax, the rate of which is the same for everybody. Summing the tax bills over the individuals confirms that

$$p = \alpha(\overline{Q})\sum y^i + \sum \gamma^i(\overline{Q}) = \sum v^i(y^i, \overline{Q}),$$

which is the first-order condition given by Samuelson. If utility functions are known, this equation may be used to solve for $\overline{Q}$, and the individual tax bill equations then solve for the Θ^i's.

6.3   The preference revelation problem

By itself, Lindahl's thought experiment only solves the problem of securing an efficient allocation of resources in a public goods economy by evading a crucial problem, that of the informational requirements for attaining the Lindahl equilibrium. Here the analogy with competitive equilibrium in a private goods economy breaks down. In that world, all that each individual has to know is his or her own preference ranking—or, if a producer, his or her technology—and the prices confronting him or her in the markets. As the number of individuals in the economy becomes larger, the *scope for individual dissembling is reduced,* and in the limit each acts as a price-taker; the result is a competitive equilibrium that is Pareto optimal. The public goods world is rather different, and, if anything, *the scope for profitable dissembling increases* with the size of the community. Consider again the two-person economy, and suppose that the tastes of individual 1, hence his or her true Lindahl reaction curve, L_1L_1, are common knowledge. By contrast, the only person who knows individual 2's preferences is individual 2. His or her true preferences, unknown to us, are reflected in the continuous indifference curves $i_2'i_2'$ and $i_2''i_2''$ in Figure 6.3. There is a true Lindahl equilibrium at E_L; however, attainment of this presupposes revelation of individual 2's true preferences. As far as individual 2 is concerned, L_1L_1 represents the offer curve facing him or her, the most-preferred attainable allocation being a point of tangency between L_1L_1 and one of his or her true indifference curves, $i_2''i_2''$ in Figure 6.3. This point can be sustained as a Lindahl equilibrium if individual 2 acts as if his or her preferences are given by the reported, or revealed, indifference curve $i_2^r i_2^r$. Even if others are behaving honestly, it pays a given individual to dissemble. Of course, the same incentive is at work on all potential contributors to the public good. This problem may be termed informational easy riding, to distinguish it from microlevel and systemic easy riding discussed in Chapter 5. Again, "easy" is more appropriate than "free," since it is not necessarily in the individual's interest to deny any desire whatever in the public good.

Clearly, in assessing any public goods allocation mechanism, its ability to cope with this problem is an important aspect to consider. Other things held equal, incentive structures that encourage individ-

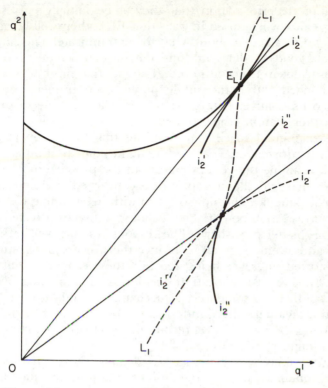

Figure 6.3

uals to reveal their true preferences are desirable. It is hardly an exaggeration to claim that this general problem, of designing mechanisms that make it an individual's interest to reveal truthfully information only he or she possesses, is one of the most important recurring themes in economics. Even the standard private goods economy is not immune from inefficiency arising from individuals misrepresenting their tastes, as Hurwicz (1972) has shown. Unless there is strictly a continuum of consumers, the typical individual can influence the equilibrium relative prices in his or her favor by sending false messages to the Walrasian auctioneer. Policy makers have a more difficult job than the mythical auctioneer, and are faced with the general task of securing socially desirable outcomes through the design and implementation of mechanisms that do not presuppose their possession of information concerning the technology and tastes of individual members of the economy. If those individuals are asked to communicate information that they alone initially possess, and that they realize will be used in ways that affect their well-being, they will think very carefully about what to communicate. The single, or pure, public goods model is only one of many in which the preference-revelation problem is encountered. The fact that most of this literature is couched within the single public good framework can be ascribed to its relatively simple structure, allowing one to progress rather further than in other contexts.

Before examining specific mechanisms that have been proposed to cope with informational easy riding in the context of public goods, we should examine the general nature of the problem more closely. The policy maker or Pareto-optimist is concerned with determining the optimal value Q^*, and not so much with determining the shares, Θ^h. By contrast, each potential contributor is directly affected by the value of his or her own share. The response of each will reflect this concern, and attempts by all to reduce their own share results in a set of distorted messages being fed into the mechanism that determines Q. In short, the allocation decision is contaminated by distributional conflict. If, somehow, a mechanism could be devised that makes an individual's share independent of his or her own actions, while making the overall level of output sensitive to the response of each, this might provide the key.

An early paper by Vickrey (1961) dealing with a private goods economy contains the essential insight. Suppose an auctioneer is selling an antique and wishes to auction it in such a way as to encourage each bidder to reveal his or her true valuation of the object. The common procedure of letting bidders push the price up until only one is left will not generally work. The winner buys the object at the highest bid price, which will typically fall short of his or her valuation. Vickrey's suggestion is that each bidder should be asked to write his or her true valuation on a piece of paper and submit this bid to the auctioneer. The rule is that, when the bids are examined, the object should be sold to the highest bidder, but at a price equal to the valuation reported by the *second* highest bidder. A little reflection should persuade one that revealing one's true valuation is, under this rule, a dominant strategy. That is to say, whatever one believes about the valuations of fellow bidders, one cannot do better than by reporting honestly. Reporting too low a value does not help, since it exposes one to the risk of not getting the object, while it does not reduce the price paid if one is successful. Recall that the successful bidder does not pay his or her own bid price. This simple mechanism, by destroying the link between the bid price and the price paid if one is successful, eliminates the scope for advantageous dissembling by bidders.

How can this idea be exploited in the setting of the public goods model? The problem of designing an incentive-compatible mechanism for determining the optimum supply of public goods and individual contributions is not straightforward. It is complicated by the fact that seeking the truth is not an end in itself. The objective is to determine an allocation satisfying several conditions, of which fulfillment of optimality conditions is but one. Other desirable features include the following requirements: (1) the implied cost shares should indeed cover the cost of providing the public good; (2) the determination of cost shares should pay some heed to distribution so that individuals are not bankrupted by their share of the cost, and (3) the scheme should not be vulnerable to strategic collusion by coalitions of individuals. It turns out that it is impossible to design a mechanism that simultaneously possesses all the properties considered desirable, and difficult tradeoffs seem unavoidable. We discuss one of the best known mechanisms, the so-called *Clarke-Groves demand-revealing mechanism,* in the next section. Like all such schemes, it requires a special functional form for utility functions. A significant feature of the scheme is that honest preference revelation is a dominant strategy for each individual, as with Vickrey's auction mechanism.

6.4   Clarke's demand-revealing mechanism

Our treatment of the scheme first suggested by Clarke (1971) for determining the optimal supply of public goods and individual cost shares, or tax rates, follows the analysis of Bergstrom and Cornes (1983), who use the class of preferences represented in equation (4):

$$U^i(y^i, Q) = A(Q)y^i + B^i(Q), \qquad i = 1, \ldots, n. \tag{4}$$

This is a somewhat broader class of preferences than can be found in earlier discussions. Since the function $A(Q)$ is common to all individuals, it is reasonable to suppose that $A(\cdot)$ is known at the outset. The problem is to provide incentives for individuals to reveal honest information about the functions $B^i(Q)$, which differ across individuals and therefore are initially private information. We assume that each consumer has an initial endowment, I^i, of private goods. These may be used to produce the public good by means of decreasing returns to scale technology. The cost of producing Q is given by $C(Q)$

where $C'(Q) > 0$ and $C''(Q) \geqq 0$. This reflects an aggregate technology, to which each individual's share of the input has to be determined. The set of feasible allocations is the convex set defined by

$$\sum_i y^i + C(Q) \leqq \sum_i I^i. \tag{5}$$

The mechanism requires each individual to reveal his or her functions $B^i(\cdot)$. We will denote by $R^i(\cdot)$ his or her reported function, which may or may not be the true one. The objective of the mechanism is, indeed, to provide incentives for the reported functions to be the true ones, $B^i(\cdot)$. The vector of reported functions is denoted by $\mathbf{R}(\cdot) = (R^1(\cdot), \ldots, R^n(\cdot))$.

The ultimate government objective is, we assume, to choose Q so as to maximize the sum of utilities:

$$\underset{\{Q(\mathbf{R})\}}{\text{Max}} \quad A(Q) \sum_j y^j + \sum_j R^j(Q). \tag{6}$$

Using the budget constraint (5), this may be written as

$$\underset{\{Q(\mathbf{R})\}}{\text{Max}} \quad A(Q)[\sum_j I^j - C(Q)] + \sum_j R^j(Q). \tag{7}$$

The government's choice variable, Q, is written as $Q(\mathbf{R})$ to remind us that the government has to depend on the reported functions $R^i(\cdot)$ in performing its optimization.

The heart of the mechanism is the rule determining individual i's cost share, or tax bill. Consider the following rule:

$$T^i(\mathbf{R}) = I^i - \sum_j I^j + C(Q(\mathbf{R})) - \frac{\sum_{j \neq i} R^j(Q)}{A(Q(\mathbf{R}))}. \tag{8}$$

This is less complicated than it looks. Recall that for each consumer, the amount available for expenditure on the private good is his original endowment less his or her tax payment:

$$y^i(\mathbf{R}) = I^i - T^i(\mathbf{R}). \tag{9}$$

Substituting (9) and (8) into the individuals' utility function (4) gives

$$U^i(\cdot) = A(Q(\mathbf{R}))[\sum_j I^j - C(Q(\mathbf{R}))] + \sum_{j \neq i} R^j(Q(\mathbf{R})) + B^i(Q(\mathbf{R})). \tag{10}$$

Comparison of (10) with (7) reveals an interesting property. Inspection of (10) shows that the only way in which the reported function $R^i(\cdot)$ influences i's utility is through the dependence of $U^i(\cdot)$ on Q. Varying $R^i(\cdot)$ will not affect i's share of the cost of a given level of the public good. The government's objective function, (7), and the individual's objective function, (10), are the same except that the government has to rely on the ith individual's reported function $R^i(\cdot)$. Consequently, since they are maximizing the same thing, the individual can do no better than by reporting to the government his or her true function. The government will then be maximizing (7) with $R^i(\cdot) = B^i(\cdot)$, which means maximizing the individual's true utility function (10).

The scheme outlined above encourages true reporting of preferences as a dominant strategy—no matter what others do, i's best course is to be honest. It has, however, a major drawback. There is no guarantee that the tax shares will raise enough revenue to cover the cost of the implied level of public good. This defect can be patched up but in a somewhat unsatisfactory manner. There is no way of amending the tax rule to achieve precise equality of tax revenue with the total cost $C(Q)$ without destroying some other desirable property. However, it can be amended to ensure that the revenue is at least equal to the cost. Going back to equation (8), add a term $\phi^i(\tilde{\mathbf{R}}^i)$, where $\tilde{\mathbf{R}}^i$ is the vector of reported functions of everyone except for i:

$$T^{i*}(\mathbf{R}) = I^i - \sum_j I^j + C(Q(\mathbf{R})) - \frac{\sum_{j \neq i} R^j(Q) + \phi^i(\tilde{\mathbf{R}}^i)}{A(Q(\mathbf{R}))} . \quad (11)$$

The presence of $\phi^i(\cdot)$ does not affect the individuals' incentives since its arguments do not contain R^i. The question is: Can we find a set of functions $\phi^i(\cdot)$ such that

$$\sum_i T^{i*}(\mathbf{R}) \geqq C(Q)?$$

Suppose for each i the government sets a target share Θ^i such that $\Theta^i \geqq 0$ and $\sum_i \Theta^i = 1$. The government now tries to fix $\phi^i(\tilde{\mathbf{R}}^i)$ so that for every i, $T^{i*}(\mathbf{R}) \geqq \Theta^i C(Q(\mathbf{R}))$. Rearranging (11) yields

$$A(Q(\mathbf{R}))[T^{i*}(\mathbf{R}) - \Theta^i C(Q(\mathbf{R}))] = A(Q(\mathbf{R}))[(1 - \Theta^i)C(Q(\mathbf{R})) - \sum_{j \neq i} I^j]$$

$$- \sum_{j \neq i} R^j(Q(\mathbf{R})) - \phi^i(\tilde{\mathbf{R}}^i). \quad (12)$$

Since by assumption $A(\cdot)$ is positive, the government's requirement will be met if

$$\phi^i(\tilde{\mathbf{R}}^i) \leq A(Q(\mathbf{R}))[(1 - \Theta^i)C(Q(\mathbf{R})) - \sum_{j \neq i} I^j] - \sum_{j \neq i} R^j(Q(\mathbf{R})). \quad (13)$$

This will be satisfied if the government chooses $\phi^i(\tilde{\mathbf{R}}^i)$ equal to the minimum value of the right-hand side of (13) with respect to Q—formally, if

$$\phi^i(\tilde{\mathbf{R}}^i) = \underset{\{Q\}}{\text{Min}} \{A(Q)[(1 - \Theta^i)C(Q) - \sum_{j \neq i} I^j] - \sum_{j \neq i} R^j(Q)\}. \quad (14)$$

Equation (14) gives an expression in which $\phi^i(\tilde{\mathbf{R}}^i)$ does not in any way depend on i's reported function $R^i(\cdot)$. It therefore introduces no incentive for individual dissembling. It also provides an expression that ensures that the total tax revenue implied by the tax rule (11) is at least sufficient to meet the cost of the implied level of public good.

A worrying problem remains. The operation of the Clarke scheme will typically result in an excess of tax revenue over the cost of the public good. Attempts to return this revenue to taxpayers will generate the very problems the scheme is designed to avoid—namely, attempts by individuals to influence their share, this time of the reimbursed taxes, by misrepresenting their preferences. The only way to avoid this problem, it appears, is to remove the excess of tax over cost from the economy altogether. In the resulting equilibrium, the economy will have thrown away real resources, while having a Pareto-optimal allocation of those resources retained. The empirical significance of the budget surplus problem is difficult to gauge. If preferences are similar across individuals, it will tend to be small. However, it does raise an awkward problem that does not appear to have received much attention. Suppose that, in the absence of the mechanism, the utility possibility frontier is *FF* in Figure 6.4, but it is suspected that without the benefit of a Clarke scheme the equilibrium would lie at a point such as X. Now a Clarke tax is introduced that implies a certain wastage of resources. Given the remaining shrunken resource base, a new utility possibility frontier may be imagined—*GG* in Figure 6.4. The new equilibrium, C, lies on the new boundary, since it is optimal with respect to the shrunken resource base. But this observation does not, by itself, enable us to rank it above X in Pareto's sense, as Figure 6.4 indicates.

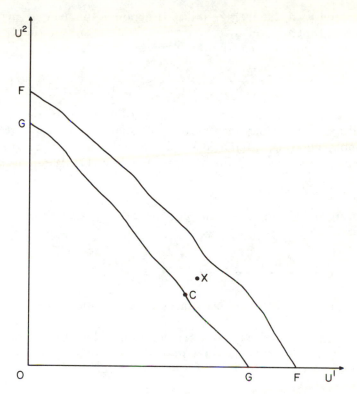

Figure 6.4

6.5 Majority voting

An alternative mechanism, somewhat simpler in operation and easier
to describe than the Clarke mechanism, involves a simple voting
scheme. Its information requirements are less exacting, but restrictive
conditions must be fulfilled if it is to have the virtue of producing
Pareto-optimal allocations. Suppose again that direct utility functions
can be represented by:

$$U^i(y^i, Q) = A(Q)y^i + B^i(Q). \tag{15}$$

The government does not know the individual $B^i(\cdot)$ functions but
has a good estimate of their average, $\bar{\bar{B}}(Q) = (1/n) \sum_i B^i(Q)$. In
effect, it knows the "average," or "representative" utility function:

$$\bar{\bar{U}}(y^i, Q) = A(Q)y^i + \bar{\bar{B}}(Q). \tag{16}$$

Associated with the average utility function is the average marginal valuation function, relating the marginal rate of substitution between Q and y^i to points in consumption space:

$$M\bar{\bar{R}}S_{Qy} = \frac{\partial\bar{\bar{U}}/\partial Q}{\partial\bar{\bar{U}}/\partial y^i} = \frac{A'(Q)}{A(Q)}y^i + \frac{\bar{\bar{B}}'(Q)}{A(Q)} = \alpha(Q)y^i + \bar{\bar{\gamma}}(Q). \quad (17)$$

Now suppose taxes are determined according to an average Lindahl schedule, under which each individual's share of the cost of the level of public good, $\bar{Q}$, is equated to his or her estimated marginal rate of substitution based on the average schedule (17). We then have

$$\Theta^i p = \alpha(\bar{Q})y^i + \bar{\bar{\gamma}}(\bar{Q})$$

or, using the budget constraint for individual i, $y^i + \Theta^i pQ = I^i$,

$$\Theta^i p = \alpha(\bar{Q})(I^i - \Theta^i p\bar{Q}) + \bar{\bar{\gamma}}(\bar{Q})$$

$$\Theta^i p = \frac{\alpha(\bar{Q})}{1 + \alpha(\bar{Q})\bar{Q}}I^i + \frac{\bar{\bar{\gamma}}(\bar{Q})}{1 + \alpha(\bar{Q})\bar{Q}}. \quad (18)$$

Equation (18) determines tax shares as simple linear functions of the endowments.

Now suppose that tax shares are determined by (18) and consumers now vote on the level of public goods. The utility of consumer i for any given level Q is simply

$$U^i(Q) = A(Q)[I^i - \Theta^i pQ] + B^i(Q). \quad (19)$$

Convex preferences imply that, given the present tax rule, $U^i(Q)$ is quasi-concave in Q, and hence is single peaked. Figure 6.5 shows utility functions for the members of a three-person economy. $\hat{Q}$ is the utility-maximizing level of Q for the ith individual implied by (19). Consider the situation of i for the given level $\bar{Q}$ of the public good. This marginal utility is given by

$$\frac{\partial U^i(\bar{Q})}{\partial Q} = A(\bar{Q})(-\Theta^i p) + (I^i - \Theta^i p\bar{Q})\frac{\partial A(\bar{Q})}{\partial Q} + \frac{\partial B^i(\bar{Q})}{\partial Q};$$

therefore

$$\frac{\partial U^i(\bar{Q})}{\partial Q} \gtreqqless 0 \text{ as } \frac{\partial A(\bar{Q})}{\partial Q}[I^i - \Theta^i p\bar{Q}] + \frac{\partial B^i(\bar{Q})}{\partial Q} \gtreqqless \Theta^i pA(\bar{Q}),$$

or recalling that

$$\frac{\partial A(\bar{Q})/\partial Q}{A(\bar{Q})} = \alpha(\bar{Q}) \text{ and } \frac{\partial B(\bar{Q})/\partial Q}{A(\bar{Q})} = \bar{\bar{\gamma}}(\bar{Q}),$$

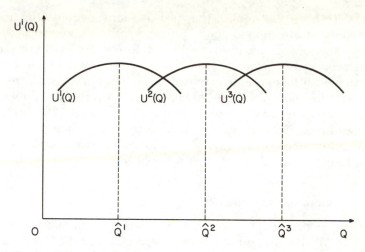

Figure 6.5

we have

$$\frac{\partial U^i(\overline{Q})}{\partial Q} \gtreqless 0 \text{ as } \alpha(\overline{Q})[I^i - \Theta^i p\overline{Q}] + \gamma^i(\overline{Q}) \gtreqless \Theta^i p. \qquad (20)$$

Now recall (18), which implies that

$$\Theta^i p(1 + \alpha(\overline{Q})\overline{Q}) = \alpha(\overline{Q})I^i + \bar{\bar{\gamma}}(\overline{Q})$$

or

$$\Theta^i p - \alpha(\overline{Q})[I^i - \Theta^i p\overline{Q}] = \bar{\bar{\gamma}}(\overline{Q}).$$

Substituting this into (20), gives

$$\frac{\partial U^i(\overline{Q})}{\partial Q} \gtreqless 0 \text{ as } \gamma^i(\overline{Q}) \gtreqless \bar{\bar{\gamma}}(\overline{Q}). \qquad (21)$$

Equation (21) tells us that individual i will find $\overline{Q}$ too low (high) if his $\gamma^i(\overline{Q})$ exceeds (is less than) the average $\bar{\bar{\gamma}}(\overline{Q})$ function implied in the government's perception of the average utility function, (16). This implies that

$$\hat{Q}^i \gtreqless \overline{Q} \text{ as } \gamma^i(\overline{Q}) \gtreqless \bar{\bar{\gamma}}(\overline{Q}). \qquad (22)$$

Now suppose that the functions $\gamma^i(\cdot)$ have a symmetric distribution. Then the mean, $\bar{\bar{\gamma}}(\overline{Q}) = (1/n) \sum \gamma^i(\overline{Q})$, equals the mean value of the

$\gamma^i(\cdot)$'s. Hence, (22) implies that just as many people want more as want less of the public good. Consequently, $\bar{Q}$ coincides with the median value of the most preferred levels, $\hat{Q}^i$. It follows that if preferences are symmetrically distributed in the sense described above, and if taxes are determined according to (18), majority voting will lead to selection of the Pareto-optimal level of the public good. This represents a slight generalization of Bowen (1943), who assumes a quasi-linear utility function. His contribution is notable also for its clear statement, usually associated with Samuelson, of the necessary condition for optimal supply of a public good.

6.6   Concluding remarks

We began this chapter with a brief discussion of the properties of the set of Pareto-optimal allocations, and followed that with an analysis of Lindahl's equilibrium concept in the presence of public goods. Once preferences have been determined, the role of Lindahl prices in sustaining a Pareto-optimal allocation is clearly analogous to the competitive price system in a private goods economy. Bergstrom (1976) generalizes the concept of Lindahl prices to more complicated externalities models and emphasizes the analogy. New and difficult problems, which, although not peculiar to public goods, are particularly severe in their presence, emerge in Section 6.3. By contrast with the world of private goods, an economy with a public good is still very susceptible to manipulation by individuals with private information concerning their own preferences, even when the size of the community is large. Clarke's demand-revealing mechanism is one of a number of schemes thrown up by the hunt for incentive-compatible mechanisms—that is, mechanisms that provide incentives for individuals to reveal their true preferences. Other schemes, differing by virtue either of the assumptions required or the desirable properties they possess, are referred to at the end of Chapter 8, since a proper appreciation is helped by some familiarity with game theory. This remains an active and controversial area of research.

CHAPTER 7

Public goods in general

The public goods model formalized by Samuelson (1955) has provided not only a starting point for countless extensions and modifications, but also a target for criticism. Early critics, such as Margolis (1955), were quick to point out the difficulty of finding situations that precisely fitted the model. It certainly envisages a particularly simple structure. If any given individual increases his or her contribution to Q by some increment, then each and every individual's consumption of Q rises by precisely the same amount. The only characteristic that distinguishes the contributor of this increment from his or her fellows is that he or she has presumably had to reduce his or her private consumption. Leaving aside the implications of the budget constraint, and concentrating on the utility function, $U^i(y^i, Q)$, one can characterize the model by observing that the distribution of individual contributions is of no consequence. A given increment of Q affects individual i in the same way regardless of its source.

The model is more general than is sometimes thought. It does not imply, as has occasionally been claimed, that an increase in the quantity Q affects every recipient in the same way, whatever that may mean. Indeed, what one person regards as a public good may be a public bad to another, so that even the sign of $\partial U^i(y^i, Q)/\partial Q$ may differ across individuals. Nothing in the basic model precludes such a possibility. Nevertheless, one can readily sympathize with those impatient to get to grips with applications. Unfortunately, the phrasing of a good deal of criticism seems to suggest a much more limited role for the basic model than it deserves. The picture is often drawn of a whole continuous spectrum of models, of which the pure public goods model is at one end, and the pure private goods model at the other. This seems to suggest that real world situations typically lie in a murky area in between, which neither extreme case can cast much light on. This is misleading. It is not the purity of the model that accounts for its simplicity and for its inadequacy as a description of many real phenomena, but rather the presence of only one public good. Armed with appropriate definitions of commodities, we can model any externalities situation as one involving public goods. Naturally, the move from one to many public goods will increase the complexity of the resulting model. But insight provided by Samuelson's famous optimality conditions remain available to us.

The models encountered in this chapter share the following structure. Each individual, in addition to consuming a pure private good, can contribute toward, or acquire, units of a second good, the public good. Each unit thereby acquired adds to the sum total of the good, which is available to all. But in addition the subscriber derives utility from his or her contribution alone. In the notation of Chapter 5, the individual's utility function has an extra term in it:

$$U^i = U^i(y^i, q^i, Q) \qquad i = 1, \ldots, n. \tag{1}$$

This modification to the pure public goods model may be thought of as one with n public goods—as, indeed, can the model in Chapter 5. Observe that i's utility function may be written as

$$\phi^i = \phi^i(y^i, q^1, q^2, \ldots, q^n) \qquad i = 1, \ldots, n, \tag{2}$$

where q^i is like a public good in that it is equally available to all. Since it is defined as i's subscription, it is a public good of which individual i is the sole provider. If a planner were now given the task of calculating a Pareto optimum for an economy of n consumers with tastes represented by (2), subject to the aggregate resource constraint, $\sum_i y^i + p\sum_i q^i = \sum_i I^i$, his or her first-order conditions would certainly be familiar:

$$\partial U^i/\partial y^i = \lambda \qquad i = 1, \ldots, n$$

$$\sum_j \partial U^j/\partial q^i = \lambda p \qquad i = 1, \ldots, n \tag{3}$$

$$\sum_j \frac{\partial U^j/\partial q^i}{\partial U^j/\partial y^j} = p \qquad i = 1, \ldots, n.$$

For both models, the set of equations provided by (3) summarizes the first-order conditions that equate the sum of marginal rates of substitution with the marginal rate of transformation. The difference is that in the pure public goods model of Chapter 5,

$$\frac{\partial U^j/\partial q^i}{\partial U^j/\partial y^j} = \frac{\partial U^j/\partial q^k}{\partial U^j/\partial y^j}$$

for all k, so that the n equations in (3) are identical, leaving one with the single Samuelson condition. In the more general case of (1), this equality does not hold if, say, $i = j \neq k$. The effect on an individual's own utility of an increment in his own subscription now contains an extra component, which makes it different from the effect on his utility of someone else's contribution.

It is not difficult to think of applications to which utility functions such as (1) are relevant. By immunizing oneself against an infectious disease, the individual confers a small benefit on one's fellows, by slightly reducing the probability of their becoming infected. At the same time, the benefit to oneself is particularly great. The acquisition of certain types of education is often asserted to have benefits for society at large, in addition to the purely private benefits generated for the student. An individual's production of academic research, or of a book on public goods, contributes generally to the reputation of his or her department—we hesitate to put a sign on this contribution—while generating additional benefits, one hopes, to that individual. The acts of charity and of saving and the activities of military alliances are a few of the many instances that have been claimed as examples of the joint production of both a public and a private benefit.

The additional scope provided by the formulation in (1) is particularly evident when one observes that Q may be interpreted as a public bad—that is, $\partial U^i(\cdot)/\partial Q < 0$. By contrast with the model of Chapter 5, this assumption is consistent with the possibility that individuals will voluntarily consume the individual quantities q^i. For a given income and given expected value for $\tilde{Q}$, the typical individual will acquire q up to the point at which

$$dU = (\partial U/\partial y)dy + (\partial U/\partial q)dq + (\partial U/\partial Q)dq = 0$$

or, using the budget constraint to remove dy,

$$dU = (\partial U/\partial q - p\partial U/\partial y + \partial U/\partial Q)dq = 0.$$

Since the first term in the brackets is positive, the individual may well prefer to make a positive contribution q. In the case of a pure public bad, for which $U(\cdot) = U(y, Q)$ and $\partial U/\partial Q < 0$, the equilibrium value of q will be zero.

This suggests that the generalization represented by (1) is considerable. Not only does it represent that class of models often termed impure public goods, but it can also accommodate congestion phenomena. The driver who, by using the highway, slightly increases the level of congestion can be fitted into the resulting model. So too can the suburban dweller who burns leaves in autumn, or uses a noisy mower to cut his or her grass. On a more global scale, the allegedly harmful effects of the depletion of the Earth's ozone layer, and the Greenhouse Effect resulting from the gradual accumulation of carbon dioxide in the atmosphere as a by-product of desired private goods, are both phenomena that can be captured by (1).

Subsequent sections of this chapter consider several models that build on the joint production model of (1). The first is the straightforward case in which both $\partial U^i/\partial q^i$ and $\partial U^i/\partial Q$ are positive—the impure public goods model. We show that it is amenable to the graphic approach used in our discussion of the pure public good. We then explore the extent to which the properties of the simpler model are affected by the introduction of intrinsically joint production of private and public goods.

7.1   Impure public goods

Our analysis of impure public goods closely follows our recent treatment in Cornes and Sandler (1984a), which draws heavily on the characteristics approach to consumer behavior developed by Gorman (1980) and Lancaster (1971). We should also draw attention to Sandmo (1973), who systematically applied this approach to public goods theory. The consumer has preferences over three characteristics—y, x, and Z. His or her utility function, $U(y, x, Z)$, is strictly increasing and strictly quasi-concave, continuous, and everywhere twice differentiable. In short, it is as convenient and as well-behaved a utility function as one could wish for. There are two marketed commodities. Each unit of the first generates one unit of y for the consumer. Moreover, the commodity has no effect on other individuals. It may therefore be thought of as identical to the characteristic y. The symbol y can consequently be used to denote either the first characteristic or the good that generates it. We use y as the numeraire in all that follows.

The second good, q, generates both x and Z. One unit of q produces a units of x and b units of Z; a and b are exogenously given coefficients reflecting a simple process, whereby x and Z are jointly produced in fixed proportions by the purchase of q. The model has one more crucial element. The total consumption by the individual of the third characteristic is

$$Z = z^1 + z^2 + \cdots + z^n.$$

Z is a public characteristic, the quantity of which is the sum of each individual's contribution, which in turn is determined by the relation $z^i = bq^i$. The acquisition by i of an extra unit of the commodity q has three effects: It increases his or her consumption of the private characteristic x, it increases his or her consumption of the public characteristic Z, and it increases the quantity of the public characteristic available to each of his or her fellow citizens.

The final elements of the model are the constraints that define the feasible consumption set from which the individual chooses his or her most preferred point. The first is the conventional budget constraint:

$$y + pq = I.$$

The second represents the individual's expectation concerning the rest of the community's generation of the public characteristic, $\tilde{Z} \equiv Z - z$. We adopt the Nash–Cournot assumption that the individual regards $\tilde{Z}$ as exogenously determined. If the parameter b is the same across individuals, this is equivalent to assuming that $\tilde{Q}$ is taken as given. The individual's utility function may then be expressed as a function of marketed commodities

$$U(\cdot) = U(y, x, Z) = U(y, aq, bQ). \tag{4}$$

Since a and b are fixed, utility can therefore be defined in terms of the marketed commodities:

$$U(\cdot) = V(y, q, \tilde{Q}) \tag{5}$$

where the individual chooses y and q subject to his or her budget constraint and the given value for $\tilde{Q}$. Equation (5) enables us to conduct the entire analysis in terms of the marketed commodities since they are the variables both in $V(\cdot)$ and in the budget constraint. The resulting model has an interesting structure. Since the original utility function $U(\cdot)$ has three characteristics as arguments, we can investigate the implications of complementarity between any two of them. In particular, we can analyze situations in which x and Z, the characteristics jointly produced by q, are close complements. Intuition suggests the conjecture that in this circumstance an increase in $\tilde{Z}$ may encourage the individual to consume more of the complementary private characteristic x. In doing so, the individual necessarily generates additional z through the acquisition of extra q, so that his or her reaction curve $q(\tilde{Q})$—or $z(\tilde{Z})$—may have a positive slope. This clearly has implications for the notion of microlevel easy riding. To explore this conjecture, we have to relate the pattern of preferences in characteristics space to the implied pattern of behavior in goods space. Our objective is to proceed through equation (5) to use the budget constraint to define preferences, for given I and p, in terms

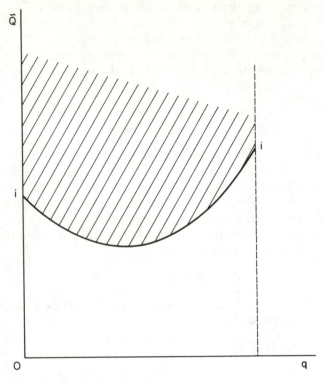

Figure 7.1

of q and $\bar{Q}$. This gives us access to a diagrammatic exposition similar to that used to analyze pure public goods.

Observe that if $U(y, x, Z)$ is strictly quasi-concave, $V(y, q, \bar{Q})$ must be quasi-concave in its three arguments, since the goods and characteristics are related in a linear fashion. Further, using the budget constraint, we may define

$$V^*(q, \bar{Q}) = V(I - pq, q, \bar{Q}).$$

Again, $V^*(\cdot)$ is quasi-concave. This means that for a given pair of values for I and p, the set of points $(q, \bar{Q})$ that are weakly preferred to any given allocation is convex. Figure 7.1 depicts such sets as the hatched areas bounded by the relevant indifference curves. The vertical dashed line that truncates the figure represents the level of q that just exhausts the individual's budget.

Suppose the individual acts as a quantity-taker. What is the shape of the implied Nash–Cournot reaction curve, $q(\bar{Q})$? In order to relate the response $\partial q/\partial \bar{Q}$ to the individual's preferences, observe that marginal rates of substitution in the characteristics and goods spaces can be linked in the following way. Equations (4) and (5) state that

$$V(y, q, \bar{Q}) = U(y, x, Z) = U[y, aq, b(\bar{Q} + q)].$$

Differentiation yields the relationships:

$$\partial V/\partial q = a(\partial U/\partial x) + b(\partial U/\partial Z)$$

and

$$\partial V/\partial y = \partial U/\partial y.$$

Taking a ratio yields

$$\frac{\partial V/\partial q}{\partial V/\partial y} = a\frac{\partial U/\partial x}{\partial U/\partial y} + b\frac{\partial U/\partial Z}{\partial U/\partial y}$$

or, expressed in terms of marginal rates of substitution,

$$MRS_{qy} = aMRS_{xy} + bMRS_{zy}. \tag{6}$$

It is useful to think of the marginal rates of substitution on the right-hand side of (6) explicitly as functions of x, Z, and u. Such functions may be derived by noting that the individual's optimizing behavior defines a restricted cost function, as discussed by Deaton and Muellbauer (1980, p. 110):

$$y(x, Z, u) \equiv \underset{\{y\}}{\text{Min }} [y \mid U(y, x, Z) \geqq u], \tag{7}$$

where the variables x, Z, and u take their equilibrium values. We assume that $y(\cdot)$ is everywhere twice continuously differentiable. Its partial derivatives with respect to x and Z yield compensated inverse demand functions, expressing the individual's marginal valuations of x and Z, respectively, as functions of x, Z, and u:

$$-\partial y(x, Z, u)/\partial x = MRS_{xy} = \pi_x(x, Z, u)$$

$$-\partial y(x, Z, u)/\partial Z = MRS_{zy} = \pi_z(x, Z, u).$$

The functions $\pi_x(\cdot)$ and $\pi_z(\cdot)$ have a number of properties that are analogous to those of conventional compensated demand functions and that prove useful in analyzing the comparative static properties of the model. The matrix of second derivatives of $y(\cdot)$,

$$\begin{bmatrix} \partial^2 y/\partial x^2 & \partial^2 y/\partial x \partial Z \\ \partial^2 y/\partial Z \partial x & \partial^2 y/\partial Z \end{bmatrix} = \begin{bmatrix} -\partial \pi_x/\partial x & -\partial \pi_x/\partial Z \\ -\partial \pi_z/\partial x & -\partial \pi_z/\partial Z \end{bmatrix}$$

is symmetric and positive semidefinite, which implies the following properties:

$$\partial\pi_x/\partial x \lessgtr 0, \quad \partial\pi_z/\partial Z \lessgtr 0.$$

$$\begin{vmatrix} \partial\pi_x/\partial x & \partial\pi_x/\partial Z \\ \partial\pi_z/\partial x & \partial\pi_z/\partial Z \end{vmatrix} \geqq 0$$

$$\partial\pi_x/\partial Z = \partial\pi_z/\partial x.$$

In what follows, we assume that the determinant is strictly positive.

Recalling that there are three characteristics in this model, we observe that the sign of the cross-effects, $\partial\pi_x/\partial Z$ and $\partial\pi_z/\partial x$, cannot be determined by a priori considerations alone. Consider what happens if, say, Z is exogenously increased while x and u are held constant. This is achieved by an appropriate change in the quantity of the numeraire characteristic, y. If, as a result of this, the individual's marginal valuation of x increases (i.e., $\partial\pi_x/\partial Z > 0$), then in the terminology of Hicks (1956, p. 156) x and Z are q-complements. On the other hand, x and Z are q-substitutes if $\partial\pi_x/\partial Z < 0$.

Armed with this definition of the relationship between x and Z, the slope of the individual's Nash–Cournot reaction curve is easily derived and interpreted. Since in equilibrium the individual's marginal rate of substitution between Q and y is equal to the price p, (6) may be written as

$$p = a\pi_x(x, Z, u) + b\pi_z(x, Z, u). \tag{8}$$

To simplify the analysis, assume that the coefficient b is the same across individuals. This enables us to write $Z = \sum_i bq^i = bQ = b(\tilde{Q} + q)$. Equation (8) may be written as

$$p = a\pi_x(aq, b(\tilde{Q} + q), u) + b\pi_z(aq, b(\tilde{Q} + q), u). \tag{9}$$

The individual's Nash–Cournot reaction curve is generated by varying $\tilde{Q}$ while holding p fixed, and using (9) to solve for the implied value of q. Differentiation of (9) yields the slope $dq/d\tilde{Q}$, which is

$$\frac{dq}{d\tilde{Q}} = \left[\frac{b(a\pi_{xz} + b\pi_{zz})}{\phi} \right] + \left[\frac{a\pi_{xu} + b\pi_{zu}}{\phi} \right] \frac{du}{d\tilde{Q}}, \tag{10}$$

where $\pi_{xz} \equiv \partial\pi_x/\partial Z$ and so on, and where

$$\phi \equiv -(a \; b) \begin{bmatrix} \pi_{xx} & \pi_{xz} \\ \pi_{zx} & \pi_{zz} \end{bmatrix} \begin{pmatrix} a \\ b \end{pmatrix} > 0.$$

The term that appears in the first set of square brackets in (10) is a pure compensated substitution response. Since the denominator, ϕ, is positive, the sign of this response depends on the sign of $(a\pi_{xz} + b\pi_{zz})$. Whereas π_{zz} is certainly nonpositive, π_{xz} may be of either sign. We have already observed that if x and Z are q-complements, $\pi_{xz} > 0$. Since the technological parameters, a and b, are independently determined, theory cannot rule out the possibility that $a\pi_{xz} > b\pi_{zz}$. In this case, an increase in $\bar{Q}$—and hence $\bar{Z}$—raises the individual's marginal valuation for the characteristic x. He or she now wishes, even in the absence of income effects, to increase his or her consumption of x. To do this, the individual must acquire more q, which has the incidental consequence of increasing z, his or her own generation of the public characteristic. In this way, strong q-complementarity between x and Z can produce a positive response $dq/d\bar{Q}$.

The total response $dq/d\bar{Q}$ includes a real income term, represented by the second term in square brackets in (10). There is a presumption that this is positive. The partial derivative π_{xu} is the change in the willingness to pay for x as real income is increased through an increase in y and x and Z held constant. One can imagine, for a given value of Z, a well-behaved indifference map in (y, x) space. The statement that $\pi_{xu} > 0$ is equivalent to the statement that x is a normal good when Z is held constant. Similar comments apply to π_{zu}.

There are, then, two forces at work that may produce a positive response in $dq/d\bar{Q}$. If either x or Z is a normal good, and the term $(a\pi_{xu} + b\pi_{zu})$ is positive, the income effect will be positive. Further, strong q-complementarity between x and Z may make the compensated response positive or, at least, less negative. The latter force is absent from the pure public good model. It raises the possibility that, even if one abstracts from real income effects, microlevel easy riding may not characterize the joint product model.

Our discussion makes it clear that, in a sense, introducing joint production of a private and public good does not radically affect the basic model. Our diagram can still be used, and can depict Nash–Cournot equilibria as well as the set of Pareto-optimal allocations. At a more detailed level, however, there are significant differences. Changes in income cannot be accommodated as easily, and the precise shape of the indifference map reflects more complicated relationships between the three characteristics over which the individual's preferences are defined. This is particularly evident if we consider systemic easy riding in the present model. As we have already seen in Chapter 5, the pure public goods model implies, in the absence of real income effects, an exacerbation of easy riding as

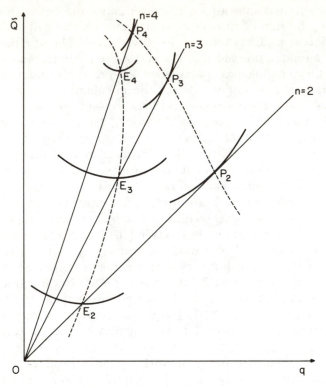

Figure 7.2

the size of the community grows. Inspection of (10) suggests that matters are not so simple in the joint production model. The representation of symmetric allocations in a community of n individuals is achieved in precisely the same way as in Chapter 5. The important difference is that both the Nash–Cournot reaction curve and the locus of Pareto-optimal allocations are influenced by additional terms, reflecting the substitute-complement relationships between the characteristics in their respective neighborhoods. Consequently, the behavior of both curves reflects a more complex structure than in the pure public goods model. In particular, one can obtain the possibility shown in Figure 7.2 of easy riding becoming quantitatively less important as n increases, and even that of an upward-sloping Nash reaction curve, without appealing to income effects.

We do not, of course, deny the possibility that easy riding may be

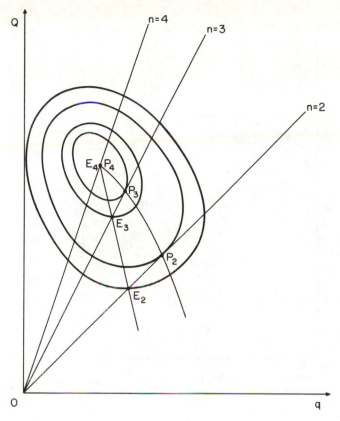

Figure 7.3

more prevalent in larger communities. We are simply pointing out that, even in the absence of powerful income effects, it is not an inevitable feature of public goods models (see Chamberlin 1974). One can construct various possible shapes for the equilibrium and optimum loci in $(q, \tilde{Q})$ space, and it is instructive to do so. An interesting special case arises if, beyond a certain level, there is satiation with respect to the public characteristic. Figure 7.3 reflects this by having closed loops for indifference curves. As n increases from 2 to 4, the equilibrium and optimum allocations converge. If one takes seriously the possibility of eventual satiation, then for values of n below the satiation level there is a presumption that E and Q will converge as n increases.

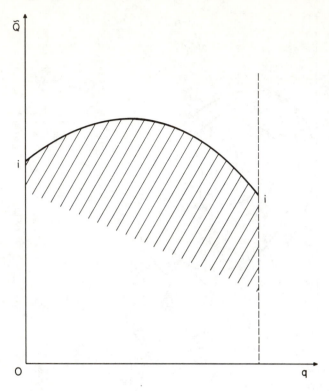

Figure 7.4

7.2   A model of congestion

We have already pointed out that the impure public good, or joint product, model may be interpreted as one of congestion. Consider the representative utility function

$$U(\cdot) = U(y, q, c(Q)), \tag{11}$$

where $c(Q)$ is a congestion function with the properties $\partial c/\partial Q > 0$ and $\partial U/\partial c < 0$. If $U(\cdot)$ is quasi-concave, it remains true that the set of points $(q, \bar{Q})$ that are weakly preferred to any given allocation is convex. This is shown in Figure 7.4, where the hatched area represents such a set. As an example, one may think of q as the amount of driving done by the individual. To explore this interpretation further, we consider a slight extension of (11). The level of congestion on the highway is dependent not only on the total amount of driving, Q, but also on the level of highway services provided, S. The congestion function may be written as $c(Q, S)$, where $\partial c/\partial S < 0$. Such an extension enables us to consider questions concerning not only Q, but also optimal provision of the congestible service, S. Consider first the characterization of an optimal allocation of resources. We assume a constant cost technology in which a unit of highway services costs ψ units of the numeraire good. The optimizing problem is

$$\left.\begin{array}{ll} \text{Maximize} & W(U^1(\cdot), \ldots, U^n(\cdot)) \\ \{y,q,S\} & \\ \\ \text{subject to} & \sum_h y^h + p \sum_h q^h + \psi S = \sum_h I^h \end{array}\right\} \quad (12)$$

where

$$U^h(\cdot) = U^h(y^h, q^h, c(Q, S)).$$

The necessary first-order conditions imply that

$$U^i_q/U^i_y = p - \sum_h (U^h_c/U^h_y)c_Q \quad (13)$$

or

$$(U^i_q + U^i_c c_Q)/U^i_y = p - \sum_{h \neq i} (U^h_c/U^h_y)c_Q. \quad (14)$$

They also imply that

$$\psi = (\sum_h W_h U^h_c c_S)/W_i U^i_y$$

$$= \sum_h (U^h_c/U^h_y)c_S. \quad (15)$$

Combining (13) and (15) yields

$$U^i_q/U^i_y = p - \psi c_Q/c_S. \quad (16)$$

Equation (16) has a straightforward interpretation. Observe first that if the total amount of driving increases by dQ, then if the level of congestion is to be kept constant, the provision of highway services must be increased by $dS = -(c_Q/c_S)dQ$. Therefore (16) states that at an optimal allocation, the marginal valuation placed by i on an extra increment of driving should equal the marginal private cost, p, plus the cost of adding enough S to maintain a constant level of congestion. In short, marginal benefit should equal marginal cost, inclusive of the external or social component. Note that the condition (16) involves, albeit implicitly, both the level of driving and the level of provision of highway services.

Now consider the consequences of Nash–Cournot behavior by the representative individual when he or she takes $\bar{Q}$ and S as exogenously given. The problem is to

$$\text{Maximize} \{U(y, q, c(\bar{Q} + q, S)) \mid y + pq = I\}.$$
$$\{y,q\}$$

First-order necessary conditions imply that

$$(U_q + U_c c_Q)/U_y = p. \tag{17}$$

Comparison of this equilibrium condition with (14) makes it clear that the individual fails to take account of the impact of the extra congestion that he or she generates for others. By contrast, the social optimality condition includes this in the extra series of terms, $-\sum_{h \neq i}(U_c^h/U_y^h)c_Q$.

How might such an allocation be sustained? Suppose that the community consists of n identical consumers, each of whom must contribute the fraction $1/n$ of the total cost of providing S. The individual's problem is then

$$\text{Maximize} \quad U(y, q, c(\bar{Q} + q, S))$$
$$\{y,q\}$$
$$\text{subject to} \quad y + pq = I - \psi S/n.$$

By itself, such a scheme does not produce a social optimum, since it does not deal with the tendency to drive beyond the socially optimal level. Consumers will still behave so as to ensure (17). Now suppose a tax, or toll, is levied on q. The proceeds of the tax go toward financing S, and any difference between the total cost ψS and total tax revenue tQ is raised from—or returned to—individuals in a lump-sum manner. The individual's budget constraint is now

$$y + (p + t)q = I - (\psi S - tQ)/n.$$

The term $(\psi S - tQ)/n$ represents a lump-sum tax that may be required to bridge the gap between the per capita cost and the per capita toll payment. In general, it could be positive or negative, as we shall see. If the consumer regards the right-hand side of this constraint as exogenous, his or her optimizing behavior will imply

$$(U_q + U_c c_Q)/U_y = p + t. \tag{18}$$

Now consider the planner's problem. The objective is to maximize the utility of the representative individual, taking proper account of external costs:

$$\text{Maximize} \{U(y, q, c(nq, S)) \mid y + pq = I - \psi S/n\},$$
$$\{y,q,S\}$$

which implies the necessary first-order conditions:

$$p = U_q/U_y + nU_cc_Q/U_y$$

or

$$p - [(n - 1)U_cc_Q]/U_y = (U_q + U_cc_Q)/U_y \qquad (19)$$

and

$$\psi/n = (U_c/U_y)c_S. \qquad (20)$$

Comparison of (18) with (19) shows that the planner can encourage utility-maximizing consumers to drive at the socially optimal level by setting

$$t = -(n + 1)U_cc_Q/U_y. \qquad (21)$$

It is interesting to consider the relationship between the revenue raised by the optimal toll and the cost of providing the optimal level of S. Suppose that the congestion function is homogeneous of degree zero in its two arguments—a doubling of the level of driving accompanied by a doubling of highway capacity leaves the level of congestion unaffected. Euler's equation tells us that

$$c_QQ + c_SS = 0.$$

Using (21) to substitute for c_Q, and noting that $Q = nq$,

$$\frac{ntqU_y}{(1 - n)U_c} + c_SS = 0.$$

Finally, using (20) to remove U_y/U_c,

$$\frac{ntq}{(1 - n)} + \frac{\psi S}{n} = 0.$$

As n becomes very large, $n/(1 - n)$ tends toward -1. Hence, in a large community,

$$\psi S = ntq = tQ. \qquad (22)$$

In this special case, then, the optimal toll kills two birds with one stone. It produces the socially optimal level of Q, while at the same time providing precisely the revenue required to finance provision of the optimal level of the service S. This is very much the knife-edge case. If a doubling of Q and S leads to an increase in congestion, then $c_QQ + c_SS > 0$, and the revenue raised by the optimal tariff is more than enough to cover the cost of the service S. Conversely, if an equiproportionate increase in Q and S reduces C, then a supplementary lump-sum tax is required from each individual. This is a well-known result that can be found in Mohring and Harwitz (1962) and Kolm (1974).

The homogeneity properties of the congestion function will depend on the particular context. Consider a problem in which $c(\cdot)$ is the level of pollution in a lake, and depends upon the ratio of pollutant, sulphur dioxide, to cleansing agent, lime. This is precisely the knife-edge case in which an equiproportional change in the two arguments of $c(\cdot)$ leaves the level of pollution unchanged. Kolm (1974) discusses other cases, one of which can be thought of as involving cleaning, or repairing damage inflicted by pollution. Here, for every unit of pollutant, any exogenously fixed level of cleansing activity is required to maintain the original value of $c(\cdot)$. Algebraically, $c(\cdot) = aQ - bS$, where a and b are exogenous coefficients. Whether the degree of homogeneity of $c(\cdot)$ exceeds, equals, or falls short of zero depends on whether aQ exceeds, equals, or falls short of bS.

7.3   Common property resources

The phrase "tragedy of the commons" is often associated with Hardin (1968). But concern with the possible overexploitation of common property resources has a much longer history. The static analysis of the problem of the commons represents another example of a situation involving interdependence but with enough structure to yield more useful insight than the trite observation that "anything can happen." As we show below, the diagrammatic approach already developed provides a simple exposition of the overexploitation result.

Examples of common property, or free-access, resources are legion. The use of air, the mineral resources of the ocean beds, fishing grounds, oil pools, hunting grounds, radio wave frequencies, and the resources of outer space have all been cited as situations involving scarce factors for which property rights are not clearly defined and that may not receive a rent from users.

Consider an industry consisting of a given number of profit-maximizing firms, each having free access to an exogenously fixed common property resource. We will refer to this resource as a fishing ground. The reader who objects to an atemporal treatment of a problem with such important intertemporal aspects is invited to replace our concrete example with another of his or her own choosing. Each firm combines the common resource with a single private input, fishing vessels, to produce an output of fish. With the size of the fishing ground fixed, the total catch, C, depends solely on the size of the total fishing fleet, R. The production function is

$$C = F(R), \quad F'(R) > 0, \quad F''(R) < 0.$$

We assume fish and vessels command exogenously fixed prices of unity and p, respectively.

The individual firm's catch and fleet size are denoted by c and r. We assume that its production function is

$$c = [r/R]F(R) = [r/(r + \tilde{R})]F(r + \tilde{R}), \tag{23}$$

where $\tilde{R} \equiv R - r$ denotes the other firms' aggregate fleet. Equation (23) represents the simplest example of the pure homogeneous common property in which individuals' catch rates are in proportion to their input levels.

The Pareto-optimal solution for the commons is found by choosing the fleet size that maximizes total industry profit, π. The maximand is

$$\pi(R) = F(R) - pR. \tag{24}$$

The optimal value of R, R^*, is uniquely determined by the first-order condition, $F'(R) = p$, being independent of the distribution of catch between firms. This is the allocation that would result from competitive exploitation in the presence of well-defined property rights. The level of profits $\pi(R^*)$ would then be the payment to owners of the rights to fish.

This solution is illustrated in Figure 7.5, where isoprofit contours $\pi_1\pi_1$ and $\pi_2\pi_2$ show combinations of r and $\tilde{R}$ corresponding to constant profit levels for the firm. As drawn, the contour $\pi_1\pi_1$ represents a higher profit level than does $\pi_2\pi_2$. The locus of Pareto-optimal allocations is the line PP, the slope of which is -1, reflecting the uniqueness of $R^* \equiv (\tilde{R} + r)^*$.

Nash equilibria are characterized by profit maximization on the part of the individual firm, and $\tilde{R}$ is treated as exogenous. The firm's problem is

$$\text{Maximize } \{[r/(r + \tilde{R})]F(r + \tilde{R}) - pr\}. \tag{25}$$
$$\{r\}$$

We have shown elsewhere, in Cornes and Sandler (1983), that the implied Nash–Cournot reaction curve is a locus such as NN in Figure 7.5 that is negatively sloped and lies everywhere above the Pareto-optimal locus except where $\tilde{R} = 0$. At that point, since there is only one firm exploiting the common property, all costs are internalized

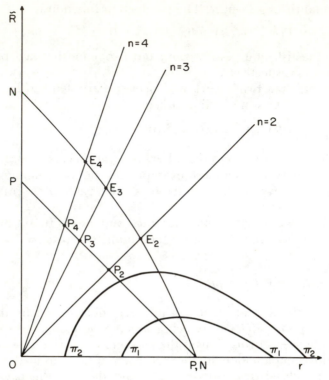

Figure 7.5

and private profit maximization is consistent with social optimality. Hence *PP* and *NN* intersect at the *r* axis.

Since it can be also shown that the slope of *NN* is numerically greater than 1 at every point, it follows that as the number of independent profit-maximizing firms increases, the ratio of equilibrium to optimum fleet size increases. In this sense, overexploitation is exacerbated by an increase in the number of firms. This is captured in Figure 7.5 by the index OE_n/OP_n, which exceeds unity and which is an increasing function of the number of firms, n. This result can be clearly seen by inspecting the first-order condition derived from (25). With a little manipulation, it can be written as

$$p = (r/R)F'(R) + (\tilde{R}/R)[F(R)/R].$$

At a symmetric equilibrium involving n firms, $r/R = 1/n$ and $\tilde{R}/R = (n - 1)/n$. Therefore the first-order condition implies that

$$p = (1/n)F'(R) + [(n - 1)/n][F(R)/R].$$

In other words, the price of a vessel is equated to a weighted sum of its marginal and average product. In the case of a single firm, $n = 1$ and the weights imply that price equals marginal product. As n tends to infinity, however, the price converges to the average product, thereby producing the standard result—discussed by Dasgupta and Heal (1979), Weitzman (1974), and Dorfman (1974)—that as the number of firms exploiting a common property resource grows large, profits tend to zero as price is equated to average, rather than marginal product.

For further discussion of the static model, the reader is referred to Cornes and Sandler (1983). Problems raised in extending the analysis to a dynamic framework are discussed in Heal (1982).

7.4 Concluding remarks

In this chapter we have tried to show how, by incorporating the possibility of joint production of a public and a private characteristic, one can significantly extend and generalize the public good model. The resulting structure, although still analytically tractable, yields a considerably richer set of possible patterns of behavior and can incorporate not only public goods, but also public bads such as congestion, pollution, and general environmental degradation. As we note in Chapter 16, it has served as the theoretical framework for empirical research, particularly in the theory of alliances, and has considerable scope for application to other topics—for example, to health and education economics, as well as to environmental studies. For some of these purposes, it may be useful to explore more general assumptions concerning the technology whereby the private and public characteristics are jointly produced. The assumption of fixed coefficients is admirably simple as an expository device but rather crude. A further possible development of the orthodox pure public good model, recently suggested by Hirshleifer (1983), concerns the broadening of the class of public goods to incorporate situations in which Q is a symmetric, but not necessarily additive, function of individual contributions. There is without doubt plenty of scope for further useful research into theoretical and empirical aspects of noncooperative provision of both pure and impure public goods.

CHAPTER 8

Game theory and public goods

Externalities and public goods clearly involve interdependence between individuals in an essential way. The benefits to an individual that result from a given course of action depend crucially on the consumption or production choices of others. So too, in general, will the individual's optimal choice. This suggests an important role for game theory in analyzing such models. Indeed, game-theoretic concepts have implicitly been used at various places in our discussion. The purpose of the present chapter is to explore the game-theoretic structure of public goods models more explicitly and systematically.

In the development of game theory since the appearance of *The Theory of Games and Economic Behavior* by von Neumann and Morgenstern (1944), it has proved helpful to categorize games into two types. Those in which the agents, or players, are able to communicate with one another and make binding agreements to act in certain ways are cooperative games, and those that do not allow such opportunities are noncooperative games. The public goods model discussed in Chapter 5 is noncooperative, since agents engage in no active attempts to coordinate their actions, but each passively forms expectations about his or her economic environment when choosing the variable under his or her own control, the individual contribution level q.

By contrast, we begin this chapter with a discussion of public goods in a cooperative game-theoretic framework. It is supposed that players can costlessly form groups, or coalitions, within which they can coordinate their actions and negotiate their shares of the benefits that accrue. In addition, each member of a coalition considers whether he or she can do better by joining some other coalition. Such a framework suggests a natural equilibrium concept, the core, which consists of that set of allocations such that no individual or group of individuals can improve their position by forming an alternative coalition. The core has proved of considerable interest in the analysis of the nature of competitive equilibrium in private goods economies. There, it has been shown that under certain assumptions the set of core allocations shrinks as the number of individuals is increased, and converges in the limit to the set of competitive equilibria. The attraction of this is that competitive price-taking behavior may be justified as the natural outcome of a bargaining process, instead of merely being assumed. It is natural to ask whether in the presence of public goods, the core shrinks and, if so, whether it converges to the set of Lindahl equilibria. It turns out that no such shrinkage occurs, and, indeed, the usual definition of the core is itself somewhat problematic in the presence of public good.

Section 8.2 returns to noncooperative games, but to a special class in which agents choose, not a continuous variable such as the level of their contribution to a public good, but rather a binary variable. It may be a choice between cooperating with others or not, tidying up one's own litter or leaving it lying around, contributing nothing to a public good or contributing one unit, and so on. Such binary choices are clearly a special and particularly simple class of public goods models, providing the simplest illustrations of their game-theoretic structure. They have also been used as a framework within which to extend the models to more dynamic, or intertemporal, formulations. An important question that the resulting literature addresses concerns whether the threat of retaliation by others in later plays of a repeated game may help to discourage would-be free riders, thereby mitigating the tendency toward suboptimal equilibrium outcomes.

In Section 8.3, we return to the model of noncooperative provision of a continuous pure public good. The nature and properties of the Nash equilibrium concept are further explored, and we discuss the problem of sustaining Pareto-optimal allocations in the presence of noncooperative behavior by individual agents. The Clarke-Groves tax scheme discussed in Chapter 6 has the property that honest preference revelation is a dominant strategy—that is, it is the best strategy for each individual regardless of what he or she expects others to do. Since the scheme has certain limitations, it is worth asking whether there are alternative mechanisms for which telling the truth is the optimal strategy for the individual only if he or she expects others to do so. The requirement that telling the truth should be a Nash equilibrium is clearly less exacting than that it should be a dominant strategy, and one might hope that by not insisting on dominance one might gain in other ways. However, we argue that serious problems may arise in the operation of such incentive structures.

Readers seeking a systematic exposition of game theory will not find it here. They are advised to consult Luce and Raiffa (1957), Bacharach (1976), Hamburger (1979), Davis (1983) or Schotter and

Schwödiauer (1980) for more substantial treatments. The first four of these provide good discussions of the basic concepts of game theory, and the last concentrates rather on its broad range of applications to economic problems.

8.1   Cooperative provision of public goods

Consider first the general notion of the core, and the role played by this equilibrium concept in the theory of competitive equilibrium with private goods. Useful expositions may be found in Hildenbrand and Kirman (1976, Chapter 1), and in Walsh (1970). Suppose there is a group of consumers, each endowed with a certain bundle of commodities. There is no production, but there is the possibility of trade, or reallocation, of commodities among consumers. If there is an allocation such that no group of consumers can come together and reallocate their initial endowments in such a way as to advantage each one of them, that allocation is said to be in the core. The set of all such core allocations is called the core.

In a two-person two-commodity exchange model the set of core allocations is that segment of the contract curve lying within the region in which both individuals are at least as well off as at their initial endowment points. Points outside that region are not in the core, because at least one of the individuals, acting as a coalition of one, can do better by remaining at his or her endowment point. Points within the region, but not on the contract curve, are not in the core because the two-person coalition can negotiate a mutually preferred allocation. This set may be large, implying substantial scope for bargaining and, indeed, an indeterminate outcome. However, it may be shown that if the economy is replicated—that is, if each of the two individuals is replaced by n economically identical individuals—then as n grows larger the indeterminacy becomes less and the set of core allocations converges to the set of competitive equilibria. That the scope for bargaining becomes small when there are many individuals will not surprise anyone who has tried to haggle with a shopkeeper over a standardized article of a type for which there are many suppliers and demanders.

Foley (1970a) provides a clear discussion of the analogues within public goods theory to the theorems of equilibrium and optimality in private goods economies. In particular, he defines a class of public goods models, of which that of Chapter 5 is a special case, for which Lindahl equilibria exist and are not only Pareto optimal but also in the core. Core allocations, by contrast to Lindahl equilibria, do have a claim on our attention as outcomes of plausible political processes. Consequently, if it could be shown that under certain circumstances the set of core allocations converges to the Lindahl equilibria as the number of agents grows, this would provide a justification for the latter as a natural equilibrium concept for a public goods economy with many agents.

Unfortunately, such convergence does not survive the introduction of public goods. It is difficult to provide an accessible formal demonstration, but Muench (1972) and Ellickson (1978) provide examples to show how the core can expand as the number of individuals grows. Foley (1970a) provides an intuitive explanation. For an initial allocation to be improved upon, a coalition must exist such that its members, by suitable reallocation among themselves of their own initial resources, can do better for themselves by comparison with the initial allocation. In the presence of a public good, the restriction to reallocations "of their own resources" is typically interpreted to mean that members of a coalition cannot enjoy public goods produced by nonmembers. Either there is exclusion, or the members of the coalition are very pessimistic or risk averse. Clearly, if the assumption is that any coalition has to rely entirely on its own members' contributions to the public good, and forego the benefits of public goods provided by others, the task of improving upon allocations is made much harder. One can readily accept that the class of core allocations may remain large as the number of individuals grows. An alternative intuition, suggested by Ellickson, ties in more closely with Arrow's discussion of externalities, which we dealt with in Chapter 3. Consider each individual's consumption of a single pure public good as a separate commodity. The provision of national defense in an n-person economy may be interpreted as the joint production of n commodities each with its own personalized, or Lindahl, price. Then as the number of individuals increases, so too does the number of commodities. Each has only one demander, so that there continue to be thin markets, in contrast to the meat-and-hides model of jointly produced private goods.

In focusing on maximin behavior—that is, requiring coalitions to consider the best they can do in the worst possible environment—this analysis certainly loads the dice heavily in favor of the arbitrary reference allocation. Suppose we consider two mutually exclusive and exhaustive coalitions, K and K'. In considering whether they can improve upon a given allocation, members of K assume that the complementary coalition K' will produce no public goods, even though this is not the most preferred allocation for members of K'. However, as Roberts (1974) points out, the task of developing alternative definitions of core-type equilibria is not straightforward.

The task of delineating the feasible strategies available to a coalition is particularly tricky in the presence of a public bad, or detrimental externality. Shapley and Shubik (1969) present an example in which, in the presence of a detrimental externality, no core allocations exist. This might suggest that the existence or nonexistence of the core depends on whether an externality is beneficial—as in the case of a public good—or detrimental. Starrett (1973) argues that this is misleading. Consider a cigarette smoker. One interpretation of the condition that he or she "use his or her own resources" in seeking improvement is that, given a cigarette and a lighter, that individual may do what he or she likes with them, wherever and whenever he or she wishes. Starrett calls this the possession rule. However, one might argue that if this individual smokes in a crowded room where there are nonsmokers who dislike cigarette smoke, he or she is, by inflicting smoke on them, using a further resource, namely the atmosphere, as a dumping ground. A more stringent interpretation is that he or she has to absorb his or her own resources, including undesirable byproducts of his or her actions. If everyone has a right to a clean environment, smoking in a public place without the consent of others becomes an inadmissible action. Under such a convention, which Starrett calls the common rule, it may be shown that externalities, whether detrimental or beneficial, are consistent with the existence of the core. Its failure to exist in the Shapley-Shubik model is the consequence, not of the detrimental nature of the externality, but rather of the particular assignment of property rights and the implications of such assignment for the set of admission strategies available to coalitions. Bergstrom (1975) provides a further example in which, if the possession rule is adopted, core allocations exist but do not contain the Lindahl equilibrium, whereas under the common rule the Lindahl equilibrium is contained in the core.

In contemplating this literature, one cannot help wondering whether, in the presence of many agents, the core is an empirically relevant solution concept. Its implied level of cooperation presupposes costless bargaining and coordination, which is increasingly difficult to justify as the number of agents becomes large. For this reason, it seems worthwhile to return to the model of noncooperative behavior.

8.2   Noncooperative binary choice models

Discussions of public goods and collective action by such political scientists as Taylor (1976) and Hardin (1982) devote a good deal of attention to examples of noncooperative games involving binary choices. Such examples, in which each of two players chooses between a pair of strategies, and obtains a payoff that depends on both players' choices, reveal simply and explicitly strategic aspects of social interactions in a way that has caught the imagination not only of economists and political scientists, but also of philosophers, sociologists, biologists—in particular, sociobiologists—and novelists.

The two-person two-strategy game can be presented in a simple matrix such as Figure 8.1(a). Each row represents a strategy open to, say, player A, while B's strategies correspond to the columns. Each of the four possible outcomes is associated with a pair of numbers representing, respectively, the payoff or net benefits accruing to A and B as a result of that pair of strategies. In a noncooperative game, there is no opportunity for the players to communicate with one another and secure mutually binding agreements as to their choice of strategy. The pattern of payoffs in Figure 8.1(a) is consistent with many popular discussions of public goods problems, and indeed has become such a focus of attention that it has a name—the Prisoner's Dilemma. Before discussing its properties, we should mention that Figure 8.1(b) has been drawn simply to show the consistency of the preference ordering with our earlier discussions of continuous choice situations. One can interpret the current thought experiment as involving a continuously variable public good, with individual preferences represented by the indifference curves in Figure 8.1(b), but in which an unspecified institutional constraint limits individual contributions to the values zero and unity. Five minutes with pencil and paper should persuade the reader that it is not the only ordering consistent with those discussions. However, more of that later.

We denote by $[C, N]$ the situation in which A chooses to contribute, while B remains a noncontributor. Examination of Figure 8.1(a) reveals a number of facts. Let us momentarily interpret utility as a monetary payoff. Then if there were cooperation and the ability to redistribute the payoff, the players could not do better than alight upon $[C, C]$. After all, if A were to propose $[N, C]$, B could offer a bribe to move to $[C, C]$. If, however, such transfers cannot take place, it is less clear that any single outcome commands our attention. However, among the four situations, three of them constitute Pareto-

B's STRATEGY / A's STRATEGY	DO NOT CONTRIBUTE	CONTRIBUTE ONE UNIT OF PUBLIC GOOD
DO NOT CONTRIBUTE	2, 2	4, 1
CONTRIBUTE ONE UNIT OF PUBLIC GOOD	1, 4	3, 3

(a)

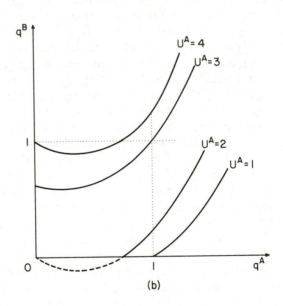

(b)

Figure 8.1

optimal outcomes, whereas the fourth, [N, N], is clearly not, being dominated by [C, C].

Interestingly, it is precisely the Pareto-suboptimal situation [N, N] that stands out as a candidate for equilibrium of the noncooperative game. The distinguishing feature of the Prisoner's Dilemma is that there is one strategy—in this case, not to contribute—that dominates all others, regardless of the choices of others. If B were not to

B's STRATEGY / A's STRATEGY	DO NOT CONTRIBUTE	CONTRIBUTE ONE UNIT OF PUBLIC GOOD
DO NOT CONTRIBUTE	1, 1	4, 2
CONTRIBUTE ONE UNIT OF PUBLIC GOOD	2, 4	3, 3

(a)

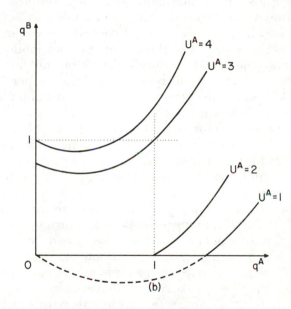

(b)

Figure 8.2

contribute, A is better off not contributing. If B contributes, A is still better off being a noncontributor rather than contributing. The same argument applies to B. Furthermore, pursuit of the dominant strategy by each leads to $[N, N]$, the one suboptimal social outcome.

The binary public goods problem doesn't necessarily conform to the Prisoner's Dilemma. It is easy to construct a ranking such that to contribute is both a dominant strategy for each player and a Pareto-optimal outcome. Then there are other, more complicated, situations in which no dominant strategy exists. One such situation—often called "chicken"—is depicted by Figure 8.2. If *A* expects *B* to contribute, he or she prefers to take a free ride and be a noncontributor. On the other hand, *A* prefers to contribute if he or she believes that *B* will not. As Figure 8.2(b) shows, this situation is also consistent with the model of a continuously variable public good introduced in Chapter 5. As in the Prisoner's Dilemma, each agent regards contributions by others as goods. The difference lies in the reversal in the ranking of the worst and next-to-worst outcomes as perceived by each. Retaining the equilibrium concept put forth by Nash, we see that there are two equilibria, [*C*, *N*] and [*N*, *C*]. However, neither player has a dominant strategy, and can equally well imagine behavior that leads to an alternative outcome. Suppose each player, not confident about what the other will do, acts so as to maximize his or her payoff in the worst of all conceivable circumstances. Player *A* can obtain a payoff of three units by contributing, whereas failure to contribute could produce a payoff of only one unit if his or her companion chooses likewise. Such logic, applied to both players, would lead to the outcome [*C*, *C*]. Such maximin behavior, in which each maximizes his minimum conceivable payoff, clearly does not lead to an equilibrium in the sense of Nash. It leads to an outcome such that each player, on observing the decisions taken by others, regrets his or her own decision. One can imagine yet further criteria that might guide players in their choice. An incurable optimist, for example, might adopt a maximax strategy—choosing the highest among the maximum possible payoffs. In the present example, this leads, ironically, to the worst possible outcome for both, and is again not a Nash equilibrium. It may be shown, however, that in games for which each player has a dominant strategy, a unique Nash equilibrium is implied by maximin and maximax behavior.

Our discussion makes it clear that even in a two-person two-strategy noncooperative game with a symmetric payoff table, there are subtle problems in identifying rational individual behavior and probable social outcomes. Where does this leave a particular equilibrium concept, such as that suggested by Nash? Johansen (1982) argues strongly that in a game with complete information—that is, in which each player knows all the information in the payoff matrix—the Nash equilibrium strategy is the only one that is consistent with a certain plausible set of rationality axioms, and therefore should be accorded special status as the natural noncooperative equilibrium concept.

There are at least three directions in which one might wish to extend the analysis of the 2 by 2 model in the context of public goods while retaining the binary choice assumption. First, the number of players should be allowed to exceed two. Second, consideration of repeated games raises new issues that considerably complicate the model. Finally, one might want to examine more closely the assumptions underlying Johansen's strong defense of Nash equilibrium strategies, and to consider the possibility that alternative assumptions may lead to departures from Nash behavior as part of a rational strategy.

Several recent attempts have been made to generalize the Prisoner's Dilemma to an n-player setting, the most notable being Taylor (1976) and Schelling (1973). Taylor also provides a lengthy discussion of repeated games, or supergames. He considers a model in which at each discrete point in time the players are confronted with an ordinary Prisoner's Dilemma. In choosing a strategy, each is aware that his or her present choice may influence the future choices of others, and hence his or her own future payoffs. Even in this special case, it is difficult to obtain strong conclusions. Taylor (1976, Chapter 5) summarizes this main result.

A particularly interesting question is whether repetition may encourage cooperative behavior. For example, suppose one of the two players follows a tit-for-tat strategy—adopting at each round the choice that the other player adopted in the previous round. This has the effect of punishing the other player for failure to contribute, while rewarding him or her for contributing. Taylor shows that, under certain conditions, mutual cooperation is an equilibrium. However, this depends on the numerical value of the discount rate used to weight future payoffs vis-à-vis the present, and other equilibria are possible. It is also the case that the one-shot solution, with its implied inefficiency, remains a Nash equilibrium in repeated play, regardless of the value of the discount rate. More recently, Axelrod (1984) has investigated the evolution of cooperation in repeated games in a study that draws on the results of a computer tourney, in which he invited contestants to submit computer programs to play a repeated Prisoner's Dilemma. In general, it appeared that a simple tit-for-tat strategy performed extremely well, by virtue of its ability to secure cooperation from the other player. Such a result is certainly interesting, although its relevance to public goods problems is debatable. For one thing, we have pointed out that, even within the binary choice framework, the public goods problem may not conform to the Prisoner's Dilemma. Second, n-player games are more complicated than two-player games. Axelrod's tournament consisted of rounds of two-player contests, whereas our ultimate interest is in public goods models with many players. It is not clear that it makes much sense for an individual to punish or reward 99 others to secure their cooperation in later plays of the game.

A natural context in which the binary choice model arises concerns the decision by a firm whether or not to adopt a particular technology. Such a decision generates benefits or costs for others, and a firm's optimal choice in turn depends on what it expects others to do. For example, firms in the video-recorder industry have in recent years had to decide which of the VHS and the Beta technologies to adopt. Whatever the intrinsic technical merits of either, it is expensive to adopt the technology that proves unpopular with other producers. Recent game-theoretic analyses of such choices are provided by Dybvig and Spatt (1983) and also by Palfrey and Rosenthal (1984). The pace of technical innovation, together with the magnitude of the resources that have to be irreversibly committed to develop and to commence commercial production of new commodities, suggests that this is an important area of application for binary choice models.

8.3   Noncooperative continuous choice models

We now return to situations in which the issue at stake is the aggregate level of a continuously variable public good. We retain the assumption of noncooperative behavior. At risk of sounding repetitive, we begin with a more formal and abstract statement of Nash behavior than we have provided hitherto. Let the payoff, or utility, of player h in an n-person noncooperative game be $U^h(a^1, a^2, \ldots, a^n)$, where a^j is the action, or decision, of player j. Johansen (1982) proposes four postulates as characterizing rational behavior. These are

I: A player decides a^h from a set of feasible actions A^h on the basis of, and only on the basis of, information concerning the sets of feasible actions of all players, $A^1, \ldots, A^n$, and the preference functions of all players, $U^1(a^1, \ldots, a^n), \ldots, U^n(a^1, \ldots, a^n)$.

II: In making a decision, a player assumes that others are rational in the same sense as he or she is rational.

III: If some decision is the rational decision to make for an individual player, then this decision can be correctly predicted by the others.

IV: Being able to predict the actions to be taken by other players, a player's own decision maximizes his or her preference function corresponding to the predicted actions of others.

Johansen goes on to argue that fulfillment of these four postulates implies a fifth:

V: A decision is rational if the player, after having observed the decisions taken by other players and the outcome of the game, does not regret the decision he or she has made.

This leads to the Nash noncooperative equilibrium, in which the chosen actions, $\hat{a}^h$, satisfy the condition

$$U^h(\hat{a}^1, \ldots, \hat{a}^h, \ldots, \hat{a}^n) \geqq U^h(\hat{a}^1, \ldots, a^h, \ldots, \hat{a}^n), \quad h = 1, \ldots, n,$$

for any feasible alternative action a^h.

This review of the Nash equilibrium concept has been kept deliberately abstract. In particular, the actions have not been interpreted in any specific way. In Chapter 5, our description of the subscription equilibrium interpreted the actions as contributions to a public good. This game, as we saw, has a Nash equilibrium that is not generally Pareto optimal. In general, its players do not have dominant strategies. Our discussion of the Clarke-Groves demand-revealing mechanism in Section 6.4 concerns a different game, in which the actions are messages, or reported functions—recall that each player is asked to reveal some aspect of his or her preferences. The resulting game implies a dominant strategy for each—tell the truth, regardless of what others are doing—and hence a unique Nash equilibrium in which the Pareto-optimal level of public good is identified. It has the drawback of producing a budget surplus. An interesting question remains, which continues to attract much attention. Can one devise alternative incentive structures, or games, in which pursuit by individuals of Nash equilibrium strategies—not necessarily dominant strategies—implies a Pareto-optimal outcome without the problem of generating an unbalanced budget?

Groves and Ledyard (1977) suggest a scheme, of which Feldman (1980, Chapter 6) provides a clear exposition, in which agents are confronted with a tax formula and invited to submit information concerning their preferences for a public good. More specifically, agent h is informed that the rest of the community has reported a preference for, say, 100 units of the public good. He then reports how much more (or less) he desires. This scheme has the property that, if all other agents report their preferences honestly, agent h is best advised to do likewise. Honest preference revelation, then, is a

Nash equilibrium strategy. However, in contrast with the Clarke-Groves scheme, it is not a dominant strategy. From this fact flow potentially serious disadvantages. Since the whole context of the game presupposes incomplete information, one cannot jump straight to the Nash equilibrium, as one could if truth telling were a dominant strategy. It is a moot point whether an iterative procedure can be devised for which convergence to a Nash equilibrium consistent with the Groves-Ledyard scheme is guaranteed. Furthermore, Bergstrom, Simon, and Titus (1984) show that even if attention is confined to preferences representable by the Gorman polar form direct utility function, there may be many Nash equilibria. This fact alone may create incentives for individuals to behave strategically so as to push the outcome to an equilibrium more favorable to themselves. Much of the recent literature on this topic, which is surveyed by Groves (1982), avoids this problem by making the more restrictive assumption of quasi-linear utility functions. We have already argued in Chapter 6 that this is not a very attractive assumption.

There is an alternative approach, which, instead of concentrating on the properties of a Nash equilibrium, explores alternative iterative processes that rely at each stage on local information regarding individual preferences. Starting with early papers by Malinvaud (1971) and by Dreze and de la Vallee Poussin (1971), a number of such dynamic processes have been suggested. Tulkens (1978) provides an extensive survey of much of this work, while Green and Laffont (1979) give a critical assessment of both this local dynamic approach and also the global static procedures associated with Clarke, Groves, and Ledyard.

CHAPTER 9

Departures from Nash–Cournot behavior

In the noncooperative subscription model of Chapter 5, it was shown that if the strategies were defined as the quantities chosen by each individual, the resulting Nash equilibrium behavior generally implies a Pareto-suboptimal outcome. In Chapter 8, we referred to Johansen's argument that in a game of complete information played once, the Nash equilibrium strategies have a strong claim as reflecting rational behavior. Attempts to explore mechanisms with superior outcomes, dealt with in Chapter 6, typically rely on some exogenously imposed, supposedly benevolent enforcement agency, such as a government, which presents the players with the rules of the game and ensures compliance. There remains an important question. Are there institutional settings in which individual contributions may, without the degree of communication and cooperation assumed in discussions of the core, and without the supervision and coercion of a referee, depart from those implied by the model of Chapter 5? Furthermore, how do the resulting equilibria compare, from the point of view of efficiency, with the Nash equilibrium?

We should emphasize at the outset that the quantitative significance of easy riding and of its welfare implications is an empirical matter. Indeed, even the Nash equilibrium of the pure public good subscription model can, under certain circumstances, lie on the locus of Pareto optima. Figure 9.1 shows such an extreme situation, which is associated with kinked indifference curves in (y, Q) space. Moreover, as we argued in Chapter 7, the introduction of joint production of a public good with a private good can provide an incentive for the Nash equilibrium to approach Pareto optimality, as in the models of Sandler and Culyer (1982), Murdoch and Sandler (1982), and Cornes and Sandler (1984a). What Chapters 5 and 7 show is a theoretical presumption that the Nash equilibrium will imply too low a level of provision of a public good, the empirical significance of which depends on the numerical values of certain parameters.

There are several ways in which one might want to go beyond the Nash equilibrium subscription model. First, while retaining the Nash equilibrium concept, one can apply it to variables other than the

145

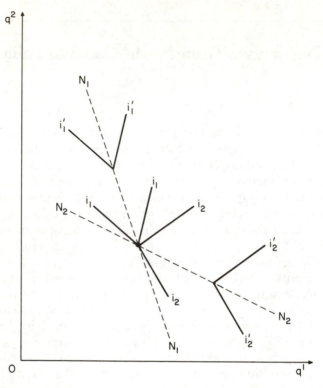

Figure 9.1

individual quantities contributed to the public good. Section 9.1 briefly considers a model of this type. Second, there is the possibility that nonmarket institutions may evolve to handle the problem of public good provision. The large and growing literature on such mechanisms is treated in Section 9.2. Finally, Section 9.3 considers situations in which the typical subscriber to a public good expects a nonzero response by the rest of the community to adjustments in his own level of contribution. Such behavior is relevant in situations involving repetition and incomplete information, in which agents form expectations about the reaction curve they face. The process of expectation formation and the definition of a logically coherent concept of rational or consistent conjectures equilibrium become important issues here.

9.1   Matching behavior

Students of oligopoly are familiar with the observation that the adoption of the Nash equilibrium concept does not by itself enable one to identify the equilibrium. One must also specify the variables that represent the firms' strategies. This was precisely one of the points at issue in the controversy between Cournot—who treated output as the choice variable—and Bertrand, who argued that the decision variable should properly be price. In the public goods model, output or subscription levels are a natural choice, and there is no obvious analogue to Bertrand's model. However, one can still imagine alternative variables as the subject of choice.

Guttman (1978) proposes a model in which the agents take part in a two-stage process, for each of which a Nash equilibrium is identified. Each individual's final contribution to a single public good is given by

$$q_i = a_i + b_i \sum_{j \neq i} a_j,$$

where a_i is the ith individual's flat contribution, and b_i is his or her matching rate; b_i represents a commitment to contribute a certain fraction of the aggregate flat contributions of everyone else. Guttman imagines a game in which each agent knows the utility functions of others, and chooses his or her optimal matching rate. The Nash equilibrium of this game determines all individuals' matching rates. Each agent, in choosing a matching rate to maximize utility, looks ahead at the effect of his or her choice on the outcome of the second stage of the process. This second stage determines the a_i's, again as the Nash equilibrium outcome of a noncooperative game. Matching rates are known, having been determined during the first stage, and each now chooses an optimal flat rate taking all other flat rates as given. It may be shown that, if agents are identical with zero income effects associated with the public good, the Nash equilibrium of this two-stage process is Pareto optimal. If there are many individuals and heterogeneous tastes, the outcome is no longer Pareto optimal, but Guttman shows that the divergence from optimality is less than predicted by the Nash equilibrium of the simple subscription game. Indeed, the latter is a special case of Guttman's model of matching behavior, being obtained by putting all matching rates equal to zero, instead of letting them be determined as the outcome of a noncooperative game. In a more recent paper, Guttman (1983) extends his analysis to incorporate nonzero income effects, which complicate matters and imply suboptimality at the equilibrium.

The matching process works essentially by lowering the effective price to an individual of a unit of the public good. Suppose one unit costs one dollar to produce. If I know that the rest of the community's matching rate is zero, then I also know that an extra dollar's contribution from me will increase the total supply by one unit. If, however, the matching rate is unity, then an extra dollar from me will generate two extra units of the public good. The effective price per unit is halved. It pays to choose a positive matching rate because this encourages higher flat contributions by others. Similar matching processes are regularly observed in the world around us. Federal governments will often contribute to public projects by making both a flat contribution and a commitment to match state governments' outlays at a given rate.

9.2   Nonmarket institutions and public goods

One can interpret the matching model of Section 9.1 as departing from the subscription model by introducing an element of cooperation into the picture. Agents agree to abide by the rules of the two-stage game, recognizing that if all do so then gains can be had. Within those rules, noncooperative behavior persists, the equilibrium of each stage being the Nash noncooperative equilibrium. One might then pose the question: What incentives are there for the individual to continue to play the game and not take a free ride by reverting to the Nash behavior analyzed in Chapter 5? One such set of incentives may be provided by the evolution of social and political institutions that provide an alternative framework within which public good provision is decided. Such institutions may affect the allocation decision in two distinct ways. They may simply change the values of payoffs associated with the various actions taken by agents. Individuals may agree beforehand to submit to a common set of rules, backed by punishments and rewards, which, for example, change a Prisoner's Dilemma into a game in which the Nash equilibrium is Pareto optimal. Alternatively, institutions may come into being that create new actions. A system of representative government presents individuals with opportunities to vote for a person or party to represent them in decisions involving, inter alia, the provision of public goods. Whatever form such institutions take, it should be emphasized that the temptation for individuals to lie about their preferences remains, and may exert an important influence on the particular set of rules that evolves.

The investigation of such nonmarket institutions raises fresh issues, such as voting theory, that take one outside the mainstream of microeconomic analysis. Their comparison with the outcomes of market structures is an important task but also a difficult one. Johansen (1977) argues that the heavy emphasis in public goods theory on the free-rider problem may be misplaced because typically a political process is involved, perhaps with a hierarchy of elected representatives or appointed bureaucrats, which produces very different outcomes from those of the individualistic subscription model. He further claims that the free-rider problem may not be empirically important in such a system. One can readily agree with his first point, but the importance of free riding and of the inefficiency of resource allocations implied by political processes is still very much an open question.

A proper assessment of the performance of alternative institutional structures in the presence of public goods requires a positive theory of their formation and behavior. This is a challenge that has been taken up by public choice theorists, with prominent contributions being made by Downs (1957), Buchanan and Tullock (1962), Niskanen (1971), and Buchanan (1975). The general thrust of much of this literature is that, contrary to Johansen's view, political processes are typically characterized by political failures, analogous to the market failures treated so extensively in microeconomics textbooks. For example, Downs (1957), Mueller (1979), and also Sandler, Cauley, and Tschirhart (1983) argue that there may be a conflict between the interests of public officials and those of their constituents, while Oppenheimer (1979) cites Arrow's impossibility theorem to support his argument that public officials may not be able to aggregate their constituencies' preferences in a coherent manner even if they wish to do so. The institution of a local government in which officials decide provision has attracted attention (see, e.g., Adams 1965; Breton 1970; Isserman 1975; Kiesling 1976; Williams 1966). Of particular interest in countries with a federal structure is the assignment of functions and the interrelations between the central government and the member states (see Oates 1972; Breton and Scott 1978). Sandler and Cauley (1977) explicitly account for transaction or "linkage" benefits and costs associated with a governmental linkage of two or more agents for the purpose of achieving a cooperative solution (see also

Auster and Silver 1973; Breton and Scott 1978). Linkage benefits include efficiency gains in approaching optimality, scale economies, and information and communication gains; linkage costs involve decision-making resources, administration expenses, enforcement expenditure, and the opportunity costs of interdependency. Co-operative agreements are *feasible* if *net* linkage benefits are positive for each potential participant. The optimal degree of cooperation or integration is chosen where marginal linkage benefits equal marginal linkage costs. In a later analysis, Sandler, Cauley, and Tschirhart (1983) present a positive public choice analysis and examine the likely workings of linkages when the policy makers' own preferences and constraints are taken into account. They conclude, as do many others, that the mere formation of a nonmarket structure need not reduce suboptimality; that is, markets may fail, but then so do governments.

In the present context, the term *institution* should be understood in a very broad sense. It refers not only to formal political and legal structures but also to the informal conventions and mores to which members of a community generally subscribe. Schotter (1981) defines a social institution as a regularity in social behavior that is agreed to by all members of society, specifies behavior in specific recurrent situations, and is either self-policed or policed by some external authority. His book represents an interesting attempt to develop a model of the organic evolution of social institutions using game-theoretic tools and applying the analysis to a wide range of problems, of which the provision of public goods is one. It is essentially a piece of positive analysis, in contrast to the normative analysis by Hurwicz (1972) and others of how satisfactorily given institutions perform according to some efficiency or welfare criterion. Schotter (1981, Chapter 5) argues, and we would agree, that the positive and normative approaches are complementary, and that a positive model is an essential ingredient in any normative comparison of institutions. This is particularly so in public goods theory. On the one hand, there is the presumption that, in some sense, provision of public goods by the market institution involves inefficiency, so that one might expect development of institutions that do better and make available the free lunch implied by the Nash–Cournot subscription equilibrium. On the other hand, we do in fact observe a bewildering array of informal and formal institutions that govern the provision of public goods. As we suggested in Chapter 3, the evaluation and comparison of institutions is not a straightforward matter, and much remains to be done in this exciting area.

9.3 Nonzero conjectures and public goods

Let us return, as promised, to the individual subscription model of provision of a public good. We suppose now that individuals do not enjoy complete information, and that the subscription decision has to be made repeatedly over time, with an equilibrium to be established in each consecutive discrete time period. In this context it has been argued, principally by students of oligopoly theory such as Frisch (1933) and, more recently, Bresnahan (1981), Perry (1982), and Kamien and Schwartz (1983), that the static Nash equilibrium, here interpreted as a zero conjectural variation equilibrium, is open to objection. The Nash assumption is that each individual expects no response by the rest of the community to variation in his or her own contribution. However, unless the reaction curve of the rest of the community is in fact horizontal, reflecting an actual response of zero, such a conjecture is not consonant with observable facts. If an individual were to experiment by making small changes in his or her contribution, then the presence of a nonzero response would in time be revealed to him or her. A truly rational individual, these authors argue, would learn from such an experience and revise his or her conjectures concerning the response of others in the appropriate direction.

This observation suggests that the model may profitably be modified to incorporate nonzero conjectures. As a first step, consider the introduction of arbitrary, exogenously imposed, conjectures. Suppose an individual expects a constant response on the part of the rest of the community's expected contribution, $\tilde{Q}^e$, to changes in his or her own contribution:

$$\frac{d\tilde{Q}^e}{dq} = \alpha,$$

where α is an exogenous constant. This can be represented by a family of expectations paths in $(q, \tilde{Q})$ space:

$$\tilde{Q}^e = \alpha q + K$$

in which K is an arbitrary constant of integration. The family of paths is generated by varying K. The zero conjectural variation model is obtained by putting α equal to zero. Positive values of α correspond to positive conjectural variations—the expectation that an increase in one's own contribution will generate an increase in $\tilde{Q}$—and negative conjectural variations are characterized by negative α. Figure 9.2

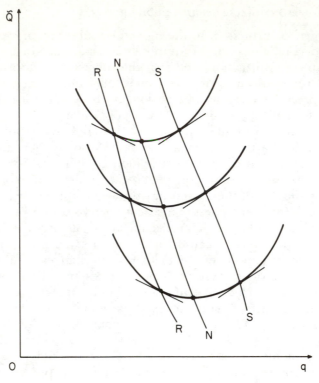

Figure 9.2

shows the consequences of different values of α for the position of the individual's reaction curve. Zero conjectural variations imply horizontal expectations paths, and their tangents with the indifference curves define the Nash reaction curve, *NN*. Positive conjectures imply positively sloped expectations paths whose tangencies with the indifference curves define the reaction curve *SS*. Observe that for any given value of $\bar{Q}$, the individual's optimal q under positive conjectural variations exceeds that implied by zero conjectures. The expectation that an extra unit of q will encourage extra contributions by others has the effect, as in the matching model, of lowering the effective unit price that the individual perceives himself as facing. This encourages a greater contribution than would be made under zero conjectures. Indeed, this is precisely the mechanism at work in Lindahl's thought experiment discussed in Chapter 6. For variations about a Lindahl equilibrium, individual h correctly perceives that q_h

$= \theta_h Q = \theta_h(\tilde{Q}_h + q_h)$, where θ_h is his or her constant, institutionally imposed, cost share. Consequently $\tilde{Q}_h = [(1 - \theta_h)/\theta_h]q_h$ and hence $d\tilde{Q}_h/dq_h = (1 - \theta_h)/\theta_h$. In Lindahl's experiment it is as if, starting at the origin where $q_h = 0$, the individual faces the conjectural variation $(1 - \theta_h)/\theta_h$. The difference between this term and α_i is one of interpretation. In the neighborhood of a stable equilibrium, a parametric increase in the value of α_i, the ith individual's conjectural variation, will lead to an increase in the equilibrium provision of the public good implied by the intersection of the appropriate reaction curves. Negative conjectural variations, on the other hand, give rise to a reaction curve such as RR in Figure 9.2, and imply lower equilibrium provision of the public good. In short, positive conjectural variations tend to mitigate the systemic free-rider problem, whereas negative conjectural variations tend to exacerbate it by comparison with the Nash equilibrium.

An alternative to given linear conjectural variations is the following nonlinear relationship:

$$d\tilde{Q}^e/dq = b(q/\tilde{Q})^\theta,$$

integration of which yields

$$\tilde{Q}^{\theta+1} = bq^{\theta+1} + K.$$

This formulation allows us to capture the idea that the less important an individual's contribution relative to $\tilde{Q}$, the less he or she expects variations in q to be noticed and to provoke a response by other contributors. Figure 9.3 shows the families of expectations contours generated by different values of b. The parameter θ is the elasticity of the conjectural response $d\tilde{Q}^e/dq$ with respect to the relative importance of the individual's contribution, $q/\tilde{Q}$. A special case of this formulation, in which $b = 1$, is treated in more detail by Cornes and Sandler (1984b). An immediate implication of this class of expectations functions is that as the number of identical individuals in a single public goods model is increased, the neighborhood of the symmetric equilibrium is characterized by conjectural variations that converge to the Nash or zero conjecture assumption.

By itself, the replacement of zero by nonzero conjectural variations does not answer the criticism that the exogenously imposed conjectures will typically be inconsistent with actual responses. One response to this criticism is to follow the example of Bresnahan (1981) and Perry (1982) and other oligopoly literature by defining a more exacting equilibrium concept. If, at some allocation, individuals' conjectures concerning the response of others are not identical with

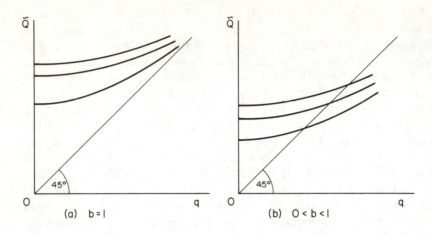

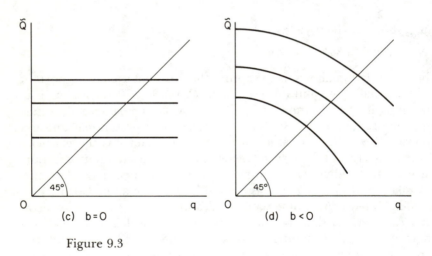

Figure 9.3

their actual responses, such an allocation cannot persist as an equilibrium, since over time individuals will change their conjectures and consequently their subscription levels. This suggests that we should introduce the notion of a *consistent conjectures equilibrium*. This is an equilibrium in whose neighborhood every agent's conjectural variation $d\tilde{Q}/dq$ is identical to the optimal actual response of the other agents. Thus, the Nash equilibrium in the two-person economy is a consistent conjectures equilibrium if and only if the reaction curves of individuals 1 and 2 are vertical and horizontal, respectively.

The general properties of such equilibria are problematic. Their existence and uniqueness are not in general guaranteed. However, if we are prepared to impose extra structure on the model, some conclusions suggest themselves. For example, if the private good and the pure public good are both normal goods, Nash reaction curves will have negative slopes. This suggests that if conjectural variations are initially zero, they will in time be revised and become negative. If a consistent conjectures equilibrium exists in this model, there seems a presumption that it will involve negative conjectural variations, which will tend to exacerbate the tendency toward underprovision. Cornes and Sandler (1983) investigate this issue in the context of the tragedy of the commons and find that there, too, the consistent conjectures equilibrium implies even greater overexploitation of a common property resource than does the Nash equilibrium.

The imposition of consistent conjectures as a defining characteristic of equilibrium in a dynamic context is not without its problems or, indeed, its critics. Friedman (1983, p. 110), discussing its use in the context of oligopoly, argues for a more full-blooded dynamic model. In the context of public goods, this is a relatively unexplored area. We have already referred, in Chapter 8, to repeated games of public goods provision with binary choice. Allowing a continuous choice variable must add difficulties to an analysis that, in the first place, has not been able to yield very strong results. Experimental work, of the kind carried out by Guttman (1983), may help to indicate the phenomena to be explained—whether, for example, the static Nash equilibrium does indeed overstate or understate the dynamic equilibrium level of provision. Again, recent work on interdependence between oligopolists may offer interesting ideas on modeling the processes of learning and adjustments over time.

PART IV

Clubs and club goods

CHAPTER 10

Homogeneous clubs and local public goods

A club is a voluntary group deriving mutual benefit from sharing one or more of the following: production costs, the members' characteristics, or a good characterized by excludable benefits. The focus of our analysis is the sharing of the last item, which we term a *club good*. A number of aspects of the club definition deserve highlighting. Clubs must be voluntary; members choose to belong because they anticipate a benefit from membership. Thus, the utility *jointly* derived from membership and the consumption of other goods must exceed the utility associated with nonmembership status. This voluntarism serves as one factor by which to distinguish between pure public goods and club goods. In the case of a pure public good, voluntarism may be absent, since the good may harm some recipients (e.g., defense to a pacifist, fluoridation to someone who opposes its use). However, harm could never befall a club member, at least usually not more than once,[1] because the right of exit is always available! For pure public goods, avoidance cost may be prohibitively high—that is, doing without fluoridated water may impose significant costs on the avoider—and hence the consumer may have to suffer harmful effects.

Second, clubs involve sharing, whether it is the use of an impure public good or the enjoyment of the desirable attributes of the members. Sharing often leads to a partial rivalry of benefits as larger memberships crowd one another, causing a detraction in the quality of the services received. Throughout Parts IV and V, *crowding* and *congestion* will be used interchangeably, implying simply that one user's utilization of the club good decreases the benefits or the quality of service still available to the remaining users. As such, crowding or congestion depends on some measure of utilization, which could include the number of members, the number of visits, or the ratio of members to the number of units provided (i.e., a measure of average utilization). Club congestion may assume sundry forms, including, among others, higher bacteria counts in swimming pools, longer travel time on highways, or increased noise levels at public performances. As membership size expands, both costs and benefits arise: Costs involve increased congestion, while benefits result from cost reductions owing to the sharing of provision expense associated with the club good. By adding a cost offset to the benefits derived from expanding membership size, crowding leads to finite memberships, a second characteristic serving to distinguish club goods from pure public goods. For the latter, *crowding costs are zero*, and therefore new users can be included always at a net benefit owing to reduced per-person assessments. Hence, the optimal sharing size for a pure public good includes the entire population of the jurisdiction.[2] Mancur Olson (1965, pp. 36–43) called such a group an *inclusive group*, since everyone should be included. Clubs sharing partially rival public goods are *exclusive groups*—for example, recreation facilities, tennis clubs, swimming pools, and highways.

A third distinguishing feature of clubs is the presence of an *exclusion mechanism*, whereby users' rates of utilization can be monitored and nonmembers and/or nonpayers can be barred. Without such a mechanism, there would be no incentives for members to join and to pay dues and other fees. The operation and provision of an exclusion mechanism, such as a turnstile or a toll booth, must be at a reasonable cost. By reasonable, we mean that the associated cost of the exclusion mechanism is less than the benefits gained from allocating the shared good within a club arrangement. Suppose that a club *augments* efficiency for a group of individuals by $1,000 a year by utilizing the exclusion mechanism to assign the proper per-visit tolls and consequently the total charges to the members. Without this exclusion mechanism, the good would be provided publicly, if at all, and its expenses paid through some form of taxation. Since the latter arrangement is likely to assign fees not truly based on marginal benefits received, efficiency losses result. In our example, these losses amounted to $1,000 a year. Therefore if the exclusion mechanism can be provided and operated *for anything less than* $1,000 a year, the costs are considered reasonable and the exclusion mechanism is justified. For a pure public good, the erection and maintenance of an exclusion mechanism may be too costly, since costs usually exceed the implied efficiency gains arising from exclusion; thus, it is better to allow the pure public good's benefits to remain nonexcludable (see Kamien, Schwartz, and Roberts 1973). To understand this point, consider the cost of erecting some type of exclusion mechanism with respect to national defense benefits. The costs, if such a mechanism were even feasible, would be astronomical. Although inefficiencies result, the pure public good must, therefore, be financed by either a specific tax or an allocation of funds from a general revenue source, such as an income, sales, or property tax.

In Chapter 7, we looked at congestion as a joint product phenomenon that can be described as an impure public good giving rise to a private output and a pure public output. The public output constitutes the congestion, a public bad experienced by other users. That analysis differs from our analysis of clubs since, in Chapter 7, membership size was not examined when provision conditions were derived—that is, congestion arose solely from utilization rates associated with a *given* set of users. This is the proper procedure whenever exclusion is not practiced because it is too costly and illegal (i.e., a constitutional constraint prohibits it), or the private benefit induces near-optimal behavior without restrictions in membership size.

A final attribute of clubs is its dual decisions. Since exclusion is practiced, members with user privileges must be distinguished from nonmembers. Moreover, the provision quantity of the shared good must be determined. Insofar as the membership decision affects the provision choice and vice versa, neither can be determined independently. For pure public goods, however, only the provision decision need be considered—membership is the entire population.

The purpose of this chapter is to present a model of homogeneous clubs in which provision and membership decisions are derived and interpreted. A homogeneous club includes members whose tastes *and* endowments are identical. If either tastes or endowments differ, then the club is called *heterogeneous* or *mixed*. Mixed clubs are studied in Chapter 11. For homogeneous clubs, the entire analysis can be carried out in terms of a representative member since everyone has the same identity. The bulk of the club literature has focused upon these so-called homogeneous clubs.[3]

The chapter is divided into six sections. A brief history of club theory is given in Section 10.1. Section 10.2 presents a taxonomy of clubs. Section 10.3 contains a theoretical model of homogeneous clubs. A diagrammatic treatment is presented in Section 10.4. Section 10.5 examines the optimal number of clubs and its relationship to Tiebout's analysis of local public goods. Section 10.6 summarizes the discussion.

10.1 A brief history of club theory

Although the majority of economic articles examining clubs have appeared since James Buchanan wrote his seminal piece, "An Economic Theory of Clubs" (1965), the origins of "club theory" can be traced to the works of A. C. Pigou (1920) and Frank Knight (1924) on tolls for congested roads. These two authors assumed the existence of two alternative commuting routes: a narrow congested road of good quality and a broad uncongested road of poor quality. By determining the tolls on the congested road, Pigou and Knight were essentially solving a club problem, since the toll would restrict users and, thereby, determine "membership size" for the congested highway.[4]

Another pioneering club model is that of Charles Tiebout (1956), whose "voting-with-the-feet" hypothesis attempted to show how jurisdictional size of local governments could be determined by voluntary mobility (or membership) decisions. In the Tiebout model, the amount of the shared local public good is fixed and distinct for each governmental jurisdiction. With costless mobility and perfect information, Tiebout envisioned the consumers partitioning themselves among the different jurisdictions according to their tastes. The resulting partition would be optimal, provided that the mix of jurisdictions and individuals could match, while achieving minimum average cost of provision in each jurisdiction. Thus, Tiebout specified a decentralized decision mechanism that could achieve Pareto optimality for local public goods. As we will demonstrate later, the Tiebout model is akin to homogeneous or mixed population situations in which individuals are partitioned into clubs, each containing *homogeneous* members.

In a private good context, Wiseman (1957) examined a club principle for sharing costs among users of a public utility. Owing to economies of scale for some public utilities such as electricity, the cost per unit of service drops as more units are provided and sold to the consumers. By coalescing a large number of customers into a cost-sharing arrangement, a public utility can take advantage of these scale economies and thus provide the service at a low per-unit charge. Wiseman called such arrangements clubs and argued that cost sharing justified these collectives. Tiebout and Wiseman were the first researchers to focus on a cost-sharing rationale for clubs.

The two most influential early club investigations are those of Mancur Olson (1965) and Buchanan (1965). Olson recognized that clubs would form to exploit economies of scale and to share public goods. He also distinguished between inclusive and exclusive clubs (1965, pp. 34–43). As mentioned previously, inclusive clubs share pure public goods and require no restrictions on the size of membership, whereas exclusive clubs share impure public goods and require a size limitation owing to crowding. Although Olson's and Buchanan's analyses appeared at almost the same time and bore some striking similarities, Olson's examination never generated the same interest as that of Buchanan. Three reasons could explain this differential influence. First, Olson's analysis of clubs was not the primary focus of *The Logic of Collective Action*, which was concerned with the effects of group size on the provision of a pure public good. In fact, Olson's work contained enough seminal ideas to overshadow his notion of clubs. Second, Olson failed to use the term *club* for a collective that shares an impure public good. Finally, Olson's (1965), pp. 22–36) club model was perhaps less clearly depicted than that of Buchanan.

Whatever the cause, the Buchanan (1965) paper generated a vast literature on clubs consisting of well over 200 articles (Sandler and Tschirhart 1980, pp. 1515–21). Buchanan introduced club theory to bridge the Samuelsonian gap between private and pure public goods (see Samuelson 1954, 1955). In the Buchanan piece, the first analytical statement of both the provision and membership conditions were derived for clubs sharing an impure public good. Moreover, Buchanan (1965, pp. 6–12) demonstrated how these two decisions interact.

Since the time of these pioneers, club theory has been extended in numerous fashions. For example, Tollison (1972) and DeSerpa (1977) examined discriminatory clubs, where notice is taken of the members' attributes and charges are adjusted accordingly. Pauly's (1967, 1970b) game-theory analysis was concerned with the stability of club membership and the optimal number of clubs for a given population. Artle and Averous (1973) and Helpman and Hillman (1977) derived the optimal conditions for clubs that exclude some population members; that is, not all members of the population belong to a club. Thus, both members' and nonmembers' utilities must be considered (see Chapter 11). Other investigators[5] have studied stochastic aspects of clubs, including demand and supply random factors. For example, a member may not be guaranteed admittance since capacity may be reached on some occasions owing to other users. Such capacity problems lead to uncertainty in utilization. In yet another extension, Sandler (1982) analyzed intergenerational clubs in which multiple generations of members share the same club good over time. Myriad other extensions are discussed in the following chapters; hence, this brief history is merely an introduction to the literature.

10.2 A taxonomy of clubs

Table 10.1 presents a taxonomy consisting of eight distinct categories. As with any taxonomy, the division is not meant to be unique or

Table 10.1. *Taxonomy of clubs*

Membership	Utilization	
	Fixed	Variable
Homogeneous (population partitioned)	A	B
Homogeneous (population not partitioned)	C	D
Mixed (population partitioned)	E	F
Mixed (population not partitioned)	G	H

best. Another taxonomy, somewhat similar to the one in Table 10.1, has been proposed by Berglas, Helpman, and Pines (1982, p. 345).[6]

Our taxonomy groups models according to the type of utilization assumed, the composition of the members, and the partitioning of the population. For fixed-utilization clubs, all members are assumed to utilize the entire supply of the shared good. If utilization is variable, however, some kind of visitation rate is involved. Clubs can also be distinguished by their membership composition into homogeneous and mixed clubs. A final decomposition concerns whether the population is partitioned into a set of clubs. This last distinction is based on the number of clubs formed and is tied to game-theoretic notions, explained later. If the population is partitioned, then every member belongs to some club sharing that good, and no member belongs to two different clubs providing the same good. When the population is not partitioned, club and nonclub members must be distinguished whenever Pareto-optimal conditions are derived. Thus, a "total-economy" viewpoint is taken, since what goes on outside the club is also relevant when optimal behavior is being determined.

This chapter is primarily concerned with Cell A in Table 10.1; however, some mention will be made of Cells B, C, and D. The variable utilization distinction is more relevant for mixed clubs in which taste differences induce individuals to utilize the shared facility to varying degrees.

10.3.　The basic model: homogeneous clubs with fixed utilization rates

In the basic model, we assume the existence of two goods: a private good (y) and a club good (X). The homogeneous members possess the same tastes and endowments. A representative member's taste is represented by a utility function,

$$U^i = U^i(y^i, X, s), \tag{1}$$

where y^i is the ith member's consumption of the private good, X is his consumption of the club good, and s is the membership size. Since the utilization rate of the club good is the same for each member, we have $x^i = X$ for all members, where x^i is the ith member's utilization rate of the club facility and X is the size of the club facility. Hence, each member is viewed as using what is available. We assume that the utility function satisfies standard requirements. In particular, increases in *either good* increase utility (i.e., nonsatiation characterizes the goods), the indifference curves are convex to the origin in goods-space (i.e., quasi-concavity), and the utility function is twice continuously differentiable. This latter assumption allows us to take up to two derivatives; hence, s is implicitly assumed to be continuous. The marginal utility derived from additional members may be positive for small memberships owing to camaraderie, but eventually crowding occurs and marginal utility becomes negative. Congestion therefore results in a decrease in utility as membership size expands beyond some point, $\bar{s}$ (i.e., $U^i_s = \partial U^i/\partial s < 0$ for $s > \bar{s}$). The existence of both a costless exclusion mechanism and congestion implies that the club good is not a pure public good in the Samuelsonian sense, even though club provision is consumed equally by all members.

Each member attempts to maximize utility subject to a resource constraint,

$$F^i(y^i, X, s) = 0. \tag{2}$$

This resource or budget constraint depends on the two goods used and the overall club membership size. An increase in either good raises cost to the individual, so that $\partial F^i/\partial y^i > 0$ and $\partial F^i/\partial X > 0$. Since everyone is identical and since club costs are equally shared among members, a membership increment reduces resource expenditures for each member—that is, $\partial F^i/\partial s < 0$. In other words, each member must pick up a smaller share of the club's total costs as membership expands and other things are constant.

The representative member maximizes utility subject to the budget constraint in (2). The following first-order conditions result from this maximization:[7]

$$MRS^i_{Xy} = MRT^i_{Xy} \qquad i = 1, \ldots, s \qquad \text{(Provision)} \tag{3}$$

$$MRS^i_{sy} = MRT^i_{sy} \qquad i = 1, \ldots, s. \qquad \text{(Membership)} \tag{4}$$

Equation (3) is the provision condition for the shared good and indicates that for each member the marginal rate of substitution (*MRS*) between the club good and the private good must be equated to the marginal rate of transformation (*MRT*) between these two goods. Thus, for the club good, members equate their marginal benefit with their marginal cost.[8] The i superscript denotes the individual, and hence MRT^i_{Xy} refers to the individual's marginal cost ratio between the two goods. If, at the margin, the club is breaking even in providing the public good, the sum of the members' marginal cost (or payments) must equal the club's marginal cost of provision (i.e., $\sum_{i=1}^{s} MRT^i_{Xy} = MRT_{Xy}$). Equation (3) then indicates that the usual Samuelson provision condition for public goods holds for the club good (i.e., $\sum_{i=1}^{s} MRS^i_{Xy} = MRT_{Xy}$). In the basic model, the provision condition of the club good does not differ significantly from that of a pure public good, except in terms of the number of individuals aggregated by the summation index *and* the interaction of the provision and membership condition.

The novel aspect of club analysis shows up in the membership condition, expressed in (4). For "within-club" optimality, a representative member equates the *MRS* between group size and the private good [left-hand side of (4)] with the associated *MRT* [right-hand side of (4)], thereby achieving an equality between the marginal benefits and marginal costs from having another club member. These marginal benefits are normally negative owing to crowding, and the corresponding marginal costs are negative owing to cost reductions derived from cost sharing. Since by assumption a whole member must be added (or removed) from the club, the membership condition may not be satisfied as an equality. That is, going from s to $s + 1$ members may reverse an inequality between the two sides of (4). When this discreteness problem occurs, members should be added, provided that marginal benefits exceed marginal costs. The membership size *prior* to the reversal of the inequality is optimal. A pure public good club could accommodate the entire population because marginal benefits from new members are zero and therefore are always greater than the corresponding negative marginal costs. Consequently, pure public goods do not require a membership restriction.[9]

It is crucial to keep in mind two aspects of the basic model. First, the provision and membership conditions must be *simultaneously* determined, since the *MRS* and *MRT* expressions in (3) and (4) depend on the same variables. Second, utility is maximized for the representative member; that is, average net benefits are maximized. This within-club viewpoint, which ignores nonmembers, may lead to Pareto optimality under certain circumstances. Specifically, the club must be replicable, and the entire homogeneous population must be a multiple of the optimal membership size determined in (4). This latter requirement means that the population can be partitioned into a set of clubs with no one left out (Cell A in Table 10.1). When this is the case, maximizing average net benefits is the same as maximizing total net benefits and no redistribution of members can improve on the net benefits of each and every club. We return to this issue in Section 10.5, Chapter 11, and Chapter 13.

Before presenting a graphic depiction of our results, we introduce an alternative model in which a specific formulation is given to a member's resource constraint, $F^i(\cdot)$:

$$I = y + C(X, s)/s, \tag{5}$$

where I is the individual's income, the price of the private good is one, and $C(\cdot)$ is the club's cost. Superscripts are dropped from now on whenever members are homogeneous. Club cost depends positively on both the size of the shared facility and the number of members; this latter influence reflects maintenance costs associated with utilization.[10] Dividing club costs by the membership size indicates that club costs are equally shared in (5).

To find the optimal provision and membership requirements, a representative member is depicted as maximizing his or her utility function, (1), subject to (5). First-order conditions are

$$(MRS_{Xy}) = U_X/U_y = C_X/s \qquad \text{(Provision)} \tag{6}$$

$$(MRS_{sy}) = U_s/U_y = [sC_s - C(\cdot)]/s^2 \qquad \text{(Membership)}, \tag{7}$$

where subscripts on the U's and the C's denote partial derivatives.

For the provision condition, the MRS between the two goods is equated with the individual's share of the marginal costs of provision. Cross-multiplying by s in (6) gives the standard Samuelsonian provision condition, equating the sum of MRSs and marginal cost. Optimal membership requires an equality between the relevant MRS and the marginal costs of increasing membership size. The latter includes increased maintenance fees (i.e., C_s/s) and reduced membership fees owing to sharing (i.e., $-C(\cdot)/s^2$). In this alternative representation, full financing always results since the budget constraint divides the club costs among the members. We will return often to this alternative model.

10.4   A graphic representation

For the reader to gain further insight into the operation of the basic model, we include a graphic representation in the four quadrants of Figure 10.1. The graphic model invokes the same assumptions as the mathematical model. Optimal provision amounts are shown for three different membership sizes in quadrant I. The quantity of the public good is measured on the abscissa, and the total cost and benefit *per* member are measured on the ordinate. The shape of the benefit curve indicates diminishing returns to consumption, and that of the cost curve reflects constant returns to scale. For a given membership size (say s_1), optimal provision corresponds to the X value (i.e., X_2) that equates the slopes of the total benefit, $B(s_1)$, and the total cost, $C(s_1)$ curves confronting a member. Hence, quadrant I equilibria satisfy (3). As membership size increases to s_2, the total benefit per member curve shifts down owing to crowding. Additionally, the total cost per member curve rotates down proportionally as more members share the costs for each facility size. When membership is s_2, optimal provision corresponds to X_3 units of the club good. Similarly, X^* is optimal for s^* members. These optima can be transferred to quadrant IV in the form of the X_{opt} curve depicting the optimal provision amount for each membership size.

For each amount of the club good or facility, an analogous exercise in quadrant II determines the membership size that maximizes per person net benefits. The benefit curves in quadrant II show the benefit per person associated with a changing membership size when the facility size is fixed at X_1, X_2, and X^* units. The shape of these curves indicates that camaraderie is eventually overpowered by crowding, and at that point the benefit per person begins to decline. In the same quadrant, the cost curves depict the cost per member when a facility of a given size is shared by a varying number of members. Owing to the equal cost-sharing assumption, these cost curves are rectangular hyperbolas. As the facility size increases, both the benefit and the cost curves shift up. For each facility size, the optimal membership results when the slope of the corresponding benefit and cost curves are equal [i.e., (4) is satisfied]: s_1 is optimal for facility size X_1; s_2 is optimal for X_2; and s^* is optimal for X^*. These optima can be transferred to quadrant IV in terms of the s_{opt} curve showing the optimal membership for each amount of provision. This transfer is accomplished via quadrant III, which transposes membership information from quadrant II to IV.

Both the provision and the membership conditions are satisfied in

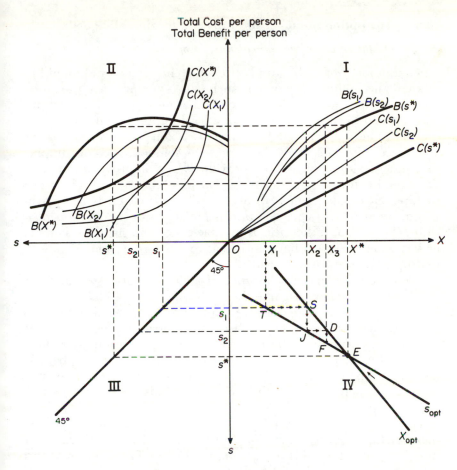

Figure 10.1

quadrant IV at point E where the s_{opt} and the X_{opt} curves intersect. If public good provision is X_1, a series of iterations shown by path $X_1 TSJDF \ldots E$ eventually forces the club to achieve optimal membership and the associated optimal provision at E. Three of these iterations are shown in quadrants I and II. For example, the club desires a membership of s_1, when output is X_1; however, a larger facility size X_2 is required to maximize average net benefits (in quadrant I) when membership is s_1. And so it goes until equilibrium is reached (see the darker curves in quadrants I and II for the equilibrium).

10.5   The optimal number of clubs and local public goods

On the core and the optimal number of clubs

When a number of clubs supply the same club good, one would like to know the optimal number of such clubs. For practical purposes, such an answer might indicate the optimal number of local jurisdictions needed to provide education, a local impure public good, to a country. The optimal number of clubs is integrally related to the game-theoretic concept of the *core*. As a solution, the core implies that no individual or set of individuals can improve upon their situation by forming a different partition. Since no individual's welfare can be augmented at a core solution, a core is necessarily Pareto optimal. If a core solution is obtained for a collection of m clubs, $(S_1, \ldots, S_m)$, then this is a stable collection, since no member or set of members will have an incentive to transfer among clubs or to drop out and form new clubs.

The conditions for the existence of a core are discussed in detail in Chapter 13, where a game-theory formulation of clubs is given. For now, we simply state the core solution found by Pauly (1967) for a homogeneous population. Pauly demonstrated that the core would consist of a partition of the population among a collection of clubs, each of which maximizes average net benefits. Since the membership and provision amounts satisfying (3) and (4), respectively, maximize average net benefits, each club must be of this membership size if the solution is in the core.

To find the optimal number of clubs, we must divide the optimal membership size associated with (4) into the population size. If an integer results, then this integer represents the Pareto-optimal core solution for the number of clubs. When an integer does not result, however, the core does not exist[11] since an excluded person has an incentive to trade places with a member, That is, an omitted individual can always bid his way into a club by offering to accept a payoff lower than that of a club member. The rejected member is then on the outside and free to bid his way into a club. This shuffling never ends.

Community size and the Tiebout Hypothesis

In his celebrated article, Tiebout (1956) specified a model in which "voting with the feet" for the various public good packages, as represented by the different communities, circumvents the preference-revelation problem and, in so doing, achieves a Pareto-optimal allocation. Hence, a decentralized decision process can reach alloca- tive efficiency for local public goods. To ascertain this result, Tiebout (1956, p. 419) invoked some limiting assumptions regarding the *continuity* of choice, public good provision, income, and costs. He assumed that a sufficiently large number of communities exists, each with its own *fixed* public good package. Additionally, all individuals live on dividend income, have full knowledge of available public good packages, and can move costlessly between communities. For each community, an optimal size exists in which the cost per person for the public good package is at a minimum. Communities below this size will attract residents, whereas those above will repel residents, since public good costs are assumed to be shared equally. Finally, all intercommunity spillovers are zero; perfect exclusion for the com- munity club is possible.

Under certain assumptions, the Tiebout Hypothesis is identical to the type of homogeneous club depicted in Cell A or B, since the hypothesis requires a population to be partitioned into different clubs or communities. A worthwhile exercise is to specify these restrictive assumptions in order to determine to what extent Tiebout follows the standard club model. We begin with the most restrictive scenario and then relax assumptions where possible, drawing on the work of Berglas (1982, 1984), Berglas and Pines (1981), McGuire (1974a), Pauly (1970b), and others.

Up to now, the clubs have provided a single product; hence, we initially assume, unlike Tiebout, that each community provides a single public good. We further require cost sharing between com- munity members and a nonvariable utilization rate. With these restrictions, McGuire (1974a) has replicated the basic Tiebout result with the following club model:

$$\max_{\{y,X,s\}} \quad U(y, X)$$

$$\text{subject to} \quad I = y + C(X, s)/s, \tag{8}$$

where the variables are identical to those defined previously. This model differs slightly from the alternative model in Section 10.3. The cost function now captures not only provision cost, but also congestion cost; that is, C_s refers to crowding cost resulting from the number of members.

The first-order provision condition is again the sum of the *MRS*'s equals the marginal cost; but the membership requirement is

$$C_s = C/s, \tag{9}$$

which is the Tiebout requirement that per-person average cost be minimized. In (9), this follows, because the marginal cost per person equals the average cost per person that can only occur at the minimum point of the average cost curve. If everyone in the population is identical, then a collection of communities, all of size s^* associated with (9), should form. When s^* divides evenly into the population size, the implied solution is Pareto-optimal.

What happens if population is heterogeneous? On this issue, McGuire (1974a), Pauly (1970), and Berglas and Pines (1981) have demonstrated that homogeneous communities should form, so that *each homogeneous subset of the population is partitioned* into clubs or communities of size s^*, sharing the same amount of the local public good. However, the public good's quantity should vary between communities according to taste; that is, taste differences between communities are adjusted through the provision of the local public good, and hence the tax levy. Communities with the same taste share the same amount of public good. When each homogeneous subset of the population can be partitioned into a collection of homogeneous communities, and no one is left out (i.e., there is no "integer" problem), Pauly (1970b) and others have shown that this solution is in the core.

Next, we examine the implications of relaxing the fixed utilization requirement, allowing instead for a variable visitation rate. Again we assume a homogeneous population. Consider the following model of Berglas and Pines (1981):

$$\begin{aligned} \max_{\{y, X, v, s\}} \quad & U(y, X, v, sv) \\ \text{subject to} \quad & I = y + C(sv, X)/s, \end{aligned} \tag{10}$$

where v is the number of visits of an individual, and sv is the total visitation rate. The budget constraint is like the alternative model in which the visitation rate gives rise to maintenance cost ($\partial C/\partial(sv)$). Crowding considerations are included in the utility function, where $\partial U^i/\partial(sv) < 0$. Optimization yields a Samuelsonian provision condition, a visitation or user fee condition, and a membership condition. The visitation condition requires the user fee to equal the sum of marginal maintenance cost and marginal crowding cost. The membership condition indicates that, at an optimum, average cost *per visit* (i.e., C/sv) equals the marginal cost per visit. Again minimum average cost is implied, but now the average cost per visit is minimized. Partitioning the population as before, so that each community minimizes average cost, yields a Pareto optimum. This solution corresponds to Cell B in Table 10.1. Heterogeneous populations can also be treated as previously explained—that is, partitioned into homogeneous groupings.

These simplified representations clearly illustrate an analogy between club theory and the Tiebout hypothesis; however, some important aspects of the Tiebout model have been ignored. Foremost is the multiproduct or public good package assumption; all of the above models contain a single public good. Recently, Berglas (1984) and Berglas and Pines (1981) have extended the above analysis in an interesting fashion to multiproducts. We intend to present and to comment on these multiproduct models in Chapter 17, where multiproduct clubs are discussed. The two models also differ with respect to provision: Public good provision is held fixed in the Tiebout model, but not in the club model. Thus, the provision and membership decisions are not really simultaneously determined in the Tiebout model; instead, a population chooses among the alternative, *but given*, packages. A final difference involves the membership decision. Membership (or community) size is based solely on cost sharing in the Tiebout model, whereas size is also based on camaraderie in the club model.

The Tiebout model has a number of existence problems. First, the number of communities must be sufficiently large so that all individuals can locate a public good package ideally suited to their tastes. Failure to have a sufficiently large choice of communities results in a nonconvexity in the form of holes in the production or consumption set (see, e.g., Ellickson 1979; Richter 1978; Westhoff 1977; Wooders 1985). Second, the entire heterogeneous population must be partitioned into homogeneous groups, one group in each community, such that the cost per person for the public good package is a minimum. The mix of people may not be consistent with the mix of communities for this to happen. Third, the provision decision must be more closely tied to the membership decision if Tiebout solutions are truly optimal. Finally, local amenities of the communities must also be "right" and consistent with tastes.

10.6 Summary

This chapter has presented the essential theory of homogeneous clubs. As we extend the theory to more involved situations, the basic models of Section 10.3 will be used as a benchmark for comparison. We will discover that some extensions will not change results much, whereas others, such as uncertainty, will modify the analysis significantly.

For a cost-sharing club in which everyone is identical, the rules derived above would be relatively easy to institute. Tolls or membership fees would equal the cost of the club divided among the members. Provision equilibrium would equate the sum of the MRSs (marginal benefits) to the marginal provision cost. Since everyone is identical, the sum of the MRSs is equal to the number of members times the MRS of any member. Hence, any member's marginal benefit can be used to determine the club's marginal benefit from provisions. In the McGuire model, membership corresponds to minimum average cost per person. For mixed clubs, these calculations will not be so straightforward.

This chapter has given the history of club theory and has provided a taxonomy. Two basic models have been presented. Additionally, we have briefly examined the optimal number of clubs. Finally, we have presented the relationship between club theory and Tiebout's analysis of local public goods. As shown in Chapter 16, the analysis of homogeneous clubs has spawned a large volume of applied studies concerning local public goods.

CHAPTER 11

Clubs in general

This chapter extends the analysis of clubs begun in Chapter 10. Inasmuch as club analysis forms the underlying theory of local public goods, the study of these goods is also indirectly extended here. The previous chapter focused on homogeneous-member clubs. Of the eight categories listed in Table 10.1, Cells A and B were of primary interest in Chapter 10. This chapter focuses on the remaining six cells, C–H. The case in which some population members of homogeneous clubs are excluded is studied. This leads us into a more detailed discussion of the within-club and total-economy distinction, which depends on whose utility is included in the objective function. We are primarily concerned here with mixed clubs, especially those in categories G and H in which the population is not partitioned, that is, categories in which a predetermined number of clubs exists (see Berglas, Helpman, and Pines 1982).

The chapter contains seven sections. Section 11.1 focuses on the within-club and total-economy distinction. Section 11.2 presents a club model in which members are homogeneous, utilization rates are variable, and the population is not partitioned. Mixed clubs are investigated in Section 11.3. Alternative representations for mixed clubs models appear in Section 11.4. In Section 11.5, the optimal number of mixed clubs is discussed. Other issues in club theory are presented in Section 11.6. These issues include club discrimination, exclusion costs, and self-financing of clubs. A summary section concludes the chapter.

11.1   Club viewpoint and the partitioning issue

The distinction between partitioned populations and nonpartitioned populations is integrally tied to the within-club and total-economy dichotomy alluded to in Chapter 10. When the economy's population is not fully partitioned into a set of clubs, some individuals are excluded from clubs that provide the shared good. In this situation, Artle and Averous (1973) and Ng (1973) indicated that Pareto-optimal membership determination can only follow from an objective function that takes into account both members' and nonmembers' utilities. Such a representation is termed a total-economy viewpoint, since everyone's well-being is included. In contrast, the within-club models present only the viewpoint of members; hence, either a representative member's utility is maximized, as in the case of homogeneous clubs, or a social welfare function including only the members' utility levels is maximized, as in the case of mixed clubs.

A number of aspects of the within-club and total-economy viewpoints are worth emphasizing. First, the form of the objective function hinges on the viewpoint under consideration. Second, the relevant viewpoint is not determined by the type of membership; each viewpoint is relevant for mixed and homogeneous clubs, based upon whether the population has been partitioned or not. Third, a club's total net benefits are maximized whenever the total-economy viewpoint is taken. Average net benefits per member are relevant if a within-club viewpoint is used and all individuals are identical. Maximizing average net benefits need not imply optimizing total net benefits. For example, consider a club in which total net benefits are $16 for four identical members but are $18 for six members. Thus, average net benefits are greatest at $4, corresponding to four members. A six-member club involves an average net benefit of $3 and a total of $18. If a total-economy viewpoint is taken, then clubs of six will form. When a within-club viewpoint is relevant, however, clubs of four will form. Which approach yields Pareto optimality depends simply on the partitioning issue (see Section 11.3 and Chapter 13). Fourth, we should point out that the proper viewpoint is related to the distinction between a predetermined and a variable number of clubs. For a predetermined number of clubs, the total-economy viewpoint is best whenever the clubs' combined capacity cannot accommodate the entire population. In the variable number of clubs case, however, the within-club viewpoint is best, provided that the population is an integer multiple of the optimum club size.

11.2   Homogeneous members: a total-economy viewpoint

For the sake of generality, we consider a homogeneous club where the visitation or utilization rates are variable; thus, the visitation rate, v, is a choice variable along with provision and membership size. The visitation rate represents some continuously differentiable measure of utilization, such as time spent on highways or the number of miles traveled. The model below characterizes the Pareto-optimal equilibrium for a predetermined number of clubs, say a single club, when the population includes homogeneous individuals and the membership size, s, is large relative to the entire population, $\hat{s}$; i.e., $0 < \hat{s}/2 < s < \hat{s}$. A member's utility function is represented by

$$U[y, v, c(sv, X)], \tag{1}$$

where superscripts have been dropped since everyone is identical and $c(sv, X)$ is the congestion function, which depends positively on total visits, sv, and negatively on the club's capacity. In (1), the congestion function can be viewed as a quality index for the shared good, much like a characteristic in the household production approach (see Deaton and Muellbauer 1980, Chapter 10). An increase in total utilization, sv, augments congestion (i.e., $\partial c/\partial(sv) > 0$), whereas an increase in provision reduces congestion (i.e., $\partial c/\partial X < 0$). Utility depends positively on both the private good and visits, but negatively on congestion. The congestion function is employed throughout much of Part IV. Many different forms for the congestion function exist, including the identity mapping used in Chapter 10. Each representation has its own implications on such issues as self-financing through tolls. The form given in (1) is quite general.

To find the Pareto-optimal club requirements from a total-economy perspective, both members and nonmembers must be considered since some individuals are by assumption nonmembers. A nonmember's utility function, $\tilde{U}$, is

$$\tilde{U}(\tilde{y}, 0, 0), \tag{2}$$

where $\tilde{y}$ is his or her consumption of the private good. Since a nonmember is excluded from club services, he or she experiences no visits or congestion. Optimality conditions are derived by maximizing[1]

$$sU[y, v, c(sv, X)] + (\hat{s} - s)\tilde{U}(\tilde{y}, 0, 0) \tag{3}$$

with respect to s, y, $\tilde{y}$, v, and X, subject to a strictly convex transformation function, $F[sy + (\hat{s} - s)\tilde{y}, X] \leq 0$.[2] Upon rearrangement and simplification, the first-order Pareto-optimal conditions are[3]

$$(sc_2)MRS_{cy} = MRT_{Xy} \qquad \text{(Provision)}$$

$$MRS_{vy} = -(sc_1)MRS_{cy} \qquad \text{(Visitation or toll)}$$

$$\left[\frac{U(\cdot)}{U_y} - \frac{\tilde{U}(\cdot)}{\tilde{U}_y}\right] = -(svc_1)MRS_{cy} + (y - \tilde{y}), \qquad \text{(Membership)}$$

where $c_1 = \partial c/(sv) > 0$, and $c_2 = \partial c/\partial X < 0$.

The provision condition for facility size is the usual Samuelsonian one, requiring the sum of the *MRS*s to equal the marginal rate of transformation between the club good and the private good (MRT_{Xy}). In this condition, the *MRS* involves the tradeoff between congestion and the private good and is weighted by sc_2, which represents the effect on club congestion resulting from a unit increase in provision. For the toll condition, the per-visit toll equates a member's marginal valuation of a visit (i.e., MRS_{vy}) with the marginal crowding cost that a visit imposes on the entire membership (i.e., $-(sc_1)MRS_{cy}$). This condition holds for each member by equating the toll to the right-hand side. Thus the congestion externality becomes internalized; that is, a member must pay for the marginal congestion cost associated with each of his visits. Each member's total toll payment can be found by multiplying the toll by the number of visits. Finally, the membership condition, in conjunction with the satisfaction of the other conditions, determines the optimal s, thereby deciding the proportion of the population to exclude. The left-hand side is the *net gain* in utility, evaluated in terms of the marginal utility of the private good, that the marginal member derives from club inclusion and is expected to be nonnegative, thus providing a rationale for voluntary membership. The right-hand side represents the marginal costs resulting from the entrant's entire utilization of the shared good, in which the first term is the associated crowding costs and the second is the reallocation of the private good, required to maintain the private good's marginal benefit to the entrant both before and after membership. If being a member alters the marginal benefit of the private good (i.e., $\partial^2 U/(\partial v \partial y) \neq 0$), then a reallocation of the private good is required for optimality. A marginal entrant who views the private and shared goods as complements in the Edgeworth-Pareto sense (i.e., $\partial^2 U/(\partial v \partial y) > 0$) should receive more of the private good when becoming a member (i.e., $y > \bar{y}$), whereas an entrant who views these goods as substitutes should receive less of the private good when becoming a member.

Hillman and Swan (1983) view the $(y - \bar{y})$ as a *compensating variation* (*CV*) that maintains an entrant's utility at the preentry level. They employ a membership charge equal to this *CV* and deduct this fee, in real terms, from y in the utility function (p. 60). As such, members and nonmembers may have the same utility level, and thus there is no utility change term. This is, indeed, an interesting interpretation, but it may not be entirely consistent. Berglas, Helpman, and Pines (1982) have shown that if utility levels *are maintained at the same level* for members and nonmembers, then the quasi-concavity of utility assumption forces the club to be inclusive. The idea is that the quasi-concavity assumption induces people to seek a combination of goods, thus making it difficult to bring nonmembers who only consume the private good up to the utility level of a member. In fact, Berglas, Helpman, and Pines (1982) show that there should be no excluded individuals. We leave the reader to check on the particulars in their proof.

There are a number of interesting features of the total-economy optimal conditions to emphasize. First, by utilizing a Benthamite social welfare function, our solution yields a single Pareto-optimal point on a Pareto frontier. To generate the entire frontier, a different objective function would be required (see Hillman and Swan 1983, and Section 11.4). Second, the form of the membership condition implies a cardinal solution, since changes in utility are involved. Third, the discreteness aspect of membership has not altogether disappeared, even though utilization is a continuous variable. This aspect shows up in the discrete changes in both utility and private good consumption that membership entails. In some instances, the membership condition cannot be satisfied at any membership size and an inequality is necessary. Fourth, for fixed utilization, the visitation condition would drop out, since v is eliminated from members' utility functions. Visitation rights are then implied by membership.

11.3   Mixed clubs: total-economy viewpoint

We turn now to the case of mixed member clubs with members drawn from a heterogeneous population. As above, we present a total-economy viewpoint, thus assuming implicitly a predetermined number of clubs; that is, the model applies to Cell H in Table 10.1. For the sake of generality, we allow for a variable utilization rate, $v(i)$, for the ith individual. In this model, $v(i)$ may represent the visitation rate or some other measure of utilization (e.g., time spent on a highway). The basic problem can be presented in alternative ways, depending upon the form of the objective function. We give the "Benthamite" representation, leaving our discussion of other representations to the following section. For this Benthamite cardinal formulation, a weighted sum of the members' and nonmembers' utilities is maximized subject to a set of constraints that determines the feasible convex set.

When analyzing heterogeneous individuals, we require further notation to provide a rigorous statement of optimality. In particular, the population is assumed to be uniformly distributed over the interval [1, $\hat{s}$] so as to form a continuum of traders, thus permitting the membership size to be continuously differentiable. Members are indexed by $i \in [1, s]$, and nonmembers by $i \in [s, \hat{s}]$. To derive an unambiguous statement of optimal membership size, population members are rank-ordered along [1, $\hat{s}$] by their net willingness to pay for the club, as measured by their net gain from membership. This ordering is assumed to be invariant to the level of use and the degree of congestion.[4] The utility function of a member is now denoted by

$$U[y(i), v(i), c\left(\int_1^s v(i)di, X\right), i] \qquad i \in [1, s], \tag{4}$$

where the i's refer to the individual and the Lebesgue integral, $\int_1^s v(i)di$, is the club's total visitation rate. The Lebesgue integrals permit us to differentiate s as though it is a continuous variable almost everywhere. Throughout our presentation, the reader is invited to replace our integrals with discrete summation signs. When this is done, differentiation with respect to s must be approximated in terms of discrete changes. For nonmembers, their utility function is

$$\bar{U}(\bar{y}, 0, 0, i) \qquad i \in [s, \hat{s}]. \tag{5}$$

Optimal provision, toll, and membership conditions are derived by maximizing a Benthamite social welfare function,

$$\int_1^s w(i)U(\cdot, i)di + \int_s^{\hat{s}} w(i)\bar{U}(\cdot, i)di \tag{6}$$

with respect to X, s, $y(i)$, $\bar{y}(i)$, and $v(i)$, subject to the strictly convex transformation function,

$$F\left(\int_1^s y(\cdot)di + \int_s^{\hat{s}} \bar{y}(\cdot)di, X\right) \leq 0 \tag{7}$$

and subject to the impurity constraints,

$$v(i) \leq X \qquad i \in [l, s]. \tag{8}$$

In (6), $w(i)$ are welfare weights that may all equal one. The impurity constraint requires a member's utilization rate to be less than or equal to the shared good's capacity. This constraint allows members to have individualized utilization rates less than capacity. Changing this condition to a strict equality for all i alters the model to that of fixed utilization. In the conditions below, we have implicitly assumed a strict inequality for this constraint. Forming a Lagrangean[5] and taking first-order partials yield the following optimal conditions:

$$c_2 \int_1^s MRS_{cy}(i)di = MRT_{Xy} \qquad \text{(Provision)}$$

$$MRS_{vy}^j = -c_1 \int_1^s MRS_{cy}(i)di, \qquad j \in [1,s] \qquad \text{(Toll)}$$

$$\left[\frac{U(\cdot,s)}{\partial U(\cdot,s)/\partial y(s)} - \frac{\tilde{U}(\cdot,s)}{\partial \tilde{U}(\cdot,s)/\partial y(s)} \right] = -v(s) \int_1^s c_1 MRS_{cy}(i)di + [y(s) - \bar{y}(s)].$$

(Membership)

These conditions have analogous interpretations to those given in Section 11.2 and, except for two remarks, require no further discussion. Though members differ in their response to congestion, an identical toll, equal to the right-hand side of the toll condition, is charged per visit; however, total tolls paid by various members differ according to one's revealed intensity of utilization (e.g., the number of visits made). It is the monitoring of visits or utilization that allows clubs to circumvent the preference-revelation problem through a quasi-market type of arrangement. Our second remark concerns the derivation of the membership condition that requires the use of the Leibnitz rule for differentiating an integral with variable limits, here the limit s. To derive the proper membership condition, the limits on the integral must not be ignored. This error appears to have been made by Ng (1973) when deriving his membership condition.

The form of the congestion function is crucial to answering many questions associated with clubs. In (4), members have different tastes for utilization, the private good, and congestion. Congestion is treated as a technical phenomenon that depends on provision and total utilization, so that each individual faces the same congestion function. This setup means that tastes for facility size affect utility *indirectly* through congestion, thus allowing the crowding-internalizing toll to adjust fully for taste differences. If, however, people's tastes for facility size affect utility directly, as in the utility function,

$$U = U(y(i), v(i), \int_1^s v(i)di, X), \qquad (9)$$

then mixing would be suboptimal since people with different tastes for X are forced to consume some compromise standard. In Section 11.6, we demonstrate that the form of the congestion function also determines whether the toll can be used to self-finance the club.

The essential difference between the homogeneous and mixed club models for a predetermined number of clubs lies in the toll payments. In homogeneous clubs, everyone pays the same total tolls owing to their identity. For mixed clubs, members pay the same rate of toll, but their total toll payments differ in relation to tastes.

11.4   Alternative representations

In addition to the Benthamite approach, there are at least five other representations of the total-economy viewpoint for mixed clubs. Each representation may or may not alter the membership condition; however, the toll and provision conditions are invariant in form with respect to these alternative specifications. In the case of homogeneous membership, representations cannot show such variety owing to everyone's identity. When members are heterogeneous, however, the identification of the marginal entrant has an important bearing on the membership condition. Thus, heterogeneity of membership adds the likelihood of ambiguity to the membership condition *unless* some means of rank ordering is at our disposal.

A second representation maximizes the utility of an *arbitrarily designated* member's utility subject to the constancy of the other individuals' utility levels. Since the marginal entrant is not necessarily the designated individual, his or her utility is probably held constant; thus the ΔU term drops out of the membership condition. In this case, Δy is the CV. This depiction was proposed by Hillman and Swan (1983). It is an ordinal representation, but begs the question by assuming preknowledge about one individual's membership status prior to optimizing. Moreover, the optimal condition will differ depending on who is initially designated as a member—ambiguity is not circumvented.

A third approach is to maximize the utility of a member's utility subject to the constancy of other members' utility levels, where membership size and status are exogenously given (Oakland 1972). This approach yields just a toll and provision condition, since membership size is given. Oakland interprets his utilization condition as a membership condition, but this is clearly incorrect. Oakland's approach is not optimal with respect to membership determination. Exogenously given membership size representations correspond to the congestion models presented in Chapter 7.

Hillman and Swan (1983) present two variants of an ordinal depiction based on CV. In the first, they found the CV measure associated with club participation and use this CV measure to rank order individuals. The *CV* measure is designated the membership fee. The new utility functions are

$$U[\bar{y} - d, v, c(\cdot)],\tag{10}$$

where $\bar{y}$ is the initial endowment of the private good and d is the *CV*. In the Hillman-Swan representation, a member's utility, in the form of (10), is maximized subject to the constancy of other individuals' utility levels. The resulting membership condition does not contain a ΔU term owing to the *CV* charge. An equivalent alternative representation is to optimize the sum of the net *CV*'s over all club participants (Hillman and Swan 1983, pp. 59–61). These authors seem to forget that in this second approach they are assuming preknowledge of club participants—this is the same error made by Oakland, whom they reprimanded.

A fifth variant is to sell lottery tickets for club membership to the population, so that members pay both a lottery fee and a *CV* charge. Maximizing total expected utility of the population yields a membership condition identical to that in Section 11.3. This approach produces the entire Pareto ex-ante frontier as shown by Hillman and Swan (1983).

Which approach is best depends upon the information available. Each has its strengths and weaknesses, however, although the weaknesses are usually not mentioned by the researcher proposing a particular approach.

11.5   Mixed clubs: the replication issue

The issue of replicating mixed clubs is a hotly debated topic in the literature.[6] A reader studying the various arguments and counter-arguments would probably come away quite confused. Sandler and Tschirhart (1984b) have argued that replicating mixed clubs is optimal under certain circumstances, whereas Berglas and Pines (1981) have stated that replicating a mixed club is nonoptimal. Sandler and Tschirhart (1984b)[7] have shown that this issue hinges on the way that provision levels affect utility. Quite simply, if provision adds indirectly to utility through its effects on congestion, and if the congestion function is the same for everyone, then mixing is optimal since the toll arrangement, depicted in Section 11.3, fully internalizes taste differences through total toll payment. Replicating the mixed club is also optimal and might lead to a partition of the population (Cells E and F in Table 10.1) under fortuitous circumstances. When provision levels influence utility directly, however, there is no way to adjust for taste diversity and mixing is nonoptimal. It is interesting to note that Berglas (1984) has come around to this same conclusion in a recent paper, though he denied this very point in a reply to Sandler and Tschirhart (1984b; see Berglas and Pines 1984).

11.6   Other issues in club theory

Discrimination and clubs

In the non-game-theory literature, discriminatory clubs refer to those sharing arrangements in which members consume both the shared good and the characteristics or attributes (e.g., race, religion, appearance, presence) of the other members.[8] Each member has a fixed vector of characteristics that is made available to the other members according to his utilization rate of the club. Heavier users provide the club with a larger amount of their attributes than less heavy users. The total available quantity of any membership attribute depends upon the aggregate utilization rates of all members and the amount of that attribute associated with each member. By varying the utilization rate, a member determines his or her consumption of the other members' characteristics as well as that of the shared good; a jointness in consumption exists.

Members' characteristics may be viewed by the other members as generating either an increase (e.g., beauty, congeniality, intelligence) or a decrease (e.g., race, rudeness) in utility. Crowding can be treated as one characteristic of the membership that arises from the mere presence of the other members. Thus, the basic model in Section 11.3 can be extended to include discrimination, provided that a vector of membership characteristics is generated by the utilization rates and one characteristic corresponds to congestion.

The provision condition of the discriminatory club model remains essentially unchanged from that of Section 11.3; however, the utilization and membership conditions change as members consume a *club package* consisting of the shared good and the members' characteristics. A member utilizes the club until the marginal benefits that he or she derives from the club package equal the associated marginal costs (or value) that the club experiences from the member's utilization. Unlike our basic model, the tolls differ between members owing to their different attributes. The membership condition must also include both aspects of the club package. Some members with desirable traits may be paid to join, since they generate enough positive characteristics to offset any crowding caused by their presence. The analysis of discriminatory clubs allows for a study of the pure taste for association rationale for club formation.

Exclusion costs

A number of investigators[9] have examined exclusion costs associated with the erection, maintenance, or existence of a mechanism to limit club utilization or membership. At least three different approaches to exclusion costs exist in the literature. In one approach, waiting costs can result from the exclusion mechanism, and these waiting times are a *pre-utilization* crowding or queuing cost, which depends on the number of users.[10] In this case, the basic model of Section 11.3 remains basically unchanged, except for the interpretation of crowding costs, which now include pre-utilization and utilization crowding.

A second approach concerns the resource costs of the exclusion mechanism and is best illustrated by Oakland's treatment (1972, pp. 351–5). Oakland assumed that these exclusion costs rise as the quantity of the shared good increases, but they fall as the average utilization rate, k, increases, where k is the ratio of total utilization to provision. On the average, this latter measure shows the utilization rate of each unit of the shared good. As k increases, a smaller number of potential users must be excluded. In order to represent these exclusion costs, the basic model's transformation function must include k as an additional argument with a negative influence on resource costs.

When exclusion costs are introduced in this manner, the optimal provision amount is reduced, whereas optimal utilization and membership are increased (see Oakland 1972, pp. 353–4). For provision, the marginal benefits from reduced crowding must be equal to the *sum* of marginal production costs and marginal exclusion costs. Since this sum is greater than marginal production costs alone, marginal benefits from provision must be correspondingly larger for optimality; optimal provision falls. Moreover, utilization rates increase because the resulting marginal net damage must equal the marginal exclusion costs of utilization. This marginal net damage is the difference between marginal crowding costs and the user's marginal benefits from utilization. Without exclusion costs, optimal utilization is reached when marginal net damage is zero—all users fully compensate for damages inflicted on the club. With exclusion costs, utilization is expanded even when marginal net damages are positive, provided that these marginal net damages are *less* than marginal exclusion costs. In this situation, exclusion is more costly than the uncompensated damage. These exclusion costs can increase utilization rates, and, in an analogous fashion, membership size.

A third technique of handling exclusion costs is that of Kamien, Schwartz, and Roberts (1973, pp. 225–9). These authors have determined the optimal degree of exclusion in the transformation function. Their optimal exclusion condition compares the marginal benefits of utilization (i.e., nonexclusion) with the marginal exclusion costs.

Self-financing and efficient tolls

An important question, "Can efficient tolls self-finance optimal provision of the shared good?" has been often asked.[11] To answer this question, we intend to modify the crowding function presented previously. In particular, let

$$c = c(k), \qquad k = \int_1^s v(i)di/X, \tag{11}$$

where $c_k > 0$, $c_X = \partial c/\partial X = -(kc_k)/X < 0$, and $c_v = c_k/X > 0$. This respecification implies that an increase in average utilization augments crowding, and that an increase in provision reduces crowding. Finally, greater utilization increases crowding, ceteris paribus. This particular specification characterizes much of the literature. Using this congestion function only changes the weighting factors on the MRS's in the provision, toll, and membership conditions listed in Section 11.3. That is, $-(kc_k)/X$ replaces c_2 and c_k/X replaces c_1; otherwise everything remains unchanged. When the per-unit toll (T) is set equal to the left-hand side of the new toll condition and the result is substituted into the new provision condition, the finance condition,

$$kT = MRT_{Xy}, \qquad \text{(Finance)}$$

results.

This condition indicates that the sum of the tolls paid on a unit of the shared good suffices to finance *marginal* costs of provision; the toll is multiplied by the average utilization rate when determining toll revenues on a unit of the shared good because each unit can be utilized more than once. Even though an efficient per-unit toll serves to finance marginal costs, the toll fails to self-finance the shared good whenever average provision costs exceed marginal provision costs— that is, increasing returns to scale are present.

Deviations from this financing result are usually traceable to the form of the congestion function. If crowding depends upon k *and* the provision amount, the new financing condition is

$$[1 - (Xc_X/kc_k)]kT = MRT_{Xy}. \tag{12}$$

When congestion costs are homogeneous of degree zero in utilization and provision, marginal costs are financed because c_X is zero and the new financing condition degenerates to the previous one. Otherwise self-financing is not necessarily assured whenever c depends on k and X. In an interesting article, DeSerpa (1978) analyzed three alternative crowding functions and showed how self-financing is responsive to the form of this function.

When increasing returns characterize the production of the shared good, a two-part tariff can levy a fixed membership charge and a utilization fee. The fixed charge attempts to recover the deficient revenue needed to self-finance provision. Some form of outside intervention (e.g., government subsidies) is required for financing purposes when a fixed charge is not assigned.

Some club models avoid the self-financing issue altogether by imposing a constraint requiring membership revenues to equal provision costs. Such models may yield second-best results owing to implicit full financing.

11.7   Concluding Remarks

We have covered a great deal of ground in this chapter, focusing on the total-economy viewpoint that excludes some population members. Mixed and homogeneous clubs have been studied and compared. The models of Sections 11.2 and 11.3 form the basis for our analysis of uncertainty in club participation and intergenerational clubs in Chapters 14 and 15. Prior to that discussion, we will examine institutional issues and game-theoretic aspects of clubs. The latter allow us to investigate the partitioning issue in more detail.

The general principles of club theory are applied in Chapter 16 to diverse real-world cases. To motivate the reader, we indicate a few possible applications here. Since alliances share a defense arsenal possessing congestion possibilities, an optimal sharing size can be determined using club theory. Club theory can also be applied to recreation studies when deciding tolls, utilization rates, and provision. Thus, the study of wilderness areas and national parks can profit from club analysis. Similarly, club theory can yield insight into a host of local public goods decisions having to do with highways, communication systems, mass transit, and the like.

CHAPTER 12

Institutional forms and clubs

Up to now, we have implicitly assumed that members owned and operated their clubs, either using the congestion toll to finance provision, or else instituting a two-part tariff when self-financing was not possible. For the case of replicable homogeneous clubs (Cells A and B in Table 10.1), we demonstrate that a competitive industry in which each firm corresponds to a club would meet the same optimality conditions as those indicated in Chapter 10. Thus, there is no necessary reason for member ownership. That is, under ideal circumstances, any of a number of institutional forms can operate the club efficiently. Monopolistic and oligopolistic provisions are also discussed and related to the total-economy viewpoint. In addition, government or public provision is analyzed.

This chapter is divided into four sections. Market provision of clubs is presented in Section 12.1, and public or government provision is examined in Section 12.2. Other institutional considerations are taken up in Section 12.3. Some real-world examples and concluding remarks are presented in Section 12.4.

12.1 Competitive and noncompetitive market provision

Competitive provision

To find a case in which a competitive market can provide the shared good, we must return to *replicable* homogeneous clubs whose utilization rates are either fixed or variable.[1] We focus our remarks on the variable utilization case, leaving the fixed utilization case for the reader to explore.

If each club is owned by the members, then the representative member faces the following optimizing problem,

$$\begin{array}{ll} \max\limits_{\{y,\, v,\, s,\, X\}} & U[y,\, v,\, c(sv,\, X)] \\ \text{subject to} & I = y + C(sv,\, X)/s, \end{array} \tag{1}$$

where $c(\cdot)$ is the congestion function and $C(\cdot)$ is the cost of provision and club maintenance. Equal cost sharing among the members is assumed. The solution to this problem was discussed in Section 10.5, but its form was not explicitly given. For comparison purposes, we list the first-order conditions here:

$$sc_2 MRS_{cy} = MC_X \quad \text{(Provision)}$$

$$MRS_{vy} = -sc_1 MRS_{cy} + MC_m \quad \text{(Toll)}$$

$$-svc_1 MRS_{cy} + vMC_m = C(\cdot)/s, \quad \text{(Membership)}$$

where $c_2 = \partial c/\partial X$, $MC_X = \partial C/\partial X$, $c_1 = \partial c/\partial(sv)$, and $MC_m = \partial C/\partial(sv)$. MC_X is the marginal provision cost and MC_m is marginal maintenance cost. These three conditions have already been interpreted and require few additional remarks. The provision condition corresponds to the Samuelsonian public good condition. The toll or per-visit price, P_v, is set equal to the right-hand side of the toll condition; hence, the toll collects for marginal crowding cost and marginal maintenance cost. The membership condition requires the costs that the marginal entrant imposes on the club to be equal to his benefits from membership.

If these multiple clubs correspond to firms in a competitive industry, then each firm would maximize its profits, π, subject to a constraint that members must be as well off as under membership ownership. Since we are comparing institutional forms, competitive market provision must be at least as good as the alternative structure; thus, the previous solution forms a lower bound to alternative institutional structures. Each firm faces the following problem:[2]

$$\begin{array}{ll} \max_{\{s,v,X,P_v\}} & P_v sv - C(sv, X) \\ \text{subject to} & U[I - vP_v, v, c(sv, X)] \geq U^*, \end{array} \quad (2)$$

where U^* corresponds to the optimal utility level associated with the solution to (1), $P_v sv$ is the revenue collected from visitation fees. Forming a Lagrangean and taking partials yield the following first-order conditions:

$$P_v: \quad sv - \lambda U_y v = 0 \quad (3)$$

$$X: \quad -C_2 + \lambda U_c c_2 = 0 \quad (4)$$

$$s: \quad vP_v - vC_1 + \lambda U_c c_1 v = 0 \quad (5)$$

$$v: \quad sP_v - sC_1 - \lambda U_y P_v + \lambda U_v + \lambda U_c c_1 s = 0, \quad (6)$$

where subscripts on C, c, and U denote partial derivatives (e.g., $U_v = \partial U/\partial v$) and λ is a Lagrangean multiplier. Using (3)–(6) to eliminate

λ yields a provision, membership, and toll condition *identical* to those associated with problem (1). Thus, P_v^* must equal the sum of marginal crowding cost and marginal maintenance cost, just as before. This is clearly seen from an inspection of (5). In long-run equilibrium, profits must be zero, so that $P_v sv = C(\cdot)$, which implies that $P_v = C(\cdot)/sv$ in long-run equilibrium; hence, each member must pay a toll equal to the average cost per visit. At the long-run equilibrium, this toll is also equal to the marginal cost per visit. The membership condition for problem (1) can be rewritten to show that this long-run equilibrium solution holds for the optimum s. Hence, a competitive industry is capable of running the various clubs, and there is no need for a nonmarket structure.[3] However, remember that sufficient replicability of clubs is required for this result.

If members are heterogeneous, and if a large number of replicable clubs are formed, a perfectly competitive industry can still efficiently allocate resources to the shared good. This extension holds, provided that utility depends indirectly on X and sv via a congestion function that is the same for everybody, so that *total* toll payments can differ between individuals according to tastes.

In the above formulation, fees were collected as a per-unit toll rather than as a membership fee. Berglas (1976, p. 119) has shown that this is more efficient than charging a membership fee, even one set equal to C^*/s^*, in which case an individual will utilize the club until the marginal benefit from visiting is zero (i.e.,, $MRS_{vy} = 0$), since each additional visit effectively costs nothing once the membership fee is paid. Thus, the toll condition is violated and suboptimality results. Many real-world clubs, such as country clubs, use membership fees rather than visitation fees and are, in the absence of transaction costs, inefficient. This arrangement may be justified, however, when the transaction costs of collecting visitation fees are included. If these transaction costs exceed the loss in efficiency associated with collecting membership fees, then the membership fee approach is best.

Noncompetitive provision

Noncompetitive provision is more appropriate as an alternative institutional structure for those cases in which the population is not partitioned, since a predetermined number of clubs will form and this number may be quite small, as little as just one. If only one club is optimal, then a monopoly might correspond to the alternative industrial structure, provided that *monopoly power* is present in the form of a low elasticity of demand for the club good. The mere presence of a single firm-operated club does not necessarily imply monopoly, since other clubs might exist that provide a near substitute, thus reducing monopoly power. The within-club viewpoint is more appropriate to the competitive solution owing to the large number of clubs, while the total-economy viewpoint may be more in keeping with the monopoly or oligopoly solution. Monopoly or oligopoly need not imply large inefficiencies where clubs are concerned, since the member-owned alternative limits the amount of rent that the monopoly or oligopoly can capture. Hence, the monopoly or oligopoly solution will correspond to the member-owned and operated club solution. This point is missed by Hillman (1978) when he argues that monopolies will restrict club output and will raise P_v. Our conclusion is analogous to the contestable market argument, currently in vogue among industrial organization economists. Extending the analysis to monopoly requires the monopolist to choose v, P_v, X, and s so as to maximize profits subject to the optimal utility level, associated with the total-economy problem depicted in Chapter 11. Monopoly must do as well as member ownership or it is not a viable institutional structure; but it need not do as well as perfect competition where multiple clubs form. A similar conclusion would hold for oligopoly.

Of course, our analysis is based on the absence of transaction costs. Since transaction costs will probably differ among institutional forms, monopoly rents and exploitation may be feasible whenever monopoly can save on transaction costs. We turn to this issue in Section 12.3.

12.2   Government provision of club goods

Since we have already seen that member-owned and firm-owned clubs operate efficiently, one must wonder why government-operated clubs are needed at all. At least two factors may justify government provision. First, significant scale economies in provision may eliminate competitive provision as an option. Moreover, these scale economies might not allow the members to support the club with congestion-internalizing tolls (see Oakland 1972). Hence, only monopoly or government provision are then options, and the absence of member-owned alternatives might lead to monopoly exploitation, thereby justifying government provision. Second, constitutional constraint might mandate government provision—for example, interstate highways and national defense.

Highways, zoos, and national parks are a few examples of club goods provided by local, state, and federal governments. Each of these goods is a club good, since exclusion is feasible at a low cost and benefits are partially rival. Unlike market provision, a government does not have to compete against alternative institutional forms such as member ownership. Thus, there is no reason to believe that members' utilities will be as high for government provision as those associated with member operation.

A second problem restricting government efficiency is the public access problem; all citizens must be allowed access, and hence membership size cannot be restricted. Of course, capacity limits may reduce use at a given time owing to queuing costs. These queuing costs would add a deadweight loss. A third problem has to do with the inability of governments to vary congestion fees, since any possible claim of discrimination must be avoided. Once a fee is determined, that fee stays the same; thus, the toll cannot vary on the basis of crowding conditions. Since most clubs do not charge user fees according to congestion conditions, the third problem may not detract from the *relative* performance of government-operated clubs.

Perhaps the greatest difficulty for government-operated clubs is trying to ascertain what the members really want in terms of provision, maintenance, and fees. These decisions must be made prior to citizen utilization, a utilization that reveals preferences. In a member-owned club, members have an incentive and an ability to reveal their preferences for provision during meetings. Governments may be more interested in pleasing constituents with large political influence than in setting up an efficient public club. We return to this issue in Chapter 15.

12.3   Other considerations

Transaction costs

Part of the expense of operating a club includes transaction costs; billing, administration, and meetings all require resources. Most of these transaction costs are independent of the level of use and provision; however, others may vary with membership size or provision. For example, larger memberships need bigger meeting rooms and may entail larger administration costs. The inclusion of transaction costs requires a number of alterations, the exact specification of which depends on variability of these transaction costs. If transaction costs depend on sv and X, then the formal problem faced by the representative member stays the same, except for the interpretation of the cost function. When these costs are independent of sv

and X, the cost function of the club must include an exogenously given fixed amount, which corresponds to transaction costs. The first-order conditions do not change, but the level of maximum utility will be reduced owing to these additional expenditures. The interesting change comes when we look at market provision, because the constraining utility level in (2) has fallen. Furthermore, the club's cost function, $C(\cdot)$, may vary between institutional forms. These alterations imply that competitive provision need not correspond to the solution associated with member ownership. To choose between alternative institutional arrangements requires an explicit comparison of transaction costs and the welfare levels implied by different institutional structures. Therefore, a monopoly may be desirable if what is lost in welfare owing to restrictions in output is more than compensated by a reduction in transaction costs. With differential efficiencies in transactions, monopoly rents need not dissipate with time.

Authority structure

A topic that has received scant attention in the literature is the authority structure in a club. Most club models treat all members symmetrically, the most notable exception being the game-theoretic representations in which payoffs may differ between members.[4] For example, Sorenson, Tschirhart, and Whinston (1978a) distinguished a club as containing two types of participants: a proprietor and consumers. The proprietor's payoffs and authority are greater than those of the consumers. Pricing and other club-type decisions were then presented. Once members are differentiated by either payoffs or authority, homogeneous representations are no longer appropriate because *average* net benefits are not maximized; that is, members from different categories obtain different goals. Game theory representations appear best for examining membership differentiation, since they allow for discrimination. Moreover, game theory shows that the extent of discrimination is limited, because the discriminated individuals always have the option of leaving and forming or joining a new club (Sandler and Tschirhart, 1980, pp. 1500–1). We return later to the question of membership game-theoretical representations of clubs.

Moving toward membership discrimination permits us to differentiate between founding members and other members, especially when founding members reap greater benefits. Once classes of members are distinguished, the study of institutional form becomes more interesting, since an institutional form implies a particular hierarchical structure. For example, authority is probably more evenly spread for member-operated clubs than for firm-operated ones. We leave further discussion of the authority issue to our future research.

12.4   Some examples and concluding remarks

How do real-world clubs operate? Three different approaches are seen. Some clubs use membership fees and do not discriminate between heavy and light users. This is clearly the cheapest and easiest scheme to administer. Even in the absence of transaction costs considerations, this arrangement is efficient whenever members are homogeneous and utilization differences are not discernible. An alternative approach has clubs monitoring utilization rates and charging a fixed per-visit fee. This fee usually does not change with the actual crowding experienced, since such an efficient scheme is difficult and costly to institute. Telecommunications clubs, however, distinguish between peak and off-peak hours. American Telephone & Telegraph and the British Telecommunications System make numerable different time period distinctions in an attempt to account for crowding variability. Utilization units are based on the number of seconds or minutes of use. A third method is that used by governments in allocating resources to their club goods. Governments may levy user-type fees, such as gasoline taxes for highways or daily fees for national parks, but much of the club's revenues come from general funds collected through general tax instruments. Such a scheme is not efficient, inasmuch as nonusers subsidize users whenever general funds supplement club revenues.

An interesting example of a club is INTELSAT,[5] which links some 80 nations in an external communication network carrying approximately two-thirds of all transoceanic messages. Currently, the system consists of eight geostationary satellites positioned some 22,300 miles above the equator. At this altitude, the satellites orbit the Earth in the same time interval that the Earth rotates about its axis, and hence the satellites remain stationary over a point on the Earth's surface. This high-altitude geosynchronous or geostationary orbit means that only three satellites are required to provide point-to-multipoint service almost everywhere on the Earth (except near the poles), because each satellite can communicate with the microwave transmitters and receivers on one-third of the Earth. Four satellites are positioned over the Atlantic, and two each are positioned over the Pacific and Indian Oceans. Since the largest flow of messages transverses the Atlantic Ocean, this region requires more communication satellites than elsewhere. Of the eight satellites, four serve as spares and increase the system's reliability to better than a 99.9 percent effectiveness rate. INTELSAT satellites receive weak radio signals in the megahertz frequency band from Earth station transmitters. After receiving these signals, the satellite amplifies and retransmits them in the gigahertz band to Earth station receivers. Between Earth stations and other ground points, signals travel via microwave links and cables.

INTELSAT qualifies as a club good, since access to the network can, for the most part, be restricted by coding or scrambling signals and the network can be simultaneously used. As utilization of the communication system increases, the benefits per signal transmitted diminish owing to congestion (e.g., interference or noise) as more signals share the same frequency band. A club arrangement can optimally allocate utilization rates on the basis of congestion considerations. This arrangement consists of voluntary participants agreeing to pay a user fee (or toll) per unit of utilization.

The current structure of INTELSAT conforms closely to that of an economic club with firms and governments as members (see Edelson 1977; Sandler and Schulze 1981). Members pay fees according to their utilization on a per-unit basis, and voting in the Board of Governors is weighted according to members' utilization rates and investment shares. Although the other bodies of INTELSAT, such as the Assembly of Parties, the Meeting of Signatories, and the manager, make policy recommendations, the Board of Governors is the decision-making body of INTELSAT. A weighted voting scheme based on utilization appears to promote optimality, since heavier users will be serving more individuals (whose marginal benefits and costs must be aggregated), and consequently, these users account for a greater share of the costs and benefits resulting from policy changes.

Another real-world example of a club is a military alliance in which allies share an arsenal whose conventional weaponry is subject to *thinning* (a congestion phenomenon) as it is spread over a longer perimeter. In Chapter 16, we discuss the NATO alliance in detail since it allows us to apply the principles developed in Parts II–IV.

We view our remarks about institutional forms as an initial discussion of this important, but relatively ignored, issue of clubs. A ripe area for future research lies here.

CHAPTER 13

Game theory and club goods*

This chapter presents the game theory formulation of club goods. By introducing game theory we can finally address a number of unanswered questions concerning club formation and operation. In particular, a game formulation allows for a determination of the optimum number of clubs; that is, an optimum partition of a population into a system of nonoverlapping clubs can be devised. A by-product of this determination is a more complete answer to the question posed in Chapters 10 and 11 concerning what constitutes the optimum club size. The stability of clubs can also be examined with game-theoretic notions, in which the membership composition and payoffs can be related to the *core* of a game. In a stable system of clubs, the membership composition remains fixed, since reshuffling between clubs does not improve an individual's net benefits.

Game theory also permits us to reexamine institutional form in terms of the ψ-stability function, which can account for transaction costs. Furthermore, by placing bounds on the extent of discrimination of payoffs between members, game theory can be related to the differentiation between membership subgroups, alluded to in Chapter 12 when authority was mentioned. Cost allocation schemes can also be elucidated with game theory.[1] Thus, clubs deriving their benefits from cost sharing, as in the case of goods whose production is characterized by increasing returns to scale, can be analyzed with game theory.

N-person game theory, developed by John Von Neumann and Oskar Morgenstern (1944), provides a natural formulation of club problems. In game theory, players have an incentive to form coalitions because of the payoffs available from playing the game, whereas in club theory members form clubs to partake of the available benefits. When clubs are investigated, n-person cooperative games are most appropriate, since all can benefit through voluntary membership. If a member does not benefit from club membership, then he or she

---

* Portions of this chapter are revised versions of material presented in the Sandler and Tschirhart (1980) survey on clubs. With Tschirhart's permission, we have included revised excerpts here.

always has the option of defecting. Our underlying rationality assumption implies that nondefectors are better off in the club. Cooperative agreements, such as toll payments, are made binding through the threat of expulsion. For pure public goods and many types of externalities, however, private and group incentives conflict, thereby inducing individuals to pursue noncooperative or defector strategies (e.g., easy riding). Hence, noncooperative games, such as the Prisoner's Dilemma or the game of chicken, were employed in Chapter 8 to study the provision of pure public goods.

This chapter is made up of six sections. The basic concepts and notation needed for a game-theoretic formulation of clubs are presented in Section 13.1. This formulation is applied to both the determination of the optimum club size and the calculation of the optimum number of clubs in Section 13.2. Section 13.3 compares the game and the nongame formulations of clubs. Game-theoretic notions are applied to the institutional structures issue in Section 13.4. Section 13.5 examines the use of game theory to decide cost allocation, and Section 13.6 presents some concluding remarks.

13.1 A game theory formulation

Game theory helps to establish the optimum number of clubs and their stability of composition, although, as will be shown in Section 13.3, some generality is sacrificed in the formulation since provision determination is pushed to the background. The set of players in a game involving club formation is typically the entire population; thus, both club and nonclub members are considered for all possible partitions of the population into multiple clubs. The analysis therefore corresponds to cells A, B, E, and F of Table 10.1.

An essential concept of game theory is that of the core, a concept used in Chapter 8 when contrasting private goods and public goods equilibria for various group sizes. For clubs, the core is used to examine the stability issue. The core is a less general solution than a Pareto optimum, since a partition may be Pareto optimal but not in the core, whereas a partition in the core is always Pareto optimal. Lloyd Shapley (1971, p. 11) states that "the core of an n-person game is the set of feasible outcomes that cannot be improved upon by any coalition of players." In other words, once a core is achieved, no realignment of players into another set of coalitions can augment the payoffs to the participants. That is, no different set of coalitions can form to block the coalitions associated with a core.

The characteristic function used in n-person game theory indicates the total benefits available to all potential coalitions of players and can be used in club theory with some modifications. If $\hat{S} = \{1, \ldots, \hat{s}\}$ is the set consisting of the entire population, and $S = \{1, \ldots, s\}$ is some subset of the population, then the nonnegative characteristic function is denoted $v(S)$ for all subsets S of $\hat{S}$. This function represents the total net benefits available to a club consisting of the members in S.[2] If the club includes the entire population, then the associated characteristic function is $v(\hat{S})$.

In game theory,[3] the characteristic function is defined to be *superadditive*, that is $v(S' \cup S'') \geqq v(S') + v(S'')$ for all mutually exclusive subsets S' and S'' of $\hat{S}$. The term $v(S' \cup S'')$ does not necessarily mean that the players in $S' \cup S''$ are acting as a single decision unit, for if the two sets can do better apart than together, they will stay apart and $v(S' \cup S'') = v(S') + v(S'')$. In club theory, however, $v(S' \cup S'')$ implies that the two sets do act as a single decision unit (i.e., one club). If the two sets could do better forming separate clubs rather than a single club, it must be the case that $v(S' \cup S'') < v(S') + v(S'')$. Thus, club characteristic functions may be *subadditive* to allow for this possibility (Pauly 1970b, p. 55). Clubs may therefore be subadditive owing to congestion and/or transaction costs. Such costs may mean that a finer partition of the members (i.e., smaller clubs) may improve net benefits.

Each person in the population is interested in the net benefit or payoff available to him or her from possible club participation. If **b** $= (b_1, \ldots, b_{\hat{s}})$ is any vector of these net benefits available to the population, then *individual rationality* implies

$$b_i \geqq v(\{i\}), \qquad \text{for } i = 1, \ldots, \hat{s}, \tag{1}$$

where $\{i\}$ is the club that just contains the ith person. This rationality requirement means that an individual's net benefit from club membership must be at least as great as the net benefit of dropping out of the club. If $b_i < v(\{i\})$, then the individual would be better off by leaving the club, especially since membership is voluntary. The rationality concept can be carried over to any set of individuals including the entire population. Thus,

$$\sum_{i \in S} b_i \geqq v(S), \tag{2}$$

for all subsets of $\hat{S}$. Net benefit vectors satisfying (2) are said to be in the core. The core is an equilibrium solution for the population, since it implies that no individual or coalition of individuals can improve upon their situation by forming a different partition.

Condition (2) includes individual rationality, condition (1), as a special case. Moreover, inasmuch as the entire population is one of these sets, a core solution implies a Pareto optimum as asserted above. If a core solution is obtained for a club consisting of the entire population, then this is a stable club, since no member or set of members will have an incentive to defect. When a core solution is obtained for a collection of k clubs, $(S_1, \ldots, S_k)$, then this is a stable collection, because no member or set of members will have an incentive to transfer among clubs or to drop out and establish new clubs. In Chapter 10, a core solution for homogeneous clubs corresponded to that which maximizes average net benefits for club members. Furthermore, the homogeneous population must be partitioned evenly into a set of clubs of identical size, leaving no individuals unassigned to a club. This result is discussed further in Sections 13.2 and 13.3.

13.2   Optimum club size and the optimum number of clubs

With a homogeneous population, the characteristic function depends only on the number of club members and not on the composition of the club's membership. In this homogeneous framework, a number of interesting results regarding club size and the number of clubs have been obtained by Pauly (1967, 1970b). These results establish the existence of a core when the population can be partitioned into a set of homogeneous clubs. Table 13.1 illustrates these results. For each membership size, the total and average net benefits for the club are listed. The average increases up to $s = 4$ because of scale economies, camaraderie, and/or the sharing of the benefits derived from the impure public good, but after $s = 4$ the average falls as these benefits give way to increased congestion and/or decision costs. The net benefits are zero for clubs beyond size 9.

The optimum club size, s^*, was defined by Pauly (1967, p. 315, 1970b, p. 56) as the one for which average net benefits are maximized; that is, $v(S^*)/s^*$ is a maximum over all s. This definition follows the Buchanan (1965) approach presented in Chapter 10 and corresponds to a within-club model. Maximizing average net benefits is not the same as maximizing total net benefits for the economy[4] and is at variance with the nongame formulation of Ng (1973), Helpman and Hillman (1977), and that presented in Chapter 11. This apparent contradiction is reconciled in Section 13.3.

Consider the case where $s^* = \hat{s}$, so that the optimum club size is the entire population. The core exists, and in one solution in the

Table 13.1. *Net benefits and club size*

Club size (s)	1	2	3	4	5	6	7	8	9	10	···
Total net benefits, $v(S)$	0.4	1.50	9	16	17.5	18	14	8	0	0	···
Average net benefits $v(S)/s$	0.4	0.75	3	4	3.5	3	2	1	0	0	···

core each club receives $v(S^*)/s^*$. From Table 13.1, $s^* = \hat{s} = 4$ and each member receives $v(\{1, 2, 3, 4\})/4 = 4$. With these payoffs, no subset of members can do better by abandoning the club; that is, the maximum net benefit to an economy of 4 is shown to be 16. No equal-sharing realignment of four people can do as well in the imaginary economy depicted in Table 13.1. Since condition (2) is satisfied, the solution is in the core.

There are, however, other core solutions that involve unequal payoffs. In that event, price discrimination is being practiced, although the basis for discrimination is not the members' characteristics, as in Chapter 11. Obviously, characteristics do not vary among identical individuals. The core places bounds on the extent of this price discrimination, thereby limiting payoff distinctions between founding fathers and other members (see Section 4). For example, suppose member 1 is being discriminated against, and the payoffs are $\mathbf{b} = (0.4, 5.2, 5.2, 5.2)$. Member 1 could do no better by dropping out of the club, since $b_1 = 0.4$ is the most he or she could attain alone (see Table 13.1). Nor could he or she persuade any other member or two members to join in a club of size 2 or 3 because the net benefits would be less than those currently received. Consequently, the $\mathbf{b} = (0.4, 5.2, 5.2, 5.2)$ payoffs represent a core solution. When two members are discriminated against in a like manner so that $\mathbf{b}' = (0.4, 0.4, 7.6, 7.6)$, however, members 1 and 2 could either abandon the club and form a new club of two, or they could be joined by either member 3 or 4 in a new club of three. Their situation improves in both cases. In general, a core solution must satisfy the condition that if members in subset S are being discriminated against, they must receive at least $v(S)$, which denotes their opportunity cost.

When optimum club size is less than the population, the existence of the core will depend on whether $\hat{s}/s^*$ is an integer and whether equal sharing is enforced (see Pauly 1970b for a rigorous proof). If $\hat{s}/s^*$ is an integer, then the core is attained only if the entire population is divided into clubs of size $s*$, where each person receives $v(S*)/s*$. For this situation, there will be strong incentives for the sizes of clubs to equalize, where members in oversized clubs switch to undersized ones. To demonstrate this result, suppose that the population is eight and that Table 13.1's payoffs apply. If two clubs form with three and five members each, then at least one member in the club of five can improve his payoff by transferring to the three-member club. This transfer can improve the net benefits of the members of both clubs when there is no discrimination; per-person payoffs rise to 4 in both clubs. The transfer may even increase the members' payoffs in the presence of discrimination, provided that the discrimination is small. However, *only* equal-sharing payoffs are in the core because any club that practices discrimination will find that either the members being discriminated against are abandoning the club or the members in the discriminating group are replaced by members of other clubs. If, say, two clubs have payoffs of (0.4, 5.2, 5.2, 5.2) and (4, 4, 4, 4), then member 1 from the first club could move to the second club, or any member of the second club could replace any one of the last three members in the first club. These results suggest that a multiclub world provides safeguards against discrimination, since discriminated individuals have the option of transferring between clubs.[5] When only one club forms, however, discrimination is easier to practice, as shown earlier. Thus, the ability to distinguish between member classes depends on the similarity of the members and the existence of substitute clubs.

When $\hat{s}/s*$ exceeds one but is not an integer, the core typically does not exist.[6] An individual omitted from all clubs of size $s*$ because of the integer problem can always bid his or her way into a club by offering to accept a payoff lower than a club member. The rejected member is then on the outside and free to bid his way into a club. This shuffling never ends; thus, a stable solution is never found.

With a heterogeneous population, the optimum number of clubs is considerably more elusive. Pauly (1970b) worked with a heterogeneous population partitioned into homogeneous groups. Each homogeneous group is divided into multiple clubs in which average net benefits are maximized and there is no integer problem. Hence, the optimum club size for a given class of identical individuals must divide evenly into the total number of individuals of that class. This partitioning result is essentially the Tiebout Hypothesis, where a population partitions itself into jurisdictions with homogeneous members. Even in this restrictive model, however, little can be said. The main result is that a core exists if the clubs consist of identical members with equal payoffs and that clubs with higher average payoffs have fewer members than those with lower average payoffs. This ensures that members of larger clubs have no incentive to transfer to smaller clubs or accept members from smaller clubs (Pauly 1970b, pp. 60–4).

Sorenson, Tschirhart, and Whinston (1978a) have examined heterogeneous clubs in which the only impetus for formation is decreasing production costs. Unlike the homogeneous case, total net benefits to the club do not depend simply on the number of members, but rather on the *number* and *identity* of members. Consequently, maximizing average net benefits is not a useful determinant of optimum club size. Sorenson, Tschirhart, and Whinston (1978a) distinguished an entrepreneur from a set of consumers; thus, two classes of members are indicated. In the homogeneous case, members can evaluate their own payoff by comparing it to the average benefit, since their contribution to the club is the same as everyone else's contribution; in the heterogeneous case, this same evaluation is meaningless, since a member may contribute more or less than others. When a club consists of the entire population, a core can exist for a membership greater than that corresponding to where the average benefit is maximized. A sufficient condition for core existence is that the provision level that maximizes consumers' surplus is in the range of decreasing average cost, thereby ensuring a net benefit to all population members from club inclusion. All individuals are better off within the club. Depending on the members' demands, core existence is also possible beyond minimum average cost; but there is the possibility that for any output beyond minimum average cost, a single club is not optimal. Determining the optimum number of clubs is similar to deciding the optimum number of firms that have U-shaped average cost curves. Moreover, mixed clubs in this situation may very well be desirable.

The existence of a core for partitioning a population into a system of *mixed* clubs of the type described in Chapter 11 is an unsettled issue. Sandler and Tschirhart (1984b) have shown that multiple mixed clubs can be optimal, provided that provision affects utility indirectly through a congestion function (see the discussion in Chapter 11). Moreover, this congestion function must be identical between individuals, thus implying that crowding is a technical phenomenon. In this situation, the optimal toll would fully internalize the crowding externality; taste differences are then accounted for through the *total* toll payments of the members. However, these authors have not demonstrated that if the optimal membership size divides evenly into the population that the resulting partition is in the core. We suspect that this may be true, but must leave its demonstration to our future research. Clearly, an integer problem would lead to the nonexistence of the core as it did for homogeneous clubs, because of the shuffling of omitted individuals.

13.3   A comparison of the game and nongame formulations

A direct comparison of the game and nongame formulations of club theory is complicated by the different assumptions used. The game formulation *does not admit* a well-defined interaction between the provision and toll conditions. The nongame formulations have a provision condition that is separate from the membership condition, and the toll condition requires that marginal-cost pricing be adopted. For a homogeneous population, each club member's total payment is identical and consistent with his demands, since provision and toll conditions are found simultaneously. In the game formulation, there is unlimited bargaining among the population regarding payments to support the club. The payoff, b_i, represents the ith member's benefit, net of a lump-sum charge. The characteristic function implies nothing regarding the distribution of these charges among members. For any b vector, a level of provision follows; but another vector would imply different demands and therefore a new level of provision. Provision is relative to charges. Since the game formulation does not account for these charge-sensitive provision changes, the $v(S)$ function must be understood to be associated with an optimum membership S. Otherwise, as bargaining proceeded, provision would change.

Essentially, the game formulation allows the membership, provision, and finance conditions to be solved simultaneously, while the toll condition is solved afterward. There is latitude in solving the toll condition, since different tolls are compatible with a single solution to the other three conditions. This is clearly different from the nongame formulation, which solves simultaneously everything, including tolls. Another difference arises with respect to the finance condition: Game solutions require full financing, whereas nongame solutions involve marginal-cost pricing that may not finance the good. For the nongame approach, self-financing depends upon the presence of increasing returns and/or the form of the congestion function (see Chapter 11).

Authors who have used a game-theoretic formulation have approached the provision question differently. Pauly (1970b, p. 55) avoided the issue and simply stated that $v(s)$ reflects net benefit from the quantity of good chosen. Littlechild (1975, p. 118) abstracted from the level of provision and was concerned only with whether the good is produced at all. Basically, provision demands are perfectly inelastic and insensitive to charges, provided that the fee to a member does not exceed his or her benefit. In an approach that used elastic demands, Sorenson, Tschirhart, and Whinston (1978b) defined $v(S)$ as the maximum consumers' surplus available to S. Provision was determined by the interaction of the aggregate downward-sloping demand curve and the marginal-cost curve. This yields a unique provision level for each membership size, which corresponds to the level attained under marginal-cost pricing. However, the membership lump-sum charges may be greater or less than the amount that would be collected if marginal-cost pricing is used. To ensure that these charges do not alter aggregate demand, zero income elasticity must be assumed. Finally, Ellickson (1973) maximized the sum of individual utilities subject to a transformation function with a single crowded public good and single private good. This is very similar to the nongame approach. The solution produced provision conditions for the public good and the total amount of the private good. Ellickson then solved each member's utility-maximization problem to find demand functions and tolls that support these provision levels. A problem arises, however, when more than one distribution of the sum of utilities are considered. Each distribution must be associated with different tolls to satisfy the derived demand functions. But different tolls imply different demands and provision levels, and the sum of utilities will change. The sum cannot reflect a constant provision level with changing toll conditions and at the same time remain compatible with the demand functions.[7]

In spite of the differences between the game and nongame formulations, there are parallels between these formulations. When the entire population is equal to the membership size that maximizes average net benefits, the game and nongame frameworks lead to the same core solution for membership size. Namely, everyone must be included in a single club. In Table 13.1, this solution corresponds to $\hat{s} = s^* = 4$. Another similarity between the two approaches arises because both are interested in provision, membership size, and toll charges; however, as we have seen, each formulation determines these requirements somewhat differently.

Another parallel may arise regarding the optimum number of clubs for the homogeneous membership case, *if the number of clubs is a variable*. First, we consider the differences in the two approaches

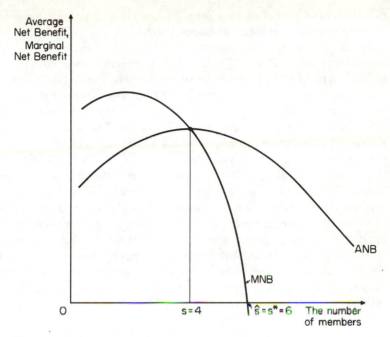

Figure 13.1

when the number of clubs is *predetermined*, again using Table 13.1 for illustrative purposes. The one-club constraint may yield a Pareto optimum in some cases. Suppose that the population contains six individuals. The core does not exist because there is an integer problem. Maximizing total net benefits yields a Pareto-optimal club of 6, while maximizing average net benefits yields a Pareto-inferior club of 4, as shown in Table 13.1. The integer problem brings into question the definition of the optimum club size as that which maximizes average net benefits. For Pareto optimality, an integer problem may require the club to go beyond the membership that maximizes the average net benefit. In Figure 13.1, the number of members is measured along the horizontal axis, and the average net benefit (*ANB*) and marginal net benefit (*MNB*) per member are indicated on the vertical axis. If $\hat{s} = 6$, maximizing *ANB* implies s^* = 4, and maximizing total net benefits implies $s^* = 6$, where *MNB* = 0 and the entire population is in the club. Thus, the integer problem is shown to push the club beyond the membership size associated with maximizing *ANB*. Unfortunately, there seems to be no single correct answer to the definition question, since there are two different points of view: the within-club viewpoint (maximizing average) versus the total-economy viewpoint (maximizing total).

For $\hat{s} > 6$, requiring one club becomes too restrictive for Pareto optimality[8] (see Table 13.1). If $\hat{s} = 8$, however, a one-club constraint yields a size of 6; but two clubs of 4 each are Pareto superior and in the core. When $\hat{s} = 12$, maximizing total net benefits in a one-club framework again yields a club of 6. Two clubs of 6 each are Pareto inferior to three clubs of 4 each.[9] Thus, to obtain an economy-wide Pareto optimum, the number of clubs must be treated as a variable. Comparisons must be made for each alternative partition of the population to achieve a Pareto optimum and possibly a core solution. When this is done and the core exists, maximizing total and maximizing average net benefits *converge to the same result*: a Pareto-optimum solution in the core. Total net benefits are maximized when each club is maximizing average net benefits and everyone is in a club (e.g., $\hat{s} = 12$ with three clubs of 4 each). Hence, true parallels between the two approaches exist when homogeneity of members is assumed and the number of clubs is variable, as in the Buchanan (1965) approach depicted in Chapter 10.

13.4   Game-theoretic formulation and institutional structures

The game-theoretic approach allows us to augment the discussion of club institutional form, begun in Chapter 12. The analysis of Section 13.2 demonstrates that differentiation between *homogeneous members* in terms of payoffs is indeed limited. In fact, a small degree of discrimination is only possible for the single-club case where the entire population is included in the club. In a homogeneous multiclub world, stability of equilibrium eliminates any possibility of payoff discrimination. Thus, *significant* benefit distinctions between classes of members, such as founding fathers and others, must occur in mixed rather than homogeneous clubs. Researchers using a Buchanan-type multiclub model were therefore correct in ignoring membership class distinctions.

Wider latitude for differentiation and payoff discrimination is available to mixed clubs. Sorenson, Tschirhart, and Whinston (1978a) showed that the core can be quite large when heterogeneity and discrimination prevail. Thus, if institutional structure is to be examined with the use of game theory, mixed rather than homogeneous, clubs must be scrutinized. Payoffs to different homogeneous classes of members must be studied to set the bounds for discrimination in keeping with such stability concepts as the core. This boundary issue should provide a fertile ground for future research.

Introducing the notion of ψ-stability permits the discussion of transaction costs to be carried further.[10] Suppose that τ includes sets of coalitions arranged according to different partitions. For example, for a population of four where individuals are indexed by $i = 1, 2, 3, 4, \tau$ might include the following partitions of coalitions:

$$(\{1\}, \{2\}, \{3\}, \{4\}), (\{1,2\}, \{3,4\}), (\{1,3\}, \{2,4\}), (\{2,3\}, \{1,2\}),$$

$$(\{1,2,3\}, \{4\}), (\{1,2\}, \{3\}, \{4\}) \text{ and } (\{1,2,3,4\}),$$

where each partition is denoted between the parentheses. Then the rule ψ indicates all *permissible* coalitions that can form from the coalition structure τ. Such a mapping is denoted by $\psi(\tau)$ and can rule out coalitions in which the transaction costs of decision making are too high. Inhibitive transaction costs might eliminate clubs either above or below a certain size from forming. Thus, $\psi(\tau)$ indicates those coalitions that can form, while improving its members' welfare. With ψ-stability, rationality requires that

$$\sum_{i \in S} b_i \geqq v(S) \qquad \text{for every } S \text{ in } \psi(\tau). \tag{3}$$

Thus, every feasible coalition delineated by $\psi(\tau)$ must possess the rationality requirement.

Suppose that the population consists of four people and that transaction costs limit club size to just three members owing to decision-making costs, setup costs, and/or communication considerations. In this case, only the three different three-member clubs must be considered when determining stability of club membership; only these three clubs are in the set of coalitions denoted by $\psi(\tau)$. Clearly, the possibility for member discrimination is altered whenever $\psi(\tau)$ restricts the feasible set of coalitions, since the opportunities of omitted individuals are limited even in a multiclub environment. For example, if singleton clubs cannot form because of setup costs, then a discriminated member does not have a positive opportunity cost of going it alone, as in the examples derived from Table 13.1.

In their study of cost allocation for a regional wastewater treatment system in the Meramac River Basin, Loehman et al. (1979) restricted the system of feasible coalitions owing to transaction and production costs considerations. In particular, coalitions between members located at opposite ends of the basin were eliminated.

Transaction costs affect not only club feasibility through the choice of ψ, but also club payoffs. In this second role, transaction costs affect the total net benefits to be distributed between members.

13.5   An application: cost allocation

Increasing returns to scale in production are an impetus for the formation of clubs. Members can aggregate their demands and attain a given provision level at less cost than if they obtained the good on their own. Aggregation, however, gives rise to problems of cost allocation: Tolls equal to marginal provision cost result in a deficit. Therefore, if members are to cover total cost, another pricing arrangement is required. If a member is assigned a disproportionate share of the cost, he or she may choose to go it alone. This would be a loss to the remaining members, since they are less able to take advantage of the scale economies. The same concept also applies to any set of members. Thus, a member or set of members must not be overcharged if scale economies are to be fully exploited. The concept of coalitions of members being charged acceptable sums suggests game theory and the core as a working framework.

Using a game-theoretic characteristic function with transferable utility implies that demands must be insensitive to tolls if a unique provision level is associated with each membership size. The assumption employed in the game-theoretic applied work is that demands are perfectly inelastic over some range of tolls. The characteristic function is defined as

$$v(S) = \sum_{i=1}^{s} C(x^i) - C\left(\sum_{i=1}^{s} x^i\right), \tag{4}$$

where $C(x^i)$ is the cost of serving member i alone and $C(\sum_{i=1}^{s} x^i)$ is the cost of serving all members in S together. Equation (4) is the net benefit of cost savings available to group S. Provided that the cost function is subadditive, $v(S)$ is positive. Once $v(S)$ is calculated for all relevant subcoalitions, game-theoretic solutions can be used to determine payoffs in the core.

The core may, however, contain more than one solution, much like the core in a private good economy (e.g., the contract curve in an Edgeworth-Bowley box). The selection of any particular core solution hinges upon the ethic or social welfare function that one employs. Two of the most commonly used solutions are the Shapley (1953) value and the nucleolus (Schmeidler 1969). When certain conditions are satisfied,[11] the Shapley value, $\phi(v)$, equals

$$\phi(v) = \sum_{S \in I_s} \gamma_s(s)[v(S) - v(S - \{i\})], \tag{5}$$

where $\gamma_s(s) = [(s - 1)!(\hat{s} - s)!/\hat{s}!$ and I_s denotes the list of population members. In (5), the bracketed term corresponds to the game value derived from all coalitions containing the ith person. Shapley value is therefore a weighted sum of the incremental gains derived by all coalitions containing i as a member. Luce and Raiffa (1957, p. 246) demonstrated that Shapley value is a generalization of the minimax value. Its value may be best described as a payoff to the coalition members according to their average contribution. The nucleolus is much like the Rawlsian maximin principle according to which the payoff to the least well-off coalition is maximized. The choice of solution is a distribution issue. Since both the nucleolus and Shapley value are core solutions, a choice between them is a decision between two Pareto optima.

Dermot Gately (1974) studied the problem of electric power production in India. The club members were different regions within India that could enjoy savings through cooperation in planning investments. Some of the solutions explored include the Shapley value, nucleolus, the von Neumann-Morgenstern, and payoffs that minimize the tendency to disrupt the club. The nucleolus was used by Suzuki and Nakayama (1976) to allocate the costs of water projects in Japan where the club membership included cities and agricultural associations. The capital cost of airport runways at Birmingham Airport, England, was assigned to aircraft types by Littlechild and Thompson (1977). They examined the Shapley value and variations of the nucleolus and showed that the charges, which include a price per landing and takeoff and a lump-sum fee for common costs, are an example of the club principle used in public utility pricing.

13.6   Concluding remarks

The chapter has presented the game-theoretic representation of clubs. This representation is crucial in examining the stability of club composition and the optimum number of clubs. When combined with the nongame formulation, the game approach sheds light on what constitutes a Pareto-optimal solution for club size—the within-club viewpoint or total-economy viewpoint. The analysis demonstrated that the answer crucially depends upon whether the optimum club size divides evenly into the population, whether the members are homogeneous, and whether the number of clubs is variable.

The game approach was also applied to the question of institutional structures. In particular, the degree of discrimination between members was shown to be limited by multiple clubs and members' homogeneity. The use of ψ-stability allowed for an investigation of transaction costs. Finally, costs allocation was examined using game-theoretic notions.

CHAPTER 14

Uncertainty and club goods*

In Chapters 10–13, we examined club behavior when membership status, club utilization, club fees, and the operation of club facilities are known with certainty. Many important examples of clubs experience random use or random breakdowns in facilities, which lead to the type of uncertainty analyzed here. For example, drivers entering a highway do not know the level of traffic (congestion) or road conditions that they might experience on a given trip. Thus, transit time, an important cost of highway use, might vary from one day to another. Allies do not know ahead of time where the alliance troops might be deployed when they are needed to repel an attack. Additionally, community members cannot determine beforehand whether police or fire protection will be available when required. Many club and local public goods must therefore be allocated under conditions of uncertainty. In addition to the examples already given, tennis courts, golf courses, and swimming pools face stochastic elements on both the demand and supply sides.

Uncertainty can affect clubs, their members, and potential members in at least five ways. First, a potential member might be uncertain as to whether he or she will be admitted to membership; membership slots are limited and not all individuals seeking membership are therefore successful. Second, a member might be uncertain about the availability of the facilities during a given visit; capacity constraints might keep some members from utilizing the facilities. Third, members might not know the exact monetary costs of club participation, and fourth, members might not know the degree of crowding that they will experience during a particular visit. Fifth, uncertainty might characterize the club on the supply side; facilities might suffer operational difficulties owing to insufficient maintenance, overuse, or breakdowns.

* This chapter has profited from discussions with Roy Adams, Doug Gegax, Fred Sterbenz, and John Tschirhart. Some of the material presented here has been developed through joint research with Fred Sterbenz and John Tschirhart, and draws from Sandler, Sterbenz, and Tschirhart (1985), published in *Economica*. Portions of this chapter are taken from Sandler, Sterbenz, and Tschirhart (1985).

In this chapter, we examine all five types of club uncertainty. Much of the chapter's analysis will, however, focus on uncertainty in club utilization, where the number of users is a random variable. Stochastic utilization can lead to uncertainty with respect to the availability of the facilities, the fee charged, and the degree of congestion experienced during a visit; hence, uncertainty cases 2–4 above apply. The introduction of uncertainty adds significantly to club goods analysis. For example, members' risk attitudes can be introduced and related to the choice of capacity and provision. The analysis here demonstrates that the optimality conditions and their interpretations for uncertainty differ fundamentally from those associated with certainty.

Since the details of the models are available elsewhere (see e.g., Sandler and Tschirhart 1984a; Sandler, Sterbenz, and Tschirhart 1985), only the structure and the results of the models are given here. The body of the chapter contains five sections. Participation or membership-status uncertainty is examined in Section 14.1, utilization uncertainty in Section 14.2. Section 14.3 presents the effects of risk attitudes on the choice of provision and capacity size. Supply-side uncertainty is analyzed in Section 14.4. Concluding remarks appear in Section 14.5.

14.1   Participation uncertainty

The first case of club uncertainty concerns membership uncertainty, whereby prospective members must participate in a lottery to determine whether they will be admitted to the club. Once admitted, club utilization is then certain. Hillman and Swan (1979) first introduced this type of uncertainty. For example, people wanting to secure a ticket to a rock concert or to a sporting event must apply for the privilege, but space constraints mean that not all those who want to go are given a ticket. Publishing in economics journals serves as another example. All scholars submitting papers want to become a member of the journal's club of contributors, but page constraints limit entry and make membership status uncertain.

To model participation uncertainty, we employ some simplifying assumptions that could easily be relaxed. We assume that a homogeneous population is seeking membership rights to a club whose utilization rates are fixed (i.e., x^i or v^i equals X). Each prospective member has an equal chance of being chosen as a member. If the club membership size is s, then the probability of securing membership is $s/\hat{s}$, where $\hat{s}$ is the entire population. Since the entire homogeneous population participates in the membership lottery, the economy's transformation function,

$$F[\hat{s}y + (s - \hat{s})\bar{y}, X] \leqq 0, \tag{1}$$

is the relevant constraint. In (1), $\bar{y}$ corresponds to the private good consumption of a nonmember. The objective function is the expected utility of the population $[\hat{s}E(U)]$, where $E(U)$ is the expected utility of a representative individual.[1] This latter expected utility weights the utilities associated with the two states of the world (i.e., membership and nonmembership status) by the relevant probabilities:

$$E(U) = \frac{s}{\hat{s}}U[y, c(s, X)] + \frac{(\hat{s} - s)}{\hat{s}}U(\bar{y}, 0). \tag{2}$$

In (2), the notation corresponds to that of Chapters 10–13. The conditions for membership size and provision are found by maximizing $\hat{s}E(U)$ with respect to s, X, and y, subject to (1). This model is analogous to the total-economy model depicted in Section 11.2, except for a fixed visitation rate; hence, the first-order conditions are essentially unchanged from those presented there. For provision, the sum of *MRS*'s must be equated to the *MRT*. The membership condition equates the net gain in utility to the marginal cost resulting from an entrant's entire utilization of the shared good. This marginal cost includes marginal crowding costs and the necessary reallocation of the private good (see Chapter 11). Since utilization is fixed, there is no utilization condition.

Clearly, this first representation of membership uncertainty does not add greatly to the study of clubs. To make their uncertainty analysis more interesting, Hillman and Swan (1983) extended the model to include a lottery ticket price, t. In applying for membership, potential members have to pay a nonrefundable fee. The lucky individuals who are chosen for the club pay both the lottery fee and a membership fee, d; the unlucky individuals just pay the lottery fee. The basics of the model remain the same; the objective function is still the expected utility of the population and the constraint is $F(\cdot)$ (Hillman and Swan 1983, p. 62). The required alteration occurs *within* the utility and transformation functions to account for the fees. For example, the utility associated with membership status is now

$$U[\bar{y} - t - d, c(s, X)],$$

where $\bar{y}$ is the individual's initial endowment of the private good.

For the utility function corresponding to nonmembership status, only t needs to be subtracted from $\bar{y}$. A similar type of adjustment to account for fees is needed in the transformation function.

The first-order conditions are derived by maximizing $\hat{s}E(U)$ with respect to s, X, Y, t, and d, subject to the transformation function. The resulting conditions are identical in form to those described above and depicted in Chapter 11. The basic difference in interpretation is that endowments are endogenized through the lottery fee. Each change in this fee will give another Pareto optimum; thus, this representation is capable of generating the entire ex ante Pareto frontier. A more direct approach for deriving this frontier is to use a Benthamite social welfare function with unequal weights as the objective function in a total-economy club model. Varying the welfare weights will then generate the Pareto frontier; there is no need to appeal to uncertainty if deriving the frontier is the goal of the analysis.

As currently formulated, membership or participation uncertainty is of limited interest because uncertainty drops out once the first-order conditions are derived. Therefore, the effects of risk attitudes on club choices cannot be examined. Moreover, few clubs require prospective members to pay a fee to be considered for inclusion. Some examples do exist, including college application fees and journal submission fees. In most real-world clubs, membership is certain once fees are remitted, but capacity constraints may limit the number of members who can be accommodated at any given time. Utilization is then uncertain. This case is examined next.

14.2   Utilization uncertainty

The second model concerns clubs whose participants are certain about their membership status but are uncertain about the congestion that they will experience on any particular visit. When certain capacity limits are met owing to a high visitation rate, members must either be denied entry or else be forced to queue. The analysis here will concentrate on the case of the member who must be turned away. For these clubs, a queue is not possible. Fire protection is clearly an example—when a house is burning any queuing would lead to widespread destruction. Police and military protection are other instances in which queuing is not feasible. Even recreation facilities might not permit queuing if operating hours are limited. In other club examples, queues are possible. The analysis of McCormick and Adams (1983) is a useful source in this regard.

Members are turned away only when visitation rates exceed capacity. If visitation is less than capacity, however, additional members can easily enter. Club utilization on any given visit therefore depends on the number of other members present, which is a random variable. If a user charge is levied each time a member succeeds in using the club, then the cost of participation is also uncertain prior to the visit.

To simplify the analysis, the population is assumed to be homogeneous, so that each individual has the same tastes and endowments. Utilization rates are assumed to be fixed. Furthermore, the optimum membership, s^*, is hypothesized to divide evenly into the population, thus allowing the set of optimum clubs to partition the set of individuals. Game-theoretical results then imply that maximizing the utility of a representative member will yield a Pareto-optimal solution that is in the core. The choice of membership therefore determines the optimum number of clubs—that is, $\bar{s}/s^*$. Thus, this exercise corresponds to Cell A of Table 10.1.

A representative member must choose the total membership (s), the number of members permitted to enter at one time ($\bar{s}$), and the size of the club facility (X). The number of members that visit at one time is given by the random variable n.[2] Clearly, n is nonnegative and no greater than s. When n exceeds $\bar{s}$, then $n - \bar{s}$ members cannot enter. Assuming that members behave independently, and if the probability that a member visits is denoted by p, with $1 - p$ being the probability of not visiting, then n is binomially distributed. However, for convenience, the binomial distribution is approximated with a normal distribution and n is treated as a continuous random variable. Thus, the probability density function of n is written as

$$g(n; \mu, \sigma^2) \equiv g_s(n), \tag{3}$$

where

$$\mu = sp \text{ and } \sigma^2 = p(1 - p)s. \tag{4}$$

The member's problem is to maximize expected utility given by

$$E[U] = (1 - p)U(W^*) + p \int_0^{\bar{s}} U(W_s^i)g_s(n)\,dn$$
$$+ p \int_{\bar{s}}^{s} \left[\frac{\bar{s}}{n} U(W^i)_{n=\bar{s}} + \frac{n - \bar{s}}{n} U(W^o) \right] g_s(n)\,dn, \tag{5}$$

where $U(\cdot)$ is a von Neumann-Morgenstern utility function. In (5), the three terms on the right-hand side correspond to the three states of the world: (1) not visiting, (2) visiting and entering, and (3) visiting and possibly entering. The two terms within the last integral account for the fact that at full capacity the member may or may not be admitted with probabilities $\bar{s}/n$ and $(n - \bar{s})/n$, respectively. Arguments W^*, W^i, and W^o are net wealth equivalent measures over the three states defined as

$$W^i = w^i(n, X) - f(X)/s - c(n, X) \qquad 0 \leqq n \leqq \bar{s} \qquad (6)$$

$$W^o = w^o - f(X)/s \qquad \bar{s} < n \leqq s \qquad (7)$$

$$W^* = w^* - f(X)/s \qquad 0 \leqq n \leqq s. \qquad (8)$$

The first right-hand term in (6) is a monetary equivalent of the member's utility from all nonclub goods and the use of the club, where the latter depends on n and X. Presumably, as n increases, ceteris paribus, $w^i(n, X)$ decreases owing to increased congestion, although the model allows for the possibility that $w^i(n, X)$ increases in n over some range due to camaraderie. Also, as X increases, ceteris paribus, $w^i(n, X)$ increases because of decreased congestion. The first right-hand term in (7) is the monetary equivalent of the member's utility from all nonclub goods only, since in this state of the world the member is unsuccessful in entering the club. In (8), w^* is the monetary equivalent of the member's utility from nonclub goods when the member is not visiting. The second term, $f(X)/s$, in (6), (7), and (8) represents the fixed membership fee per period and must be paid regardless of the state of the world. The numerator, $f(X)$, is the fixed provision cost of the facility, and is assumed to be continuously differentiable with a positive first derivative ($f' > 0$). The $c(n, X)$ term in (6) is the variable user charge to the member, which is collected only if he or she gets in and depends on the number of visitors present and the facility size. This latter term captures any maintenance and other variable costs that depend on usage, and is assumed to be continuously differentiable in X and n.

The two-part tariff structure in (6) is indicative of the scale economies associated with many club goods (e.g., highways).[3] The lump-sum charge, $f(X)/s$, is levied on members independent of their usage, while $c(n, X)$ is levied according to usage. This would seem to be an accurate description of the way many clubs actually finance their operations. In other uncertainty models such as insurance models, the charges levied create wealth transfers from the more desired to less desired states of the world, thereby mitigating the losses in the latter states. In our model of clubs, these same types of transfers occur via the provision and capacity choices. This feature is made clear in Section 14.3.

In summary, the member faces the following problem: he or she maximizes expected utility, (5), with respect to membership size (s), the entry cutoff or capacity, ($\tilde{s}$), and the facility size (X). Larger membership sizes are associated with both decreased costs per member as provision expense is spread over more members, and a decreased probability of a successful visit. When the representative member chooses the entry cutoff point, two influences are present, since a larger $\tilde{s}$ increases both the likelihood of a successful visit and the probability of reduced utility for successful visitors. The latter influence results from the possibly larger number of other visitors with whom a successful member might have to share the facility. Greater facility sizes are associated with both increased enjoyment of the facility and increased maintenance and provision fees for successful visitors. Moreover, an increase in X increases provision fees for members, whether or not they succeed in visiting. The choice of both X and $\tilde{s}$ determines the maximum congestion possible. The member's preferences regarding congestion are captured by the $w^i(n, X)$ function.

Characterizing the optimum club

If we assume an interior maximum exists,[4] first-order conditions characterizing the member's optimum choice of s, $\tilde{s}$ and X are given by equations (9), (10) and (11), respectively:

$$p\left[\frac{\tilde{s}}{s}U(W^i)_{n=\tilde{s}} + \frac{s-\tilde{s}}{s}U(W^o)\right]g_s(s)$$

$$+ p\int_0^s\left[U'\frac{\partial W^i}{\partial s}g_s(n) + U\frac{\partial g_s(n)}{\partial s}\right]dn$$

$$+ p\int_{\tilde{s}}^s\left\{\left[\frac{\tilde{s}}{n}\left(U'\frac{\partial W^i}{\partial s}\right)_{n=\tilde{s}} + \frac{n-\tilde{s}}{n}U'\frac{\partial W^o}{\partial s}\right]g_s(n)\right.$$

$$+ \left.\left[\frac{\tilde{s}}{n}U(W^i)_{n=\tilde{s}} + \frac{n-\tilde{s}}{n}U(W^o)\right]\frac{\partial g_s(n)}{\partial s}\right\}dn$$

$$+ (1-p)U'\frac{\partial W^*}{\partial s} = 0 \qquad \text{(Membership)} \qquad (9)$$

$$p\int_{\tilde{s}}^s\frac{1}{n}\left[\tilde{s}\left(U'\frac{\partial W^i}{\partial \tilde{s}}\right)_{n=\tilde{s}} + U(W^i)_{n=\tilde{s}}\right.$$

$$\left. - U(W^o)\right]g_s(n)\,dn = 0 \qquad \text{(Capacity)} \qquad (10)$$

$$(1 - p)U' \frac{\partial W^*}{\partial X} + p \int_0^{\bar{s}} U' \frac{\partial W^i}{\partial X} g_s(n) \, dn$$

$$+ p \int_{\bar{s}}^s \left[\frac{\bar{s}}{n} \left(U' \frac{\partial W^i}{\partial X} \right)_{n=\bar{s}} + \frac{n - \bar{s}}{n} U' \frac{\partial W^o}{\partial X} \right] g_s(n) \, dn = 0$$

(Provision)   (11)

where a prime indicates a derivative and function arguments have been dropped when confusion does not result, and where

$$\partial W^i/\partial X = w^i_X - f'(X)/s - c_X \gtreqless 0 \tag{12}$$

$$\partial W^o/\partial X = \partial W^*/\partial X = -f'(X)/s < 0 \tag{13}$$

$$\partial W^i/\partial s = \partial W^o/\partial s = \partial W^*/\partial s = f(X)/s^2 > 0. \tag{14}$$

The subscripts in (12) denote partial derivatives. Equation (12) indicates that changes in provision have ambiguous effects on net wealth in state 1 owing to greater enjoyment ($w^i_X > 0$), higher membership fees ($-f'(X)/s < 0$), and higher maintenance fees ($-c_X < 0$); whereas, (13) denotes that increased provision lowers net wealth in states 2 and 3 owing to the higher membership fees. Equation (14) indicates that increased membership size increases net wealth owing to reduced membership fees.

In (9), four expressions make up the membership condition. The first term results from extending the upper limit of integration of the second integral in (5), and is the expected utility if all members show at one time. This expected utility is weighted by the likelihood that this will occur. The second expression in (9) is the expected marginal net benefit associated with increased membership size when the member succeeds in visiting prior to capacity. This integral term includes both the expected marginal benefit derived from the reduced membership fees owing to cost sharing and the expected marginal cost associated with the reduced likelihood of admittance. The latter influence stems from the changed probability distribution, resulting from the membership expansion. The next integral expression in (9) denotes the expected marginal *net* benefit associated with increased membership once capacity is reached. At capacity, the representative member may or may not succeed in visiting, as shown by the probabilities $\bar{s}/n$ and $(n - \bar{s})/n$. In either state, expected marginal benefit derives from the reduced fees, and expected marginal cost arises from the reduced likelihood of admittance. The final term in (9) is the marginal benefit from reduced fees when the individual chooses not to visit.

The condition for the optimum capacity requires that the aggregate utility loss to successful visitors due to another visitor being admitted at full capacity (first term in brackets) equals the increase in utility experienced by the admitted visitor (second and third terms in brackets). That there must be an increase upon admittance at the optimum can be seen by assuming the reverse. Suppose that at the optimum, denoted by $E[U]^*$, the marginal entrant is no better off upon entry ($U(W^i)_{n=\bar{s}} \leq U(W^o)$). Then, at the optimum values of s and X, expected utility in (3) can be shown to increase if capacity is decreased until the entrant is better off upon entry ($U(W^i)_{n=\bar{s}} > U(W^o)$). Therefore, $E[U]^*$ could not be an optimum. A formal proof is available from the authors. Thus, congestion is allowed to increase to the point where its costs to existing visitors equal the benefits bestowed on the marginal entrant. The homogeneity assumption allows for such direct comparisons of utilities.

The provision condition equates the expected marginal benefits with expected marginal costs of increased facility size. The first term in (11) is the marginal utility of a change in facility size when the member does not visit. This is negative by (13), since greater provisions only add to the nonvisiting member's costs. The second term is the marginal utility of a change in facility size when the member is a successful visitor. This may be positive or negative by (12), depending on whether the enjoyment of a larger facility outweighs the additional provision and maintenance costs. The third term is the marginal utility of a change in facility size when the member visits and may or may not gain admittance since more than $\bar{s}$ members visit. The first term in brackets is ambiguous in sign for reasons just cited above with respect to term two; however, the second term in brackets is unambiguously negative, since an unsuccessful visitor faces increased provision costs with no concomitant benefits.

A comparison of certainty and uncertainty conditions

Interesting differences distinguish the membership condition in the uncertainty model from the corresponding condition in certainty models. To understand these conditions, note that in the certainty model the total membership size, s, enters the cost and utility functions; in the uncertainty model, congestion is random and n, not s, enters these functions. Under certainty, a larger membership, ceteris paribus, unequivocally increases congestion. Under uncertainty, a larger membership, ceteris paribus, reduces the likelihood of admission and increases the likelihood of congestion. However, the maximum congestion allowed does not change, since capacity has not changed. The extent to which these likelihoods change depends on how the probability density function is altered when s increases, since s affects both the mean and variance.

To facilitate a comparison between the certainty and uncertainty representations of the provision condition, consider that under certainty the member's maximand would be

$$W^i = w^i(s, X) - f(X)/s - c(s, X), \tag{15}$$

which is the same as (6) except s replaces n. Visitation is not random and the club can accommodate all s members. The member equates the marginal benefit and marginal cost of increased provision by setting the partial derivative of (15) with respect to X equal to zero. The counterparts to this partial under uncertainty are the second term and first term in brackets in (11), the sum of which, for reasons cited above, must have a positive sign. Hence, the member does not increase facility size to the point where marginal benefits and costs of using the facility are equal, as under certainty, because doing so is too costly in terms of greater expenditure on membership fees even when the member does not visit [term one in (11)] or visits but does not enter [second term in brackets in (11)]. Under certainty, the possibility of nonadmission does not arise.

In certainty club models where average net benefits are maximized, the member is always better off in the club. For the Berglas, Helpman, and Pines (1982) certainty model, facility size is such that members are indifferent to participation. In the uncertainty model, members are always better off if they gain admittance, since the difference between the second and third terms in brackets in (10) is positive. This implies that when members are allowed to choose the maximum possible congestion, they will ensure that visitation is not pressed to the point where the club affords a bad experience. Yet, one can imagine real-world situations in which visitors are allowed admittance to the point where members are indifferent to or perhaps even worse off by visiting. For example, consider the mass transit rider who hops on a bus or train and finds standing room only. He may well wish that he had waited for a later ride. Or consider a country club member who visits the swimming pool facilities only to find an overwhelming crowd that makes him wish he had stayed home.

Two qualifications are needed to explain these situations: (1) constraining $\bar{s}$ in the maximization problem, and (2) explicitly describing the information available to the members. With regard to (1), suppose $\bar{s}$ is not a decision variable, but a parameter in (5). Then we obtain $\partial E[U]/\partial \bar{s}$ evaluated at the optimum values of s and X. By the envelope theorem, if $\bar{s}$ is fixed at a value equal to, less than, or greater than the optimum value as defined by (10), then $\partial E[U]/\partial \bar{s}$ will be zero, positive, or negative. The latter event allows for the possibility that $U(W^i)_{n=\bar{s}} - U(W^o) \leqq 0$, and visitors may be indifferent to or even worse off upon gaining admittance. The implication is that the maximum allowable congestion must be defined by the members, and not by some nonmember, perhaps a design engineer, who may be more concerned with physical dimensions and feasible crowd levels than with preferences toward congestion.[5]

The second requirement above has to do with the information available to the member when visiting. Suppose entry entails being made worse off. Since entering is voluntary, the member must not know beforehand that he would be worse off. Thus, information regarding the status of the club is imperfect prior to entry. Two conditions must be met for this to occur: First, there must be some physical reason why the member cannot observe the level of congestion (e.g., a fence around a pool); and second, the user charge is not collected prior to entry so that it does not reveal information about the level of congestion. Instead, collecting $c(n, X)$ must be done after the member is admitted, or at the end of some specified period when the member's total number of visits is tallied. This method of collection is more realistic, since collecting $c(n, X)$ upon entry implies that each entrant is charged a different fee, and prior entrants must pay more each time a new entrant is admitted. In practice, clubs that do collect upon entry usually set a constant fee, independent of n.[6]

Although our model highlights the uncertainty that members have about being admitted to the club, there are conditions under which large membership clubs tend to moderate this uncertainty. We refer to this phenomenon as an expansionary bias under uncertainty. Given our assumptions on the distribution of visitors, the fraction of the club membership wanting to use the facility at any given time is the random variable n/s, which has a mean of p. By the central limit theorem, we know that as s increases, the variance of n/s decreases and the distribution of n/s is asymptotically normal. Therefore, as membership increases, the fraction of the membership wanting to use the facility at any given time is subject to less uncertainty. This provides an incentive to form large clubs. This expansionary bias is similar to the principle behind insurance companies.

To illustrate, consider a club whose technology for producing X

exhibits constant returns to scale. By this we mean that if provision is doubled, the cost of provision, $f(X)$, is doubled. Ignoring maintenance costs for the sake of simplicity, this club can double provision and membership while keeping membership fees constant. If capacity is also permitted to double, there is no increase in fees but the probability of being admitted is increased.[7] This suggests that the optimum club would include the entire population when constant returns hold.

14.3   Effects of risk aversion

The club member's choices of facility size, congestion, and membership size will depend on his or her attitude toward risk. To examine how risk aversion affects these choices, we use a specific form of the utility function (Leland 1972, pp. 287–8). For small gambles, a risk-averse utility function can be approximated by the quadratic

$$U(W) = kW - rW^2 \qquad 0 < W < 1/(2r). \qquad (16)$$

When $r = 0$, risk neutrality obtains, and as r increases from zero, risk aversion increases according to the Arrow-Pratt measure.[8]

To isolate the effects of risk aversion, Sandler, Sterbenz, and Tschirhart (1985) substitute (16) into the objective function, (5), for $U(\cdot)$. The first-order conditions associated with the new objective are found and evaluated where $r = 0$. A comparative-static analysis is then performed from this starting point of risk neutrality by finding the changes in optimal capacity and provision when risk aversion increases; that is, $\partial \bar{s}^*/\partial r$ and $\partial X^*/\partial r$ are derived. For tractability, Sandler, Sterbenz, and Tschirhart (1985) assume that membership size is fixed and only consider the choices of facility size and capacity when analyzing the influence of risk aversion. Since facility size and capacity define the maximum-allowed congestion, their analysis examines how risk attitudes affect maximum congestion for a club whose membership is fixed at s. We refer the reader to Sandler, Sterbenz, and Tschirhart (1985) for details and derivations.

To obtain unambiguous results, they assume that W^* exceeds W^i and W^o. In such a case, the following comparative-static relationships hold:

$$\frac{\partial \bar{s}^*}{\partial r} > 0 \text{ and } \frac{\partial X^*}{\partial r} > 0. \qquad (17)$$

Increased risk aversion leads to larger facility size and capacity. More members are permitted to visit the club at one time, and the facility is expanded to accommodate the additional visitors. To explain this result, consider the type of club in which $W*$ might dominate W^i and W^o. Using the example of a fire department as the club, W^i, W^o, and $W*$ correspond to the three states in which the member's house is: (1) burning and the fire department succeeds in extinguishing the fire; (2) burning and the fire department does not come to the rescue; and (3) not burning. Certainly in this type of club, $W*$ would greatly exceed W^i and W^o since state (3) is by far the most desired state. The impetus for joining the club is to insure one's wealth. A typical feature of expected utility models is that the individual transfers wealth from the desired state to the undesired state through some type of insurance mechanism. In our model, increased risk aversion leads the member to effect this transfer by two means. First, he or she transfers wealth by choosing a larger facility, since the facility is paid for in every state. Second, by choosing a larger capacity, he or she increases the probability of falling into the second most desired state (fire extinguished) while decreasing the probability of falling into the least desired state (fire not extinguished). Hence, increased risk aversion leads him or her to increase both capacity and provision, thereby insuring against high losses.

If $W*$ does not dominate, little can be said. Increased risk aversion has ambiguous results for the choice of $\bar{s}$ and X. Clubs that provide swimming pools, golf courses, and other less vital goods would probably fall into this category.

14.4   Supply-side uncertainty

Uncertainty on the supply side may also plague club goods; club facilities may break down owing to utilization or lack of maintenance. Gegax (1984) has developed a model in which the percentage of capacity available at any time is a continuous random variable.[9] By expressing available capacity as a percentage, we can treat usable provision as a continuous variable. The distribution of the random variable is affected by both the level of maintenance, m, and the size of the membership. Increases in m reduce the percentage of unavailable capacity, whereas increases in membership size increase this percentage.

The Gegax model allows for supply-side uncertainty only; demand is certain with visitors equal to s. Members are also homogeneous in tastes and endowments. Furthermore, utilization rates are fixed and equal to the percentage of capacity available $(1 - b)$ times the amount of the club good provided; thus, $x = (1 - b)X$. The parameter b

therefore represents the percentage of capacity that is unavailable. To account for the observation that b is usually low, Gegax assumes a truncated exponential whose values range between 0 and 1. The probability density function is

$$g(b) = [\psi/(1 - e^{-\psi})]e^{-\psi b} \qquad b\epsilon[0, 1], \tag{18}$$

where $\psi = \psi(s, m)$ with $\psi_m > 0$ and $\psi_s < 0$. These partials indicate that for high levels of m, low levels of b are likely; the reverse causation holds for s.

The expected utility of the representative member is

$$E(U) = \int_0^1 U[y, (1 - b)X, s]g(b)db. \tag{19}$$

The convex transformation constraint for the representative individual is

$$F(y, X, m, s) \leq 0, \tag{20}$$

where increases in the first three arguments use scarce resources, and an increase in the fourth term reduces the use of resources owing to club cost sharing. Optimal provision, maintenance, and membership size can be derived by maximizing (19) subject to (18) and (20). The provision condition is analogous to the Samuelsonian condition, except for the appearance of expected utilities. That is, the sum of the ratios of expected marginal utilities is equated with the *MRT*.

For the maintenance condition, the covariance between utility and b is important in determining the optimum maintenance expense. The same covariance expression shows up in the membership condition. These two conditions are

$$\frac{\psi_s[-cov(U, b)]}{E(U_y)} = MRT_{my} \qquad \text{(Maintenance)}$$

$$\frac{\psi_s[-cov(U, b)] + E(U_s)}{E(U_y)} = MRT_{sy} \qquad \text{(Membership)}$$

where the subscripts on ψ and U indicate partial derivatives. Since the covariance between U and b is negative (i.e., $cov(\cdot) < 0$), a higher absolute value of the covariance term justifies greater maintenance and smaller membership levels.

The maintenance condition's interpretation depends upon the covariance term, the weighting factor ψ_m, and the relative marginal cost of maintenance (i.e., MRT_{my}). A low tolerance for facility breakdowns (i.e., $|\ cov\ (U^i, b)\ |$ is high) will, ceteris paribus, increase the associated marginal benefits derived from maintenance, thereby justifying higher maintenance. The term, ψ_m, denotes how effective an increase in m is in bunching the probability distribution toward reliable services (i.e., a low b). If the club is breaking even at the margin in financing maintenance, then a Samuelsonian-type condition can be derived once again. This result is to be expected, since maintenance is a pure public good to the club members, much like provision. Clubs providing essential services such as fire protection or ambulance would have a low tolerance for breakdowns, and therefore would maintain equipment at high levels of reliability.

The membership condition can be interpreted as equating the expected marginal costs of adding another member with the certain marginal benefit of reduced fees due to cost sharing (i.e., $MRT_{sy} < 0$). The membership condition denotes *two sources* of expected marginal costs from increasing membership size: The first involves the effects that s has on the distribution of breakdowns, and the second concerns the expected marginal costs of crowding associated with larger club memberships, that is, $E(U^i_s)/E(U^i_y)$. Only this second influence has an analogous expression in the certainty model of clubs. When members are not very tolerant of breakdowns, a small membership is indicated. Adding a new member now entails the likelihood of more crowding and the possibility of more service failures; both marginal costs must be summed and then compared to the cost savings associated with membership expansion.

The obvious next step is to include uncertainty on both the demand and supply sides. Since reductions in usable capacity affect $\bar{s}$, the interaction between the two sources of uncertainty would indeed be interesting. A reduction in $(1 - b)$ would help determine at what point members were denied entry. Increases in either maintenance or provision levels can increase the number of members the club can accommodate. We leave this exercise to our future research.

14.5 Conclusions

This chapter has examined three cases of uncertainty for club goods: (1) participation uncertainty, (2) utilization uncertainty, and (3) facility operation uncertainty. The last two types of uncertainty lead to interesting results when compared with those of the certainty analysis presented in Chapters 10–13.

The analysis of uncertainty in club utilization has produced optimum conditions for membership and provision that differ fundamentally from those of the certainty model. In particular, larger memberships affect the *likelihood* of admission and crowding for the uncertainty model. Larger memberships unequivocally increase congestion for the certainty model. With constant returns to scale, the underlying distribution assumption may produce an expansionary bias for clubs since larger memberships may reduce uncertainty, thus increasing the likelihood of admittance. Provision conditions differ in the certainty and uncertainty models owing to membership fees that must be paid regardless of whether the member visits. With uncertainty, members do not expand facility size to the point where marginal benefits and costs of using the facility are equal. Finally, risk aversion was shown to affect a member's choice of capacity and facility size. When a member's wealth in the certainty state dominates, increased risk aversion leads, under some reasonable assumptions, to increased provision and capacity as a means for insuring against risk.

CHAPTER 15

Intergenerational clubs*

This chapter is concerned with clubs in which multiple overlapping generations of members share a club good. For such *intergenerational clubs*, the life span of the shared good exceeds the membership span of the founding members, so that the good is shared between generations until the time span of the good is exhausted. Many clubs are intergenerational in character and deserve study. In particular, decisions with respect to city management, national parks, highways, and the design of school districts can profit from the principles of intergenerational clubs developed here. But the list does not end there. Universities are intergenerational clubs since multiple generations of students and faculties share the campus. Even "Spaceship Earth" can be thought of as an intergenerational club good, shared by mankind and other earth-dwelling inhabitants. This analogy holds whenever the Earth's population is endogenous. The utilization of the electromagnetic spectrum is yet another example. Fraternities, professional associations, and religious groups are still other examples.

Unlike our previous treatment of clubs, an intertemporal model must be used to examine intergenerational clubs, since costs imposed upon club members by an entrant may be *either* atemporal crowding or intertemporal *depreciation due to utilization* whenever the act of using the good can detract from the good's remaining benefits over time. Suppose that a national park is heavily utilized during a holiday weekend. People, cars, and campers crowd the park's roadways, filling the parking areas. Whenever the "carrying capacity"[1] of the park is exceeded so that car emissions and human transits deteriorate the environment, depreciation due to utilization is taking place. It is easy to see that intertemporal depreciation due to utilization (henceforth called depreciation) may involve both present and future members. In contrast, crowding cost affects only current members, since members must be contemporaries to crowd one another. To

---

* Some portions of this chapter are taken from Sandler (1982), published in *Economic Inquiry*.

account for depreciation, depreciation cost must acknowledge the existence and sequencing of future members.

An intertemporal analysis requires a great deal of additional detail. First, crowding and depreciation considerations must be separated. Second, an additional index is needed to distinguish between time periods. Third, the transformation constraint must encompass intertemporal resource allocation. Fourth, members' periods of membership must be analyzed; hence, membership decisions with respect to club status *and* with respect to membership span must be investigated. Fifth, tolls must be distinguished between periods owing to a changing composition of members; hence, crowding and depreciation costs may vary drastically from one period to another. Sixth, maintenance decisions must be distinguished from provision decisions. Maintenance expenditures can recuperate losses in a good's benefit resulting from depreciation. In our previous discussion of maintenance, the intertemporal aspects were ignored since the model was static. Seventh, a member's lifetime period must be known and indexed. Finally, a multiperiod utility function is required for each individual. This function depends on the utility received in each period of a person's lifetime.

Since such a model has been presented by Sandler (1982), we will not bother to repeat the exercise here. Instead we will briefly describe the model's basic structure and its resulting optimal conditions. The interested reader is encouraged to consult the above reference for details and notation. Much of this chapter will focus on the model's implications. In particular, we intend to explain how the optimal conditions of the intergenerational club model differ from those of the standard atemporal model. An essential purpose is to show that institutional form helps determine whether intergenerational clubs will behave myopically with respect to allocative decisions. Specifically, adequate incentives to act with foresight are shown to exist for clubs owned by either the members or a firm; however, government-owned intergenerational clubs are more likely to be myopic owing to short-run incentives and institutional rigidities that may create suboptimal tolls, maintenance and provision, and supraoptimal memberships. This myopic tendency can be partly overcome when voters and lobbyists pressure governments to preserve option demands and to account for future generations' benefits. Some tendency toward nonoptimality and easy-rider behavior is shown to characterize maintenance decisions for all but firm-owned clubs, since maintenance is purely public within a club.

The body of the chapter is organized into five main sections. The basic model is briefly sketched in Section 15.1, where the model's optimal conditions are also discussed. Section 15.2 extends the model to consider maintenance decisions. The relationship between myopia and institutional form is analyzed in Section 15.3. Other considerations are presented in Section 15.4. Applications and summary statements follow in Section 15.5.

15.1   The model

On the model's structure

The basic model is one of perfect foresight with respect to tastes, life spans, production, depreciation, crowding, and club utilization patterns. A *single* club is hypothesized in which the optimal membership size is large with respect to population; thus, the population is not partitioned. Moreover, members can have heterogeneous tastes with respect to crowding, depreciation, and the two goods consumed. The model is consequently of type H.[2] To ensure that mixed members can be accommodated optimally, the quantity of the shared good affects utility *indirectly* through the crowding and depreciation functions (see the remarks about mixed clubs in Chapter 11). Essentially, the underlying model is a variant of the general model described in Chapter 11, where we take a total-economy viewpoint and distinguish members from nonmembers.

Initially, we hypothesize the existence of a nonmaintainable impure public good provided in an initial period and remaining in existence for an exogenous and finite number of periods. For example, national parks and wilderness areas cannot be restored to their original "undisturbed" state by investment or maintenance expense once utilization or development has caused a degradation in the nature of these goods (see Fisher, Krutilla, and Cicchetti 1972, 1974). In their natural state, the life span of parks and wilderness areas are fixed by nature.

A private numeraire good, which is produced in each period and which lasts for one period, is also assumed. Both costless exclusion of nonmembers and continuous lifetime membership spans are invoked. Multiple overlapping generations of members share the public good over its lifetime. Each member is permitted to have an individualized, but known, membership (life) span. Members and nonmembers are considered so that the number of members is a choice variable. To account for the intertemporal pattern of benefits of the shared good, a multiperiod utility function that depends upon the utility received in each period is required.

A member's single-period utility function depends on his or her consumption of the club good, the private good, and the negative externalities associated with crowding *and* depreciation. Crowding in any period indicates a detraction in the consumption experience owing to an increase in the average utilization of a unit of the impure public good in that period. Except for a differentiation between periods, the representation of crowding has not changed in this model as compared to atemporal models. An increase in the average utilization rate in a given period will augment crowding, whereas an increase in provision will relieve crowding in the period of provision, *as well as in all future periods* by lowering average utilization rates. If the crowding function is indexed according to the time periods, crowding is permitted to differ between periods owing to an alteration in the method of provision, the size of the membership, or the quality of the good.

The novel feature of an intergenerational club model is the depreciation function. Depreciation is the intertemporal analogue of crowding and can be best described as a wearing down or detraction in the good's quality owing to utilization. The depreciation phenomenon may appear as reduced attractiveness, loss in operative efficiency, loss in regenerative ability, and reduced usable area. Although both crowding and depreciation depend upon the average utilization rate(s) and involve a reduction in quality, these concepts differ significantly. Crowding is atemporal so that any decrease in the good's quality is automatically restored in the ensuing period; however, depreciation is intertemporal so that a decrease remains for the good's life span unless offset by maintenance.

Depreciation in a given period depends on the average utilization rate in that period and in *all* previous periods, since depreciation is viewed as a cumulative phenomenon.[3] That is, depreciation is the cumulative quality deterioration associated with a shared good's utilization. Since the good does not replenish itself, what went on before must be reflected in the depreciation experienced in any period. Thus, an increase in the average utilization rate in *any* preceding period enhances the depreciation in the current period. In contrast, an increase in the initial provision of the shared good reduces depreciation in the current period via a decrease in the average utilization rates in the current and all preceding periods.

Table 15.1 lists the functions used in the intergenerational club model. As discussed in Chapter 11, at least six alternative represen-

Table 15.1. *Intergenerational club model*

Equation no.	Description	Method of indexing
(1)	Member's multiperiod utility function	By person
(2)	Member's single-period utility function	By person and by period
(3)	Nonmember's multiperiod utility function	By person
(4)	Nonmember's multiperiod utility function	By person and by period
(5)	Crowding function, contained in (2)	By period
(6)	Depreciation function, contained in (2)	By period
(7)	Impurity constraint ($x^{ij} \leq X$)	By person and by period
(8)	Transformation function	Not applicable
(9)	Private good production-distribution constraint	By period

tations exist for the objective function, each of which would affect the form of the membership condition but would not alter the toll or provision condition. For example, individuals can be ordered by their net willingness to pay for the club during their lifetime, as measured by their net gain from membership. Once the individuals are so ordered, either a Benthamite social welfare function of members and nonmembers can be maximized, or else the marginal entrant's utility can be maximized subject to the constancy of the utility levels of the rest of the population. Another alternative requires the maximization of an arbitrary member's utility function, subject to the constancy of the other members' and nonmembers' utility levels (see Hillman and Swan 1983). Whichever procedure is followed, the impurity constraint (7), the transformation function (8), and the private good production-distribution constraint (9) from Table 15.1 must restrict the optimal solution.

Optimality conditions: their interpretations

When the initial provision of the shared, impure public good is increased and total utilization rates are fixed, the good's average utilization rates fall in all periods, thereby reducing congestion and depreciation during the club's life span. Optimal provision requires that the sum of the marginal benefits from crowding relief *and* depreciation reduction equals the marginal cost of increased provision. These marginal benefits must account for all club members and their membership spans. In the formal conditions of Sandler (1982), the marginal benefits and marginal costs are in terms of a numeraire good and, therefore, correspond to *MRS*s and *MRT*s.

In contrast to traditional club treatments, the inclusion of depreciation considerations creates an additional source of provision benefits. Larger optimal facility sizes may therefore be justified as compared to traditional atemporal analyses owing to these additional intertemporal benefits.

An optimal utilization or toll condition determines the Pareto-efficient utilization rates of the shared good for members during each period of their membership. This condition equates the marginal benefit that a member derives from utilization with the associated marginal crowding and marginal depreciation costs imposed on the membership. By setting the toll equal to these marginal costs, the externality associated with utilization is internalized. The jth period toll therefore includes the costs of crowding and depreciation imposed at the margin on the *relevant* membership. These marginal crowding costs involve members present only within that period, since members must be mutually present to experience a crowding externality. In contrast, the marginal depreciation cost affects all contemporaries as well as all future members for the remainder of their club membership. For example, if large average utilization rates destroy the regenerative abilities of a forest, then the depreciation to be experienced in all future periods is influenced by the high average utilization rate of the destructive period. Seen in this light, the tragedy of an *intergenerational commons* may be worse than ever believed, since overharvesting in initial periods can have long-term harmful effects. Moreover, those individuals affected are not present to negotiate with the current exploiters.

Insofar as total and average utilization rates as well as membership size can differ between periods, the optimal toll between periods will also differ. Each member pays an identical toll in any given period, since the crowding and depreciation costs of an additional unit of utilization are the same at the margin to other members, irrespective of the user. *Total* toll payments, however, vary between heterogeneous members in any period according to revealed intensity of use; that is, the equality between the toll and marginal benefits received will occur at different utilization rates for heterogeneous members.

The toll for intergenerational clubs differs from conventional tolls, since the former includes atemporal crowding and intertemporal depreciation considerations. Furthermore, a member's place in the sequence of members is important in determining that member's pattern of tolls during membership. Earlier members will cause more marginal depreciation damage for a given utilization rate owing to the greater number of subsequent members who will join the club and be affected by the depreciation. Hence, the added social responsibility that earlier members have to future members is internalized by a properly designed toll sequence.

Combining the toll and provision condition as in Chapter 11 allows us to determine whether such a proposed toll scheme can self-finance optimal provision. The finance result indicates that the sum of the tolls collected over the good's lifetime suffices to finance marginal provision cost (see Sandler 1982, p. 206); but the toll scheme fails to self-finance the shared good unless average cost is less than or equal to marginal cost. With increasing returns to scale (a typical, but not necessary, public good situation), self-financing is not achieved. Toll collections must then be supplemented by either a subsidy or else a membership assessment that constitutes a second part of a two-part tariff.

The membership condition requires the *net* membership benefits for an entrant to exceed or equal the associated costs resulting from his or her entire utilization of the club during membership. These net benefits include the intertemporal gain in utility attributable to membership and any required change in the private good allocated to the entrant during membership. Since the private good must provide the same marginal benefit for the entrant, membership status may necessitate a reallocation of the good to maintain optimality whenever the two goods are related in consumption.

On the cost side, crowding caused by the entrant's membership is experienced by all members who overlap with the entrant at some point during their membership. These crowding costs involve the entrant's utilization of the club during each and every period of membership. The depreciation costs associated with membership for the entrant affect all members who either overlap with the entrant or else join after his or her death. The membership size condition differs significantly from those in the literature, since aggregation of costs includes a *changing* number of members *and* time periods, depending upon both the entrant's position in the *sequence* of members and the entrant's membership span. For example, longer-lived members can crowd a larger number of members than short-lived members, and consequently the former should expect higher cumulative membership fees.

Nonlifetime members and membership span considerations

When nonlifetime memberships are analyzed, additional indexing must be introduced to permit the increased exactness in specification required. The membership group must be redefined to represent all one-time members. Membership periods must now be distinguished from those of nonmembership for each club participant.

The provision, financing, and toll conditions remain as described above; however, a new membership condition must be derived to determine both membership size and the span of membership for each club participant. If, for at least one period, a prospective member's benefits from membership exceed or equal the associated crowding and depreciation costs, the individual should be admitted to the club. Continuous and discontinuous membership cases must be examined when the entrant's membership span is determined. For continuous membership, additional membership periods following an initial period should be allowed until the entrant's benefits from membership no longer outweigh the associated costs experienced by the club. The period prior to that in which net benefits to the club are negative determines the entrant's final membership period and, hence, his membership span. A discontinuous membership span necessitates an examination of all periods of the entrant's life span. These periods must be ordered according to the level of positive net benefits experienced by the club. Once periods are so ordered, if information permits, membership is extended until the net benefits to the club are negative.

The endogenous choice of membership spans has already become important for intergenerational impure public goods such as national parks and wilderness areas. As population continues to expand and the huddled masses of the cities acquire a taste for the outdoors, ecological carrying capacities will be increasingly reached so that unrestricted membership spans will cause irreversible deterioration of parks. One solution to meet this eventuality is to restrict lifetime membership passes to the park according to a modified form of the membership span condition, briefly described here. Markets can allow these passes to be traded in order to achieve efficiency. Another example can be found in cities with fragile environments, such as Mexico City. Membership and spans of membership may have to be allocated and traded if these cities are to survive.

One method, currently employed by the U.S. Park Service, is to stop entry on any given day once the carrying capacity is reached. Such a strategy eliminates the bulk of depreciation costs, but is not necessarily efficient since potential visitors who have been turned away may have been willing to compensate for the depreciation costs they would have caused had they been allowed entry. Of course, the desirable aspect of the current policy is its ease of administration.

15.2   The maintenance decision

In previous chapters, we followed Berglas (1976) and others in simply relating club maintenance costs to atemporal aspects of crowding. This is inadequate, of course, since maintenance has both atemporal concerns (e.g., removing garbage) and intertemporal concerns (e.g., painting walls, repairing broken facilities). The current model permits these separate aspects and allows the maintenance decision to be rightfully separated from the provision decision.

The analysis is now extended to allow depreciation to be offset, to some extent, by expending resources in each period for maintenance. Most intergenerational clubs share goods that can be maintained to regain or forestall losses in quality resulting from utilization. A highway's potholes and cracks can be filled; campus buildings can be painted or repaired; a fraternity house can be restored; and city parks and playgrounds can be replanted and resurfaced. Though many shared goods can be maintained, their life spans may be exogenously fixed by obsolescence. A highway can be repaired, but eventually increased travel demands and new technologies will make it obsolete; interstate highways are replacing the two-lane U.S. routes.

By keeping the good's life span fixed, the maintenance decision here does not consider goods whose life span is endogenous.[4] The primary alterations to the model required by maintenance have to do with the depreciation function (6) and the transformation function (8) given in Table 15.1. Both functions must now include a stream of maintenance expenditures. The depreciation function in any period must contain the current and all prior maintenance expenditures, while the transformation function must include the entire stream of maintenance expenses, since these expenses utilized scarce resources. The optimal conditions remain unaltered; however, the depreciation cost terms may fall in value owing to maintenance. That is, a well-maintained good may be better able to withstand utilization by depreciating to a smaller extent than a less well-maintained one. When this is the case, an increase in maintenance implies that optimal provision and tolls will decline, and that optimal membership size will expand. Thus, provision, tolls, and membership requirements are not necessarily independent of the maintenance decision.

Optimal maintenance in each period requires the stream of marginal maintenance benefits from reduced depreciation to equal marginal maintenance costs expended in the given period. Maintenance, however, does not affect crowding costs. When a shared good is maintained, associated marginal benefits influence current *and* future members. Current members experience marginal maintenance benefits from the period of maintenance to the end of their membership, whereas future members experience these benefits throughout their membership. As such, the maintenance decision is analogous to a provision decision; both are investment choices with intertemporal benefits.

Maintenance poses a novel dilemma for clubs, since maintenance is purely public within the club. A club can exclude nonmembers, but cannot exclude members from sharing in the nonrival benefits of maintenance. Unlike provision, the maintenance condition does not have an associated toll by which preference revelation can achieve self-financing. Instead, the club must try to estimate each member's share of maintenance costs on the basis of maintenance benefits received. One possible scheme would be to assign a fixed maintenance charge per unit of utilization so that heavier users would pay more maintenance costs. This is precisely what traditional atemporal models do. Tying maintenance payments to utilization rates can *partly* circumvent the revelation problem, since more intense users will presumably receive greater benefits from maintenance. Nevertheless, this collection procedure will not achieve efficiency because the costs and benefits of the toll condition are different from those of the maintenance condition and thus cannot serve as exact proxies (see Sandler 1982, pp. 206–7). The per-unit maintenance charge will also move utilization rates away from the efficient outcome.

The maintenance problem, discussed further in the next section, is easy to spot in the real world. With its highway system, the United States is facing a severe lack of maintenance. Some bridges have even fallen down and caused loss of life. Tolls on the nation's highways have reflected traffic and congestion considerations, but have not adequately accounted for depreciation. Thus, insufficient tolls have been collected. Large trucks have not been charged according to the destruction they cause. Typically, the higher charges for trucks internalize the crowding externality but not the depreciation externality, which grows exponentially with the weight of the vehicle. A general gasoline tax has been proposed and enacted to pay for needed maintenance. Such a tax accounts for crowding and miles traveled since both considerations are somewhat correlated with the amount of gasoline purchased. The tax also partly accounts for weight considerations; but unless weight increases gasoline consumption exponentially, the tax cannot be considered economically efficient.

15.3 Myopia and institutional form

In Chapter 12, we presented some diverse institutional forms for clubs. We now intend to relate these arrangements to the myopia issue, a crucial consideration for intergenerational clubs. It is not at all clear whether an intergenerational club can achieve the optimal, far-sighted requirements presented in Sections 15.1 and 15.2. Problems may arise with respect to those terms in the optimality conditions involving depreciation and/or future members. Failure to account for these leads to myopia.

Government provision

Can government-owned and operated intergenerational clubs be expected to grope their way to the optimality conditions described in the preceding discussion? At least two different types of governmental organizations must be considered: a representative democracy and a direct democracy. In the former, elected bureaucrats and politicians make resource-allocating decisions; in the latter, the electorate votes directly on these allocation choices. Neither is viewed as necessarily leading to farsighted results. For a representative democracy, elected officials are motivated by a desire to win reelection (see, e.g., Downs 1957), which should bias their actions toward myopic results. This follows, because the official's office span is less than the life span of the shared goods which he is overseeing. To maximize votes, officials are more interested in satisfying the present generation that makes up their constituency. As these officials decide provision, maintenance, and tolls, there are strong incentives to ignore depreciation and crowding costs involving future (nonvoting) generations so as to keep taxes lower. This action would be myopic. That is, provision and maintenance will be less than optimal because benefits to future generations are ignored, and tolls will be suboptimal because important utilization costs are excluded. Memberships will be too large as membership costs imposed on future members are ignored when entrants are considered.

Unfortunately, direct democracy may not perform better. Consider a *median-voter* model, probably the best scenario, in which the middle voter along a spectrum pertaining to the issue is the decision maker (see Mueller 1976, pp. 408–9). Unless this voter demonstrates an altruistic interest in future generations, allocative choices will not reflect future costs and benefits. Even when the median voter is altruistic, so that his utility function is

$$U^{it} = U^{it}[x^i, y^i, \ldots, U^{j,t+1}(\cdot)], \tag{1}$$

where $U^{j,t+1}(\cdot)$ is the utility function of his child or children, efficiency might not result since the median voter's altruism might not be a good proxy for future generations. Remember the median voter's preferences are merely an *average view from the current generation*.

Another technical problem inhibits direct democracies from attaining the nonmyopic efficiency conditions required of intergenerational clubs. This is the so-called multidimensional problem of social choice (see Mueller 1976, pp. 402–9). When voters must decide an issue with many dimensions, voting cannot be expected to lead to consistent social choice, reflecting the constituency's preferences. Since the median voter result applies only to single-dimensional problems, it no longer represents an escape. Intergenerational clubs require financing, provision, toll, *and* maintenance decisions, and hence multidimensional issues are involved at every decision point.

Both direct and representative democracies face yet another blockade to farsighted decision making: the legal restriction of public access giving all citizens membership rights to public projects. Since governments cannot discriminate between individuals by limiting membership, a nonoptimal membership size may result. The public access problem can sometimes be rectified by limiting spans of membership; however, this policy fails whenever members are heterogeneous, because the required discrimination is illegal.

Several possible offsets to these myopic tendencies should be noted. First, some voters and environmental lobbyists may successfully pressure governments into preserving "option demands," thereby maintaining unique environments (see, Sepassi 1983, Chapter III). Altruistic individuals and organizations may induce the government to consider future generations when making allocative decisions; certainly, the Sierra Club has been successful along these lines. How well these pressure groups will achieve the above optimality conditions depends upon the ability of these groups to proxy and to represent the tastes of future and current generations. This is a tall order.

Another offset involves the capitalization of net benefits from local government facilities into real estate values. If residents surrounding a government-owned intergenerational facility capitalize the club's benefits, then these property owners have a strong incentive to lobby and to vote for far-sighted decisions so as to maintain property values by keeping the facilities from depreciating prematurely.

Member-owned intergenerational clubs

Intergenerational clubs can be owned by the members through the use of equity stocks issued at the club's formation and traded between generations. Since the stock's price is related to the condition and remaining value of the shared good, *strong incentives exist* for any generation *to act with foresight*. If some generation behaves myopically and ignores the benefits and costs to future generations when making club decisions, the value of the equity stock drops prematurely owing to the accelerated depreciation of the good. The myopic generation therefore pays directly for its shortsightedness as the subsequent generation buys the equity stocks at a reduced price.

As an alternative, the club can borrow the initial construction funds by issuing a debt refinanced from generation to generation. The ability to refinance depends directly on the residual worth of the shared good—the collateral upon which the debt is drawn. Whenever a generation behaves myopically, less money can be raised during refinancing and, hence, the generation shoulders the burden of its shortsightedness.

A third financing strategy is to issue long-term serial bonds; this requires varying amounts of repayments geared to expected toll collections. During each generation, a sinking fund can accumulate the tolls so that the sequence of repayments is met when due. Any myopic generation will collect too little in tolls and will have to charge its members the difference to meet repayment obligations. Again, adequate incentives exist to act with foresight. Any mixture of debt and equity refinancing provides the proper incentives.

The true burden of the club is transferable between generations provided each generation sacrifices real resources. Suppose that members from each generation buy into the club when they join, sell their equity or debt at a later age, and live on their reimbursements until death; then the burden can be transferred. The subsequent generation supports the prior generation during retirement with real resources as the prior generation demands goods with its reimbursements. Futures markets can also be used to trade membership stocks in order to permit burdens to be transferred.

Incentives also exist to induce each generation to include future generations' benefits when deciding maintenance expenditures, because maintenance reduces depreciation which, in turn, increases the value of the shared good. This increase in value will be reflected in a higher price for either the equity stock or the collateral upon which debt is drawn. In either case, future generations' shares of maintenance costs can be transferred when the ownership of the club is traded to the next generation. Easy-rider problems *within* a generation may outweigh incentives to exhibit foresight, however, and suboptimal maintenance may result; that is, members may disguise their true preferences in the hope of shifting maintenance costs onto contemporary members. Although the generation as a whole is properly motivated to be farsighted, individual member's incentives conflict with those of the generation.

Firm-operated intergenerational clubs

Efficiency aspects of firm-operated intergenerational clubs depend, as noted in Chapter 12, on the industrial organization involved. If the industry is perfectly competitive with many small firms operating, then Pareto efficiency may result. Each firm can provide the intergenerational shared good and attempt to earn a profit from operating. Ownership of the firm can pass between generations by the use of equity stocks and/or bonds. All myopic owners or entrepreneurs pay for their shortsightedness in terms of reduced profits and equity. Thus, private ownership by firms should lead to nonmyopic behavior. Easy-rider problems associated with maintenance *may* disappear, since the firm's owners can attempt to shift maintenance costs onto the users as a fixed fee each period for belonging to the club.

   When the assumptions of perfect foresight and knowledge are dropped, myriad problems arise owing to the costs of information (see Oakland 1974). When information is scarce and costly, myopic results may plague any institutional form. Transaction costs of intergenerational clubs are predicted to be high because of the complex decisions that must be reached. These costs will inhibit the achievement of the first-best solutions.

15.4   Other considerations

Other approaches

The model outlined above is essentially static. Thus, optimal values are chosen for each of the choice variables. Alternatively, the intergenerational club problem could be modeled with optimal control in which time paths for both public investment and maintenance (the control variables) are chosen so as to maximize a utility functional of a representative member, assuming homogeneity of members and additivity of utility across time. The optimal control approach has been avoided because: (1) the membership homogeneity assumption (required for mathematical tractability) forces the membership and membership span conditions to degenerate to the same condition; (2) self-financing is automatic under equal cost-sharing arrangements; (3) the strong separability assumption requiring utility to be additively separable over time limits generality; (4) the optimal conditions are noncomparable to existing club results; and (5) the discreteness of provision is not captured.

There have been few dynamic analyses of clubs or public goods owing to the large number of choice variables involved. Since the value of public goods must be expressed in terms of a numeraire private good, a two-good growth model is appropriate. Such models are difficult to devise under the best of circumstances—when linear homogeneous production functions and other simplifying assumptions are employed. Artle and Averous (1973) and von Rabenau and Stahl (1974) have examined the dynamics of the telephone club. For tractability, they focused on the growth of membership (i.e., the number of phones) at the exclusion of other considerations such as maintenance. Blewett (1983) has examined fiscal externalities and residential growth controls using a dynamic theory of clubs perspective. He concentrated on the scale of plant or provision aspect. These growth approaches may be extended to intergenerational clubs.

Option value

Many environmental amenities fall into the category of an intergenerational club. An important aspect or side benefit of these amenities is *option value* or *demand,* the value that nonusers and users place on the preservation of the amenity for possible future use (see Smith 1983). Thus, a New Yorker may never visit the Grand Canyon, but still receives benefits from knowing that it is there to visit if he chooses to do so at a later date. The above analysis can be expanded to include option value by treating the shared good as providing joint products, as in Chapter 7. One joint product is purely public and corresponds to option value, and the other is impurely public and relates to user benefits. Whether these environmental clubs will operate efficiently depends on the consumption relationship of the jointly produced output. If they are complementary in consumption, solutions may not depart significantly from optimality. Some departure will occur since some receivers of the public benefits are nonusers, and consequently cannot be excluded from the excludable benefit derived from utilization. When the joint products are substitutes or unrelated in consumption, however, suboptimality problems will arise since there is no collection mechanism or preference-revealing inducement for option value. In these cases, government-operated intergenerational clubs may perform better than previously supposed (see Sepassi 1983) since they can try to adjust for option value.

15.5   Concluding remarks

The theory of intergenerational clubs differs significantly from traditional analyses of clubs. For integenerational clubs, allocative decisions include both atemporal crowding and intertemporal depreciation considerations when provision, tolls, membership size, and financing conditions are derived. These conditions must adjust for current and future members. In contrast, traditional analyses only include crowding costs to the current membership. Another difference concerns the inclusion of the maintenance and membership span conditions that were not previously examined owing to the atemporal framework used. Such a framework meant that myopic behavior of clubs could not be studied and related to institutional form. Finally, unlike traditional club analyses, the theory of intergenerational clubs places emphasis on the sequence of members since depreciation costs depend upon the period of membership, the condition of the good, and the future number of members.

The fundamental differences just mentioned must be understood by economists if they are to provide insight into club behavior because most clubs do include multiple generations of members. Four polar cases of intergenerational public goods exist with diverse depreciation and crowding possibilities. For example, the electromagnetic spectrum is subject to crowding within a generation, but does not depreciate; it is purely public between generations, and impure within a generation. This class of goods can be adequately analyzed by existing club models. The use of antibiotics is impurely public between generations, since effectiveness declines owing to utilization; however, it may be purely public within a generation, because bacteria take time to build up immunities. National parks, wilderness areas, cities, and highways are impurely public both within and between generations owing to crowding and depreciation. Previous club models cannot explicitly examine these last two categories of inter-generational impure public good, because these models do not include depreciation and multiple generations. Lastly, the removal of a mutagenic substance is purely public both within and between generations; it is an intergenerational pure public good. This last class of goods can only be examined by an extension to existing public good analyses and does not require a club model.

PART V

Applications and future directions

CHAPTER 16

Applications and empirics

In the last two decades, a great volume of applied work has been added to the literature on externalities, public goods, and club goods. These applied studies fall into two categories: applied theory and empirical analysis. We intend here to give a flavor of the types of applied investigations that have been done. Our presentation is eclectic, since a comprehensive survey would require a chapter many times the length of this one. In particular, our review focuses on three subcategories of applications. First, we review the empirical studies that estimated a demand for a public good. Both nonmarket and market techniques are considered. For nonmarket techniques, we briefly examine contingent valuation studies, experimental techniques, voting studies, and a political decision-maker model. Market techniques include the hedonic approach and travel-cost methods. Applications of club theory are presented next. These applications involve the use of club theory to examine toll schemes, provision level, and membership size for recreation areas subject to congestion. Highways and communication systems are also analyzed. Finally, applications of the joint product and pure public good models are presented. Specific applications can be found in military alliances and philanthropy. Concluding remarks complete the chapter.

16.1 Empirical estimations of the demand for public goods

A wide variety of demand estimates have been presented using both nonmarket and market data on public goods. Desvousges, Smith, and Fisher (1983) have referred to these two measurement techniques as direct and indirect. Nonmarket or direct methods generate demand data through the use of surveys, experiments, or voting results. Indirect methods use market data from private good sales to infer information about the demand for public goods, used in conjunction with the private goods. For example, money expended on travel to reach a recreation site is used to estimate recreation demand. Moreover, the existence of substitute sites with slightly different characteristics allows the researcher to impute a value to certain characteristics associated with the recreation area.

Nonmarket techniques

The contingent valuation or survey approach asks individuals to state their willingness to pay for public goods.[1] Such a technique yields a compensated valuation (CV) measure of consumer surplus for each individual, which can then be aggregated over potential users to yield a market demand for the public good. The contingent valuation approach attempts to construct a hypothetical market for the public good in order to ascertain an estimate of demand, and is especially useful in situations where market data are not available. For example, Brookshire et al. (1982, p. 165) point out that attitudes toward a remote and unique scenic vista threatened by air pollution cannot be evaluated by market data. If a power plant that will decrease visibility is contemplated, market information concerning users' responses to the reduced visibility is not available because the plant must be built before these responses will be revealed. Since an estimation of the value of visibility is needed *before* making the power plant decision, hypothetical market data must be constructed to evaluate the cost of reduced visibility. Without this information, a full cost-benefit analysis of a proposed power plant cannot be completed.

The preference-revelation problem, which plagues public good contributions, may also hamper the use of contingent valuation by inducing strategic behavior on the part of respondents. Suppose that residents near a proposed plant are asked how much they would be willing to pay in, say, extra monthly electric rates to maintain visibility levels of a certain quality. Various visibility levels are illustrated to the respondents through the use of pictures taken near the proposed site. If the respondents anticipate that their electric rates may really be raised depending on their responses, they may underestimate their true bids, hoping that others might bid more. The usual Prisoner's Dilemma arises. When respondents believe that others will be made to pay for the pollution control devices through general taxes, however, they have an incentive to overestimate their bids (see Schulze, d'Arge, and Brookshire 1981, p. 156). In either case, strategic behavior leads to biased reporting. To date, the empirical evidence has failed to support or to deny a strategic bias.

Other biases have been attributed to the contingent valuation approach. Information bias involves the type of information given to the respondent in the contingent market. For example, the respondent is usually told about substitute sites and associated costs (e.g., travel costs). Since substitutes and costs clearly influence a consumer's choice, the nature and accuracy of this information affect responses. A third potential bias involves the design of the survey instrument. The type of payment suggested by the survey has an effect on the bid. For instance, some respondents may be less concerned about a general tax payment than an increase in their monthly electric bills. Furthermore, the way in which the researcher tries to induce a final bid from the individual is also crucial. Starting-point bias concerns the amount of payment that the researcher first asks the respondent whether he or she is willing to pay. A higher starting point (e.g., "Would you be willing to pay $20 per month in higher electric bills?") may lead to larger bids. Other biases concern sampling and the hypothetical nature of the technique. In the latter case, respondents who do not believe that the suggested changes will ever be enacted have little incentive to take the exercise seriously and to give honest bids. Many of these biases could be corrected or ameliorated by the design of the survey. Others, such as strategic bias, may be more difficult to eliminate.

A second nonmarket technique for evaluating public good demands is the experimental approach.[2] In particular, experiments have been conducted to determine whether pure public goods lead to free-riding behavior. Experiments have been designed in which a group of individuals are asked to contribute to a good that yields groupwide (public) benefits greater than the (private) benefits received by the individual. Within this setting, the experimenter varies group size, per-person returns from contributing, and the number of iterations in order to ascertain the effects that these variables have on free riding (see, especially, Isaac, Walker, and Thomas 1984). Both Nash and Lindahl equilibria are determined. The position of the experimental results relative to these two equilibria is an indication of free riding.

To date, experimental results have been mixed; some have found strong evidence of free-riding behavior and others have not (Kim and Walker 1984). Some of the Isaac, Walker, and Thomas (1984) results are especially germane to the theory of public goods and joint products developed in Chapters 5 and 7. In particular, they found that increasing group size may *or* may not augment free-rider behavior as our theory predicted. A decrease in private (or marginal per capita) returns when combined with increases in group size did, however, augment free riding. The jointly produced private benefit was therefore identified as a factor affecting free-riding behavior. Increases in the private return serve to decrease free riding, as expected. Moreover, experiments showed that the effect of group size on suboptimality was not as clear-cut as once supposed by Olson (1965) and others.

We view the experimental procedure as a fruitful technique for testing a whole range of public good hypotheses, including those concerned with the effects that non-Nash conjectures would have on suboptimality. Experimental results may be an inexpensive means of judging the effects of large group size on free riding, since large number cases can be simulated with relatively few participants, depending upon the information given to the subjects. That is, subjects may be made to believe that they are interacting with many other participants, when, in fact, they are not (see Isaac, Walker, and Thomas 1984). The major drawback of experimental valuation techniques appears to be their extreme sensitivity to the experimental design. Even minor variations have produced widely divergent results.

The third nonmarket method for evaluating the demand for a public good is the voting method, based on the median-voter model of public choice (see Mueller 1979, pp. 38–9). In this model, the median voter's utility-maximizing choice for the level of the public good becomes that of the community. When decisions are unidimensional, so that only the amount of expenditures on the public good is decided by referendum, then the median voter's choice is the deciding vote. Researchers using this method to derive demand are implicitly assuming that the requirements of the median-voter model are intact.[3]

As in the case of the other nonmarket evaluation techniques, the voting model is based upon utility maximization, in which the median voter maximizes

$$U(y, Q^*),\qquad\qquad(1)$$

where y is the private good and Q^* is the level of the public good available for consumption. The budget constraint is

$$y + \tau p Q \leqq I,\qquad\qquad(2)$$

where the private good's price is one, the public good's price is p, and τ is the tax rate per unit of public good expenditures.

The two public good levels, Q and Q^*, are related by the following formula:

$$Q^* = Q/s^\gamma\qquad\qquad(3)$$

where Q represents the amount of the public good purchased and Q^* depicts the quantity of the good available for consumption *after* accounting for consumption rivalry. If the exponent on the population term is 0, then $Q^* = Q$ and the public good is purely public. When, however, $\gamma = 1$, the publicly provided good is perfectly rival like a private good. Values of γ between 0 and 1 indicate partial rivalry. The addition of this exponent allows the researcher to test for the degree of rivalry or congestion.

Empirical estimates use a variant of the following specification:[4]

$$\log(pQ) = c + \alpha \log s + \delta \log \tau + \epsilon \log I + \sum_{j=1}^{k} \beta_j X_j, \qquad (4)$$

where c is a constant, the X_j's are descriptive social and economic variables for the municipality, and the Greek letters α, δ, ϵ, and β_j are coefficients. Increases in population influence public expenditures through two avenues: rivalry and tax shares. Rivalry is tested by the value of α, which is functionally related to γ, that is, $\gamma = \alpha/(1 + \delta)$. Tax shares and income levels are those of the median voter.

Often the investigator assumes a particular utility function for the median voter (see, e.g., Dudley and Montmarquette 1981. The preferred form is the Stone-Geary utility function:

$$U = \alpha_1 \ln(y - \phi) + \alpha_2 \ln(Q - \theta), \qquad (5)$$

where ϕ and θ are minimum subsistence quantities for the private and public good, respectively. All of the parameters of (5) are positive with $y > \phi$ and $Q > \theta$. Maximizing (5) subject to the median voter's budget constraint in (2) gives first-order conditions that, after suitable transformation, yield *linear expenditure* functions. These latter functions can then be estimated with linear regression techniques.

There are a number of strong assumptions required by this voting-evaluation technique. Typically, this empirical analysis is applied to municipalities in which the voters are elected candidates whose platforms include a host of different public goods expenditure proposals. *Multidimensional* issues are therefore being decided by the referendum; but the underlying median-voter model assumes unidimensional issues. This inconsistency is a major flaw in the theoretical-empirical linkage for this technique. Another problem concerns the assumption that the median voter's income is also the population's median-income level (see, especially, Bergstrom and Goodman 1973). This assumption is not always justifiable. Although the Stone-Geary utility function is convenient for estimation, more support for its application to particular problems should be provided. Clearly, the specification of the underlying utility function influences the estimated elasticities.

A fourth nonmarket evaluation procedure for estimating public good demand has been developed by Murdoch and Sandler (1984). Their technique tests the degree of publicness associated with the jointly produced benefits derived from the military expenditures of an alliance. Alliance arsenals yield purely public benefits (e.g., deterrence), impurely public benefits (e.g., damage-limiting protection when deterrence fails), and private benefits (e.g., protection of coastal waters) to the allies. By examining the sign on the spillin term (which represents the military expenditures of the other allies), Murdoch and Sandler (1984) can test for both free riding and the publicness of defense. Their model is theoretically based on utility maximization subject to a resource constraint; but, unlike the voting model, it uses the decision maker in charge of defense decisions (e.g., the Joint Chiefs of Staff in the United States) as the utility maximizer. This model is examined in greater detail in Section 16.3.

Market techniques

As the name implies, these techniques utilize market-provided data to estimate a demand for public goods. The method is indirect, because data on the demands for private goods are exploited to draw inferences concerning the demands for consumption-related public goods. For instance, when visiting a national park, a consumer must expend money for travel costs, costs that represent expenditures on private goods (e.g., automobile maintenance, gasoline). These travel expenditures are used to derive the demand curve for the national park. Currently, there are two indirect methods for evaluating public good demands: the hedonic approach and the travel-cost approach.

For the hedonic approach,[5] an individual demands goods to use in the household production of final characteristics or commodities, which provide satisfaction. Hence, the demand for goods is a *derived demand* for inputs used to produce more basic commodities such as living space, safety, or warmth. This household production model also forms the basis of the joint product model (see Chapter 7) in which an activity gives rise to both private and public characteristics.

The hedonic approach requires two steps. First, the implicit price of a public characteristic (e.g., clean air) must be estimated, using price differentials revealed in the private goods market. Second, the implicit price must be regressed against the observed quantities of the public characteristics to estimate the demand function. Consider, for example, the determinants of the selling price for a house. The house contains a package of characteristics, which include the structural attributes of the house (e.g., the number of bedrooms, living area), neighborhood characteristics (e.g., crime levels, average income levels), and public attributes (e.g., air quality). The estimation proceeds by regressing the selling price of the house against its neighborhood, structural, and public characteristics (see Brookshire et al. 1982). If we sample price data for houses located in different parts of a city, we will find that air quality typically varies, since pollution usually differs according to location. The selling price differential between two houses whose characteristics are the same except for air quality provides a measure for the private willingness to pay for the public good of clean air. Moreover, varying the locations of the houses sampled yields different levels of air quality needed to derive the requisite demand curve.

In recent years, the hedonic approach has become quite popular and has been used not only to derive public good demands, but also to test the Tiebout Hypothesis. Although the hedonic approach is preferred by many, it suffers from a number of difficulties. First, aggregation over individuals requires strong assumptions when deriving the total demand for the public characteristic. Second, the hedonic approach assumes that competitive forces have equalized the selling prices of houses with identical characteristics. This requires the housing market to fulfill standard competitive assumptions—no impediments to trading can exist. Third, some household characteristics may be highly correlated, and thus may lead to problems of multicollinearity.

The travel-cost method is also based on the household production framework.[6] In particular, this method attempts to account for the role that a site's characteristics have on the demand for the site's services. The existence of substitute or near-substitute sites (those with similar characteristic packages) must also be acknowledged when using the travel-cost method to estimate the demand for a *specific* site. The procedure is based on estimating[7]

$$V_{ij} = V_{ij}(P_v, P_x, d_{ij}, \bar{c}, t_{ij}, h_{ij}, Q_j, I_i), \tag{6}$$

where

V_{ij} = the number of visits by the ith individual to the jth site

P_v = the toll per visit to site j

d_{ij} = the round-trip distance between the jth site and the

   i^{th} person

$\bar{c}$ = unit travel cost

t_{ij} = i^{th} person's travel time to site j

h_{ij} = the ith person's cost of traveling to site j

Q_j = the public characteristic(s) at site j

I_i = the ith individual's money income.

Alternative sites can be handled by making terms such as d_{ij} and t_{ij} into vectors. Furthermore, an equation of the form given in (6) must be estimated for each site. If a given site has more than one characteristic, then Q_j must also be a vector.

Smith, Desvousges, and McGivney (1983) have also included time spent on-site in their demand estimates for visits, and have found this time to be a significant variable. The effects of on-site congestion have also been included in some of the travel-cost demand estimates (see Freeman 1979). As club theory implies, congestion is an important determinant of both the number of visits and the degree of substitutability between sites.

As in the case of the other evaluation methods, the travel-cost technique rests on strong, and often untenable, assumptions. For example, travel to a site must be solely for the purpose of enjoying the recreational benefits. All available substitute sites are assumed to be known. Failure of these and other assumptions to hold seriously affects the validity of the travel-cost method.

The theoretical foundation for the travel-cost method is utility maximization where resource constraints include an expenditure constraint *and* a time constraint (Freeman 1979, p. 206). A choice-theoretical framework therefore underlies all of the evaluation techniques; only the exact specification varies between techniques. Thus, the analysis presented in Parts II–IV forms the basic theoretical paradigm of the empirical investigations.

A related market technique engineered by Mäler (1971), Hori (1975), and Bradford and Hildebrandt (1977) uses market observable demands for private goods to estimate demands for consumption-related public goods. For this technique to work, two requirements must be met: (1) the individual's demand price for the public good must be zero when the quantity of the private good is zero, and (2) there must be no income effects. The first requirement implies a strong demand interdependence between the private and public good, thus allowing us to infer public good demand from observable private good demand. The second requirement enables us to use a consumer surplus measure of the inverse demand function for the private good to estimate the inverse demand for the public good as the public good quantity changes.

16.2   Applications of club theory

The wide range of problems that has been addressed by the analysis of club theory underscores the usefulness of the theory in applied work. Specifically, club theory has been applied to the study of recreation areas, highways, and communications systems. By forming the basis for the Tiebout Hypothesis, club theory has been used to analyze optimal partitions of population among jurisdictions with diverse packages of public goods. A sampling of applied work is now provided to illustrate the usefulness of club theory.

Public utilities

Two-part tariffs and the club principle: A long-standing problem in public utility economics concerns pricing under conditions of decreasing average cost. Pareto optimality requires price equal to marginal cost of provision, but this results in a deficit.[8] The remedies for covering this deficit constitute the marginal cost controversy (see Ruggles 1950).

One possible remedy is to use a nonlinear price structure: in particular, a two-part tariff. The two parts consist of a lump-sum license fee for each consumer and a toll per unit of utilization. The license fees are designed to cover any deficit caused by tolls set below average cost and can be interpreted as club entrance fees, inasmuch as they must be paid prior to utilization. For public utility clubs, the members share a private good, their sole incentive for membership being the decreasing average costs of provision. Any license fee must be large enough to ensure full financing, yet not be so large as to drive away too many potential club members. That some potential members may be driven away is an old point (Lewis 1941); however, only recently have the conditions for an optimal toll and license fee been made clear (see Ng and Weisser 1974). They considered a uniform license fee across consumers and derived the Pareto-optimal toll, license fee, and membership size. The toll may deviate from marginal cost of provision and the license fee may even be negative.

Transportation and congestion functions: Roger Sherman (1967) has drawn attention to a bias in transportation. Consumers pay marginal cost for private transportation and average cost for public transportation and, therefore, favor the less expensive private alternative. To alleviate the bias, Sherman has proposed the application of club principles to transportation. Consumers would pay a license fee for the privilege of using a public transportation system, and then a toll per trip equal to marginal cost. The license fee is required for self-financing owing to increasing returns.

Other work has dwelt on the congestion costs inherent in transportation systems. Early studies of highway congestion were done by Walters (1961), Mohring and Harwitz (1962), Sharp (1966), and Johnson (1964). Mohring and Harwitz maximized the net benefit of highway travel wherein costs include both capital costs of highway construction and congestion costs given by the function $c(X, s)$. Their conditions for a maximum required: (1) that highway size be increased to the point where the marginal cost of an increment in highway size equals the marginal congestion cost saved from that increment (provision); and (2) that the level of traffic be such that the driver's cost of making a trip is equal to his travel time cost plus the marginal travel cost other drivers must bear because of the increased congestion caused by this driver. The optimum toll is set equal to the marginal congestion cost imposed on other drivers.[9] William Vickrey (1969) argued that these provision, membership, and toll conditions must be determined simultaneously for highways since congestion tolls are not only useful in the short run, but should be part of any long-run expansion plan. The similarity between these highway studies and the club analysis of Chapters 10 and 11 is clear. Congestion is not something that must be completely eliminated; rather, an optimum level of congestion must be found. Mohring and Harwitz also indicated that tolls will fully finance the highway if there are constant or decreasing returns to scale in production and if the congestion function is homogeneous of degree zero in X and s (see our self-financing remarks in Chapter 11). This last requirement implies that a doubling of both traffic and highway size does not change total congestion costs.

Communications: The telephone has received considerable attention with respect to the size of the sharing group. Artle and Averous (1973) have referred to telephone subscribers as members of a telephone club. Artle and Averous maximized the net benefits of both subscribers and nonsubscribers and, in so doing, were the first to derive the correct Pareto-optimal membership size condition for a single club. The benefit enjoyed by a subscriber includes both making and receiving calls. This was noted by Squire (1973) who used a benefit function that depends on utilization of the phone and the number of other subscribers. Squire then derived provision, membership, and toll conditions on the basis of these benefits. The growth of the telephone system was discussed in a dynamic model by von Rabenau and Stahl (1974). Rohlfs (1974) also examined telephone growth by analyzing in greater detail the demand for service. Demand for telephone service depends on the number of subscribers and also on their identity. This is like a discriminatory club in which the characteristics of the members are important. Rohlfs showed that starting the telephone club could be difficult under these conditions, since there is no incentive for the first member to join.

Sandler and Schulze (1981) have applied club principles to an examination of INTELSAT.[10] The description of the INTELSAT telecommunications system was previously provided in Chapter 12. Sandler and Schulze (1981) have argued that INTELSAT fits a club model because the system's benefits are both excludable and partially rival. Rivalry arises from signal interference (noise) as more users utilize the system. Membership, tolls per signal transmitted, and provision decisions (i.e., the number and size of satellites) can be determined for INTELSAT on the basis of the club theory.

Sandler and Schulze also demonstrated that the allocation of satellites to a given altitude band (e.g., the geostationary band) can be analyzed with club theory, since the allocation decision is essentially a membership decision. There are two congestion phenomena involved with satellites at a given band: signal interference and satellite collision. Signal interference depends on the entire satellite network's average utilization rate. Collision involves the number of satellites at a given band and their spacing, since even geostationary satellites drift up to a 100 miles. By including both an interference congestion cost and a collision cost, Sandler and Schulze derived standard club conditions for the assignment of both orbital slots and frequency bands. This somewhat exotic application is given here to emphasize how wide, indeed, are the applications of club theory.

Recreation

The use of national and state parks, forests, and wilderness areas in the United States has increased tremendously over the past two

Table 16.1. *Synoptic comparison of highway and recreation areas*

	Highway	Recreation area
Measure of congestion	Time required to complete a trip of fixed length	The number of trail and camp encounters with hikers (Stankey 1972)
Interactions between measure and membership size	A technical function relating number of vehicles and their speed (Boardman and Lave 1977)	A technical function relating number of hikers and their likelihood of encounters (Smith and Krutilla 1974; Cicchetti and Smith 1976b)
Valuation of measure	Estimate value of travel time	Estimate willingness to pay to avoid encounters

decades. Increased usage means greater congestion at these sites and a concomitant reduction in the quality of the recreational experience. This has led researchers to study optimum congestion and provision levels for these areas by using analytical techniques similar to those used in club theory.

The problem was conceptualized geometrically by Fisher and Krutilla (1972). They constructed total benefit and total cost curves as a function of user days, in which these days can be thought of as membership size. Both of these curves depend on the capacity of the recreational site. A different set of curves was constructed for each capacity level. Fisher and Krutilla proceeded to determine an optimum membership size and provision level in a manner similar to the geometric exercise in Chapter 10. Their definition of total cost also included damage to the ecological environment. This is essentially a depreciation cost, or an intertemporal cost due to utilization, which is important for clubs that have multiple generations of members (see Chapter 15).

The congestion applications to recreation parallel those in the highway studies discussed earlier. In both cases, three main steps are involved in determining the relationship between membership size and congestion costs. First, a measure of congestion is defined that links crowding with decreased utility; second, the physical relationship between this congestion measure and total membership is derived; and third, the value that members place on the congestion measure is established. In Table 16.1, we compare the highway congestion problem and one approach to the congestion problem in a low-density recreational area.

In a series of works, Cicchetti and Smith (1973, 1976a, 1976b) estimated optimal membership size for a low-density recreation area of fixed capacity. They first estimated a representative individual's willingness-to-pay function that depends on trail and camp encounters. Questionnaires were distributed to hikers to obtain the information. By differentiating the aggregate willingness-to-pay function with respect to the number of hikers, Cicchetti and Smith illustrated analytically how the optimum membership size is determined when the marginal congestion cost imposed by an additional hiker is equal to the average congestion cost to all hikers. This is identical to the membership condition of the alternative model of Chapter 10 and assumes that congestion cost falls equally on all users. When this is not the case, the optimum membership may be different, depending on the distribution of these costs.

Many other recreation studies have also applied club theory. The studies referenced here are merely a small sample of a sizable literature.

16.3   Applications of the joint product model and the pure public good model

In this section, we consider applications of the pure public good and the joint product models developed in Chapters 5–7. The joint product model is really a generalization of the pure public good model, since the former permits an activity q to produce multiple outputs that may be purely public, impurely public, or private to the agents. When the activity yields only a pure public output, the joint product and the pure public model are identical. Both models are applied here to two areas: military alliances and the theory of philanthropy.

The economics of military alliances

Beginning with the work of Olson and Zeckhauser (1966), many studies have applied public goods theory to alliances and international organizations. In the 1950s and 1960s, the North Atlantic Treaty Organization (NATO) depended primarily on deterrence (or a threat of retaliatory punishment) as embodied by the U.S. stockpile of strategic nuclear weapons. Reliance on nuclear weapons was essential

Table 16.2. *Military expenditures as a percentage of gross domestic product by country, various years*

Year	United States	France	Germany	United Kingdom	Belgium	Netherlands	Denmark	Norway	Italy
1961	9.2	6.3	4.0	6.3	3.2	4.6	2.6	3.0	2.9
1963	8.8	5.6	5.2	6.2	3.4	4.4	3.0	3.5	3.1
1965	7.6	5.2	4.3	5.9	3.2	4.0	2.8	3.8	3.1
1967	9.5	5.1	4.3	5.7	3.1	4.0	2.7	3.5	2.9
1969	8.7	4.4	3.6	4.9	2.9	3.6	2.5	3.6	2.5
1971	7.0	4.0	3.3	4.9	2.8	3.4	2.4	3.4	2.7
1973	6.0	3.8	3.5	4.8	2.7	3.3	2.0	3.1	2.7
1975	5.9	3.9	3.7	4.8	3.1	3.4	2.4	3.2	2.5
1977	5.3	3.9	3.3	4.7	3.1	3.3	2.3	3.1	2.4
1979	5.1	4.0	3.3	4.7	3.3	3.2	2.3	3.1	2.4
1981	5.8	4.2	3.4	4.9	3.5	3.2	2.5	2.9	2.5

Note: Military expenditures and Gross Domestic Product expressed in 1980 prices using the GDP price deflators for each country. Converted into U.S. dollars using 1980 exchange rates.

Sources: *SIPRI Yearbooks* (various years) and International Monetary Fund (1983).

since the conventional forces of NATO were no match for the much larger Russian forces during this era.

Deterrence comes close to fulfilling both requirements of pure publicness. If strategic forces are sufficiently large to absorb a first-strike attack and to deal a devastating retaliatory blow, then the alliance membership size is immaterial. Taking additional allies under the deterrent umbrella does not diminish the protection afforded the original allies, provided that the threat is credible. Deterrent benefits are therefore nonrival. Once strategic forces are deployed, it is not always possible to deny an ally protection. A nuclear attack on Canada would kill millions in the United States because of fallout, misses, and wind direction. Clearly, the United States could not watch a Canadian attack and fail to retaliate; thus, deterrence is nonexcludable to the Canadians. In general, nonexcludability is less likely to characterize deterrence. Nonexcludability, however, applies whenever an attack on a nation's allies inflicts unacceptable damage, in terms of fallout or the loss of foreign investment interest and military personnel, on the ally providing the deterrence. If an ally perceives its strategic forces as much superior to those of an opposing power, then the ally may also be less apt to exclude other allies from its deterrent capabilities, since it has less to fear from retaliation.

Olson and Zeckhauser (1966) viewed deterrence as purely public in the 1950s and 1960s and predicted that the larger allies would shoulder the defense burdens of the smaller allies. The size of an ally was related to its economic activity as measured by its Gross Domestic Product (GDP). Olson and Zeckhauser tested their prediction for 1964 and found a significant relationship between GDP rank and an ally's military expenditure. Thus, free riding was said to characterize NATO smaller allies. In Table 16.2, the percentages of GDP devoted to military expenditure from 1961 to 1981 are shown for the nine major NATO allies. Throughout the 1960s, the four largest allies (i.e., the United States, France, West Germany, and the United Kingdom) allocated a relatively high percentage of GDP to defense. The small allies typically earmarked smaller percentages of their GDP for defense. In Table 16.3, we have computed a different burden-sharing measure, in which a country's share of total NATO military expenditure is calculated (i.e., the nation's military expenditure as a proportion of total NATO military expenditure). This latter share measure accounts for the relative sizes of the economies and their military expenditure by making comparisons with NATO totals. Of the fourteen allies listed, the major burdens typically fall on the larger allies—the exception being Canada. Thus, Canada has remained an easy rider throughout NATO's history, as expected.

Table 16.3. *NATO defense burdens by country, various years*

Country	1955	1960	1965	1970	1975	1980	1982
United States	77.1	73.2	71.2	74.5	58.3	56.2	59.4
Canada	3.0	2.6	2.2	1.9	1.7	1.8	1.8
Belgium	.6	.6	.7	.7	1.4	1.5	1.3
Denmark	.3	.3	.4	.4	.6	.6	na
France	5.3	6.3	6.3	5.8	9.1	10.3	9.5
Germany	2.7	5.4	7.0	5.9	10.6	10.4	9.4
Greece	.2	.3	.3	.5	1.0	.9	.9
Italy	1.4	2.1	2.5	2.4	3.2	3.7	3.6
Luxembourg	0	0	0	0	0	0	0
Netherlands	.7	.9	1.1	1.1	2.0	2.1	1.9
Norway	.3	.3	.4	.4	.6	.7	.6
Portugal	.1	.2	.4	.4	.5	.3	.3
Turkey	.3	.5	.6	.6	1.2	1.0	1.2
United Kingdom	7.8	7.2	7.0	5.6	9.8	10.4	9.5

Note: Military expenditures ÷ total NATO expenditures × 100. Military expenditure expressed in 1980 prices using the GDP price deflators for each country. Converted to U.S. dollars using 1980 exchange rates. (Columns may not sum to 100 owing to rounding errors.)
Source: Stockholm International Peace Research Institute (various years).

During the 1970s and 1980s, there has been a closing of the share gap between the defense burdens paid by the rich and poor allies in NATO that cannot be explained by the pure public good model. This closing is reflected in the fact that the smaller allies have maintained their share of GDP going to defense, whereas the larger allies have decreased their shares (Tables 16.2 and 16.3). Throughout the 1960s, the United States accounted for more than 70 percent of NATO's military expenditure; by the mid-1970s, this share had dropped sharply.

To explain the closing of the share gap, Sandler and others[11] have put forth a joint product model like the one presented in Chapter 7. Military activity, as measured by military expenditure, is viewed as producing joint products of varying degrees of publicness. For example, damage-limiting protection as provided by conventional forces is impurely public. The benefits of conventional weapons are subject to thinning as the same sized forces are spread over a longer perimeter (Sandler 1977; Sandler and Forbes 1980). Thus, the addition of allies to an alliance may lead to rivalry with respect to these forces. Moreover, conventional forces can be withdrawn easily; hence, free riding is not so easily practiced. In the 1970s, the NATO alliance began emphasizing conventional forces through its adoption of the doctrine of flexible response, a doctrine calling for measured responses to threat (Murdoch and Sandler 1984). These responses involved the use of both conventional and strategic forces. In fact, Murdoch and Sandler (1984) argued that the conventional forces of the smaller allies became complementary in the Hicksian sense (see Chapter 7) to the nuclear allies' forces. The nuclear allies (i.e., the United States, France, and the United Kingdom) could still free-ride on one another even after the mid-1970s, since their arsenals contained *both* conventional and strategic weapons. Thus, the arsenals of the nuclear allies were somewhat substitutable for one another.

Murdoch and Sandler (1984) attempted to support their hypotheses by estimating the regression equation,

$$ME = \text{constant} + \beta_1 GDP + \beta_2 SPILLIN + \beta_3 D \cdot SPILLIN, \qquad (7)$$

for each of the nine allies in Table 16.2. In (7), *ME* is the military expenditure of the ally, the β's are regression coefficients, and *SPILLIN* is the military expenditure of the rest of the alliance. The latter measure is lagged by one year to account for the sequential response attributed to Nash-type reactions. A negative coefficient on the *SPILLIN* term is indicative of easy riding, since it implies that an ally cuts its expenditure in response to increased expenditure of its allies (i.e., the Nash reaction path is negatively sloped). The dummy variable term $D \cdot SPILLIN$ in (7) is added to identify a structural shift in spillin responses after 1973; hence, $D = 0$ for pre-1974 years and $D = 1$ thereafter. The statistical model in (7) was estimated for the years 1961 to 1979, using the iterative, seemingly unrelated regression technique. Murdoch and Sandler's (1984) empirical results were not inconsistent with their hypotheses. In particular, the smaller allies free-rode to a smaller extent after 1974, as shown by the positive sign of the $D \cdot SPILLIN$ term. Moreover, the nuclear allies continued to free-ride even after 1974, since the value of $\beta_2 + \beta_3$ was negative. West Germany and Italy also continued to free-ride after 1974; their strategic positions meant that they automatically received NATO troops. The regression results also showed that military expenditure was a normal good with a positive income elasticity for all allies. The β_1 coefficient was significantly different from zero for most allies sampled.

The joint product model appears to add much to our understanding of the NATO alliance. In particular, the model predicts that technological and strategical changes, associated with an alliance arsenal, can alter the mix of public benefits. This alteration may lead to structurally different spending patterns on the part of the allies. We have allocated more space to this particular application, since we believe that these techniques can be employed to study other public good problems, such as those associated with local public goods.

Philanthropy

Philanthropy has often been characterized as a pure public good, since its altruistic externality is both nonexcludable and nonrival. Sugden (1982) recently questioned the free-rider hypothesis concerning philanthropy, after noting that many charities in Europe raise huge sums of money. Sugden concluded that the pure public good model of charity was inconsistent with real-world observations, and suggested that the model be reformulated. In an attempt to provide an alternative, Posnett and Sandler (1986) have presented a variant of the joint product model, in which a contributor purchases a private good from a charity. The charity allocates the net revenues earned on the exchange to finance its philanthropic activities. Their model predicted that this revenue-generating private trading would lead to larger contributions and less easy riding than predicted by the pure public model. Moreover, Posnett and Sandler demonstrated that the charity organization had both tax and cost advantages over potential private-sector competitors. These advantages allowed the charities to generate excess revenues for public altruistic activities. An examination of the balance sheets of charities showed that more than 50 percent of their revenues came from private trading.

16.4   Concluding remarks

Only a small sampling of applications of the theory of externalities, public goods, and club goods has been presented here. Many of the pressing problems facing mankind today can be examined with the theory developed in Parts II–IV. For example, acid rain is an example of a transnational externality and can be better understood through an application of the theory of externalities. The exploitation of ocean resources (e.g., oil) and the control of ocean pollution can also be studied with the theoretical tools developed earlier. Even the study of outer space resources can profit from public good and club theory. If the current technological trend continues to bring the nations of the world into closer contact, then the theory presented in this book will find even more areas of application.

CHAPTER 17

Conclusions and directions for future research

A great deal of ground has been covered in sixteen chapters. Starting from the general notion of an externality, we have examined specific types of externalities including pure public goods, impure public goods, and club goods. For each, we have presented and reviewed optimality conditions, pertinent institutional arrangements (including preference-revelation mechanisms), empirical investigations, and applications.

In this final chapter, we draw some general conclusions, meant to give the reader a flavor of the important general principles developed. Specific conclusions are not presented, since they have already been emphasized at the end of each chapter. A second purpose of this chapter is to suggest some directions for future research in the areas of externalities, public goods, and club goods. Only those directions that we believe are the most crucial are presented here.

The chapter is divided into two sections. Section 1 contains conclusions, and Section 2 indicates directions for future research.

17.1 Conclusions

On the distinction of pure public goods and private goods

Most treatments of the distinction between pure public and private goods focus on the differences in rivalry and excludability that characterize these two classes of goods. These differences are then related to the dissimilarity in the optimality conditions, in which the sum of MRSs, rather than the MRS, is equated with the MRT for pure public goods. The difficulty of achieving the $\sum MRS = MRT$ requirement usually concludes the analysis. In our presentation, we trace these distinctions as well as others to a simple structural difference characterizing the models of private and pure public goods. This structural distinction has to do with the nature of the constraint facing a consumer in the two cases, and derives from the differences in rivalry and excludability. For private goods, a large number of traders face a *price* constraint, since none is large enough to affect the terms of trade. In contrast, an individual faces a *quantity* constraint when making a public good decision and when the number of other agents is large. That is, the individual must take the quantity of the public good as given and choose an optimal provision amount on the basis of this constraint and a resource constraint. Thus, quantity-constrained rationing underlies public good decisions. Once this essential dissimilarity in model structure is recognized, allocative *and* distributive differences associated with these two categories of goods can be more easily identified and understood.

This distinction between price constraint and quantity constraint leads to an important difference involving the Slutsky equation. For private goods, the crucial Slutsky equation is that associated with a price change, whereas for pure public goods, the important Slutsky equation is that associated with the slope of the Nash reaction path (i.e., $\partial q / \partial \tilde{Q}$ along the Nash path). This latter Slutsky equation involves an adjustment to changes in the quantity constraint. Each of these two Slutsky equations implies quite different results owing to price- versus quantity-induced changes. In Part III, the Nash reaction path's Slutsky equation for the public good was shown to equal a compensated substitution effect with value -1 and an income effect of ambiguous sign. The substitution effect is -1 since one's own public good provision (q) is considered to be a perfect substitute for the public good provided by others ($\tilde{Q}$). Along a Nash reaction path, the income effect is positive for normal goods and negative for inferior goods. For normal public goods, the Nash reaction curve's substitution and income effects therefore work in *opposite directions*, unlike the Slutsky equation associated with a price change for a private good. Hence, the Slutsky equation for the pure public good operates differently than one normally expects. When joint products are present, the Nash reaction path's substitution effect depends upon the consumption relationship of the jointly produced goods; the -1 value only characterizes jointly produced independent goods.

Another difference between private and pure public good transactions that involves the underlying constraints concerns the influence of group size on the departure from optimality associated with Nash behavior. In the case of private goods, exchanges between two people (or a finite number) may depart from Pareto optimality, since each person may reveal false preferences in order to ascertain the best terms of trade or price ratio. With few individuals, traders can influence the terms of trade. The gains from such strategic behavior are, however, reduced when group size increases, because the terms of trade become parametric. In the limit as group size expands, atomistic behavior leads to the invisible-hand Pareto optimum; that is, the core is reached for a continuum of traders. Thus when atomistic traders view private goods' prices as exogenous, their independent-adjustment maximizing behavior leads to an efficient solution. For pure public goods, the effects of group size on the departure of a Nash equilibrium from the Pareto optimum often follows an opposite pattern.[1] If a small number of agents are involved in a pure public good decision, each individual may gain sufficiently from his own provision to justify a positive contribution. This perceived gain may hold in spite of spillovers, since with small numbers the quantity constraint is less important. However, as group size increases, each individual's public good provision becomes smaller in comparison with the total provided by the rest of the group. Under these circumstances, the individual's inducement to reveal false preferences and to easy ride on the provision of others is intensified. With atomistic behavior, individuals may become true free riders, thereby withholding voluntary public good provision altogether. Such behavior would create a large discrepancy between Nash and Pareto optima. Quite simply, increases in group size usually induce more honest preference revelation for private goods and less honest preference revelation for pure public goods owing to the difference in facing a price rather than a quantity constraint.

Yet another important distinction between private and pure public goods' Nash equilibria involves this difference in underlying constraints. In Chapter 5, we demonstrated that the Nash equilibrium for private provision of a pure public good is invariant with respect to income distribution, provided that the redistribution does not alter the set of contributors. This result derives from the analogous roles that income and the public good provision of others assume in the utility function. Neither taste differences nor the number of agents affects this robust result. Thus, allocative and distributive aspects possess a degree of separability for some pure public good Nash equilibria. The same separability and invariance do not characterize private good equilibria, which are quite sensitive to income redistribution.

The importance of the reverse roles of price and quantity is also seen when identifying those situations in which allocative and distributive considerations are, in general, independent. In such a case, the optimal level of the public good is independent of the distribution of the private good, and thus implies a slope of minus one for the Pareto optimum path (see Chapter 6). For pure public goods, the *direct* utility function,

$$U^i(y^i, Q) = A(Q)y^i + B^i(Q), \tag{1}$$

implies that individual marginal valuations are independent of y^i.

Hence, the *MRS*s can be aggregated to obtain a community's demand for public goods without concern for the distribution of income.[2] In the case of private goods, the Gorman polar form, depicted by the *indirect* utility function,

$$V^i(\mathbf{P}, M^i) = F(\mathbf{P})M^i + G^i(\mathbf{P}), \tag{2}$$

ensures that allocative and distributive considerations are independent for fixed prices. In (2), $\mathbf{P}$ is a vector of prices and M^i is the individual's money income. When (2) holds, individuals' demands for a private good can be aggregated without considering the distribution of income. Clearly, the roles of quantity and price are switched in the public good and private good analyses of allocation-distribution independency. This independency is crucial for aggregation purposes.

In Chapter 5, the likelihood of immiserizing growth was shown to be greater for private good rather than public good technological advances. Public goods were less likely to experience immiserizing growth since the pre-advancement Nash equilibrium implies underprovision. Hence, within bounds, technological change biased toward the public good should improve welfare by moving the economy away from the underprovision position, a position derived from the quantity-constrained Nash choice.

Two welfare propositions characterize a private good, distortion-free world. The first states that every market equilibrium is Pareto optimal, and the second indicates that any Pareto optimum may be sustained by a suitable lump-sum redistribution of income. Since markets do not operate in a public good world, identical propositions do not hold. Nonetheless, for a public good, we saw that similar propositions apply to the Lindahl bargaining equilibrium. That is, every Lindahl equilibrium is Pareto optimal, and every Pareto optimum may be sustained as a Lindahl equilibrium by a suitable lump-sum redistribution of income. The Lindahl equilibrium was analogous to the market equilibrium, since tax shares in the former served as price constraints, so that individuals made quantity choices on the basis of parametric prices. The Lindahl thought experiment duplicated in principle the choices one faces with private goods.

On the general principles of collective action

The conventional wisdom on the collective action of pure public good provision has certain accepted propositions: (1) As group or community size increases, easy (or free) riding and its associated suboptimality also increase (Olson 1965). (2) The stability of Nash equilibrium depends solely on the sign and magnitude of an income effect (see, for example, Breton 1970, p. 891; Olson and Zeckhauser 1966; Pauly 1970a, p. 574; Williams 1966, p. 21). (3) Nash behavior always lead to inefficiency for public goods (Pauly 1970a). (4) A model with identical individuals has a symmetric equilibrium wherein everyone provides the same equilibrium quantity of a pure public good (Olson 1965). (5) There is no measure for the extent of easy riding. These are important propositions that are universally used and accepted in public finance.

In Chapter 7, we reexamined some of these propositions with a joint product model in which a marketed good jointly provides public and private outputs or characteristics. Once we admitted joint products to the study of public goods, we could demonstrate that propositions (1)–(4) no longer hold. In particular, our analysis showed that the consumption relationship of the jointly produced outputs influences the slope of the expenditure reaction paths, the stability of equilibria, and the departure of Nash equilibria from optimality (i.e., the extent of easy riding). When the joint products are complements in a Hicksian sense, particularly interesting results follow, including the possibilities of positively sloped reaction paths and of reduced easy riding as the size of the community is increased. Thus, an agent's public expenditures may *increase* in response to increased public expenditures of others, even when all goods are normal with positive income elasticities.

Even in the absence of jointness, Chapter 5 demonstrated that propositions (1) and (4) are not valid. Proposition (1) is true, however, if a quasi-linear utility function is assumed. Many of our results were demonstrated by a simple, but useful, geometric technique, analogous to the methods used to show price reactions among oligopolists. This geometric device depicts constrained iso-utility contours in $(q, \bar{Q})$ space. With this device, an index of easy riding was presented, whose existence disproves proposition (5). Additionally, the device is sufficiently flexible to examine symmetric n-person situations. Most important, the graphic device permits Lindahl, Pareto, and Nash equilibria to be examined and compared in the same diagram. The device was also employed to illustrate non-Nash equilibria (in Chapter 9) and common property problems (in Chapter 7).

The relationship of externalities, public goods,
joint products, and club goods

In Chapter 3, our concept of externality was introduced and compared with alternative definitions. Externalities were shown to imply quantity constraints (much like pure public goods), which exist owing to the absence of a market. Hence, externalities concern one agent's behavior affecting another *and* the absence of a price, by which an agent can control the quantity derived from the externality-generator. Thus, the quantity associated with the externality enters as a quantity constraint. For a general externality, the recipient's maximization problem is

$$
\begin{array}{ll}
\underset{\{y^h, z^y\}}{\text{Maximize}} & U^h(y^h, z^h; z^1, z^2, \ldots, z^{h-1}, z^{h+1}, \ldots, z^H) \\
\text{subject to} & p_y y^h + p_z z^h = M^h,
\end{array}
\tag{3}
$$

where notation corresponds to that of Chapter 3.

Pure public good problems are a subclass of externalities, in which the z's are added together; hence a sum replaces the vector of z's. That is, the pure public model is merely the externality problem with additional structure on the objective function's form. Similarly, cases of impure public goods or bads (e.g., congestion) were seen to be externality problems with more structure on the way in which the **z** vector entered the objective function. Finally, club goods were likened to impure public goods problems where both provision *and* *group size* were chosen.

Nash versus non-Nash behavior

Conjectural variations were introduced in Chapter 9 in order to analyze non-Nash behavior, whereby one agent views his public good choice as affecting the choice of others. Pigouvian taxes, consistency of conjectures, and the tragedy of the commons could be analyzed when non-Nash reactions are present. The introduction of non-Nash behavior potentially affects the stability of equilibria, the extent of easy riding, and the influence of group size on suboptimality.

The analysis of consistent conjectures, those that conform to the actual reactions experienced at equilibrium, was especially interesting. In the case of the commons, we demonstrated that only one kind of conjecture is consistent and that this conjecture implies a more profound tragedy than usually assumed. Moreover, only two firms are required to induce this consistency tragedy. Traditional Nash reactions were seen as being inconsistent when neoclassical technologies characterized the exploitation function. In a recent paper, Sugden (1985) has shown that as group size increases, consistency of expectations implies that no one would contribute anything to a pure public good. Thus, consistency or rational expectations lead to some startling, and important, conclusions for the theory of market failures.

On clubs

Part IV has been devoted to the analysis of clubs. To comprehend the diversity of models, we have identified three crucial specification parameters: membership composition, utilization option, and population division. Hence, homogeneous clubs were distinguished from mixed clubs; fixed utilization rates were differentiated from variable rates; and partitioned populations were distinguished from nonpartitioned populations. If memberships are homogeneous, then a representative member's utility function can be used, and *individualized* utilization rates can be ignored. The type of utilization, fixed or variable, is important for determining the determinants of congestion. If utilization rates are variable, then the total number of visits affects congestion. For fixed utilization rates, congestion typically depends on the membership size. Finally, the partitioning of the population determines what optimizing viewpoint is required. When the population cannot be partitioned among a fixed number of clubs, then a total-economy viewpoint is necessary in which both members' and nonmembers' utilities are considered. Hence, total benefits are maximized. If, however, the population can be evenly divided among a set of clubs, each of size s^*, then the representative member's utility is maximized. In this case, s^* corresponds to the membership size associated with maximizing average benefits.

The following general principles were derived for clubs: (1) Maximizing average benefits yields a Pareto optimum in the core, provided that s^* divides evenly into the population size. (2) Membership and provision decisions must be found simultaneously. (3) Club stability depends on whether the core exists. (4) Clubs are analogous to cooperative games, whereas pure public good groups are related to noncooperative games. (5) For a homogeneous population, a core solution is associated with either member ownership or competitive industrial provision. (6) The Tiebout Hypothesis refers to local public good clubs called jurisdictions. (7) Members must be at least as well off as nonmembers. (8) With uncertainty, membership and provision decisions are each sensitive to risk attitudes.

Applications

A final step in our presentation is to highlight the wide range of applications of the theory, presented in Chapter 16 and throughout the book. Clearly, the theory of externalities, public goods, and clubs has much to offer to public policy decisions. We have indicated applications involving alliances, education, highways, public transportation, the environment, and natural resources. The theory has much to add to important public policy tools, such as cost-benefit analysis. We applaud recent empirical applications of the theory and hope that this trend will continue.

17.2   Some directions for future research

In a volume covering so many diverse topics, any list of future directions would be quite long. To avoid presenting such a laundry list, we have focused on what we think are the most crucial extensions.

n-person asymmetric pure public good models

In Part III, *n*-person cases were frequently examined by assuming identical individuals; thus, an assumption of symmetry simplified the analysis greatly. In particular, symmetry permitted us to use our graphic technique for the *n*-person case. Much of this symmetrical analysis should be extended to asymmetric cases in which agents differ owing either to endowments or to tastes. For instance, the importance of size disparity among agents needs to be related to easy-rider behavior when group size varies. The effects of non-Nash conjectures on stability and optimality should also be extended to asymmetric cases. The logical procedure is to start with the two-person case and to extend the analysis to two groups, each with identical individuals; hence, members differ between, but not within, groups. If feasible, the graphic device should also be augmented to permit asymmetric cases to be examined. If the analysis of heterogeneous clubs is any indication, asymmetry may significantly change some of our results for pure public goods.

Joint products

The theory of jointness, developed in Chapter 7, should be extended. In the real world, joint products include more than just private and pure public outputs.[3] Clubs may provide services that are private and impurely public; e.g., alliance arsenals yield both private and impurely public outputs (i.e., damage limitation in times of war). To analyze such joint products requires combining club analysis with the study of private goods. In such a case, jointness gives rise to membership and provision decisions. Moreover, the consumption relationship of the joint products would affect not only stability, but also group size decisions. When joint products are purely private, purely public, and impurely public, then the theory of Parts III and IV must be fused together.

Another extension concerns immiserizing growth. In the case of joint products, comparative static changes can involve resource endowments, technical coefficients, and the fixed proportion coefficients. A variety of parametric alterations would require study. Presumably our results for immiserizing growth would be sensitive to the fixed proportions ratio and the consumption relationship of the jointly produced outputs.

Applied work

More applied work is needed on externalities, public goods, and club goods. Theoretical results for both externalities and public goods should be subject to experimentation. This process is beginning, but much more needs to be done. For example, no experimental economist has adequately simulated the joint product case to ascertain the effects of group size on easy riding. Few large group size experiments have been performed owing to the expense involved. The study of preference-revelation mechanisms clearly lends itself to experimental results. In a recent article, Bohm (1984) reported the results of a preference-revelation mechanism used by the Swedish government when determining public good provision. The Bohm procedure computed the willingness-to-pay measure for two groups of randomly selected respondents: One group had incentives to underreport their willingness to pay, and the other had incentives to overreport. These willingness-to-pay measures were then combined to give an average willingness-to-pay measure. Unlike previous preference-revelation mechanisms, the Bohm method was easy to employ in practice. The results from such practical applications should yield important insight into the easy-rider problem.

Very little empirical estimation has been applied to clubs; the most noteworthy exception is alliance studies (e.g., Sandler and Forbes 1980; Murdoch and Sandler 1984). For example, the relationship between members' income levels and the choice of provision and membership size has never been adequately tested. Another interesting empirical question concerns whether variable utilization clubs use tolls or membership fees when collecting revenue. The theory indicates that such clubs should use tolls rather than membership fees. In Chapter 14, the uncertainty in club utilization analysis suggests some hypotheses involving attitudes toward risk and decisions concerning provision and membership size. Do members react to this uncertainty by choosing large capacity size? This question can only be answered empirically.

Another area that can profit from empirical research involves non-Nash behavior. This requires formulating an econometric model in which the value of the conjectural variations parameter can be tested. Zero values would then mean Nash behavior, and nonzero values would imply non-Nash behavior. Furthermore, negative values indicate a greater departure from optimality than that of Nash behavior, and positive values might imply less suboptimality than that of Nash behavior. In a recent study, McGuire and Forbes (1985) have estimated the demand for military expenditure equations for Portugal, Italy, Greece, and Turkey, using a specification that allows the conjectural variations terms to be estimated. Their preliminary results showed that in the case of Greece and Turkey these conjectural variations terms were positive and significant. More studies of this kind can add greatly to our understanding of the easy-riding phenomenon.

Clubs

Finally, we conclude with some future directions for club research. With few exceptions, analyses of clubs have examined collectives sharing *only* one impure public good; however, clubs often share and provide multiple services or products. Country clubs provide a golf course, a swimming pool, tennis courts, and rooms for social events. Analysis of multiproduct clubs must answer a host of questions. Should the entire membership share in all of the services offered, or should an optimal sharing group be determined for each service, even though members are excluded from some services? Will some clubs attempt to attract members by offering just one or a few services, while others offer a wide range of services? Will self-financing of multiproduct clubs require cross subsidization between products with some products paying for others? Is complementarity in the production of multiple outputs a sufficient justification for multiproduct clubs, or must complementarity in consumption be required as well? These questions demonstrate that membership, stability, self-financing, and provision issues are more complex for multiproduct clubs.

Since communities, cities, and local governments share multiple services, an adequate study of multiproduct clubs will provide a better theoretical foundation for local public good analyses. A similar statement was made by Berglas and Pines (1981) who presented a multiproduct club model; but they introduced a constraint requiring the entire membership to share in each service. Furthermore, they did not examine cross subsidization or complementarity in production.

In a most interesting series of papers, Baumol and others presented an analysis of multiproduct firms producing private goods (see, e.g., Baumol 1977; Baumol, Bailey, and Willig 1977). These articles studied the sustainability of monopoly, cross subsidization, economies of scope (i.e., complementarity in production), and the optimal number of firms. All these issues are closely related to the above questions. A marriage between their analysis and that of club theory should produce a useful theory of multiproduct clubs. The sharing group size *for each product* must therefore be introduced into the cost functions, and the partial indivisibility of the multiple products must be accounted for.

Another suggested research direction concerns the inclusion of a spatial dimension to club analysis. A previous attempt ignored crowding when the location of members was considered (Harford 1979). Currently, the most complete specifications of a spatial club with crowding are those concerned with optimal city size (see, e.g., Dixit 1973). More work on spatial clubs appears warranted, since *no general* analysis of spatial clubs exists.

Still other areas in which more club research is needed include the study of institutional forms, hierarchical structures, and dynamic considerations. For uncertainty, demand- and supply-side uncertainty should be combined into one model.

We hope that this book will stimulate research into these and other areas of externalities. This book should have demonstrated the advantages of applying modern microeconomic concepts, such as duality, to the study of externalities. Obviously, more work along these lines is still needed.

Notes

Chapter 2 Equilibrium concepts in public finance

1 A standard reference for optimization techniques is Chiang (1984). Chiang includes the following optimization tools: unconstrained optimization, constrained optimization with equality constraints, constrained optimization with inequality constraints, and linear programming. Constrained optimization with inequality constraints is known as nonlinear programming, or Kuhn-Tucker procedures.

2 An easy-to-use reference for readers unfamiliar with game theory is Luce and Raiffa's (1957) *Games and Decisions*. This book is easy to understand, even for readers with little mathematical sophistication.

3 Expected value refers to the sum of the payoffs corresponding to the different outcomes when weighted by the probabilities associated with each outcome. If two equally likely states, a and b, are possible and the payoffs of each are 10 and 16, respectively, then the expected value is $EV = \frac{1}{2}(10) + \frac{1}{2}(16) = 13$. For a risk-neutral individual, the expected utility of the lottery or gamble equals the utility of the expected value; i.e., $U[pW_1 + (1-p)W_2] = pU(W_1) + (1-p)U(W_2)$, where U is utility, p is probability, and W_i, $i = 1, 2$, is the wealth value of the ith state of the world. Risk-averse individuals require the utility of the expected value to exceed the expected value of the utility; risk lovers require the opposite inequality. On uncertainty, see Henderson and Quandt (1980, pp. 52–61).

4 For example, see Breton (1970), McGuire and Aaron (1969), Pauly (1970a), and Sandler and Shelton (1972).

5 Nonetheless, we will later prove that each Pareto optimum can be sustained by a Lindahl equilibrium, given a suitable lump-sum redistribution of income. This result is analogous to the second fundamental theorem of welfare economics, stating that each Pareto optimum can be sustained by a market equilibrium, given a suitable lump-sum redistribution of income.

6 In the case of scramblers, new technologies have permitted entrepreneurs to develop descramblers.

Chapter 10 Homogeneous clubs and local public goods

1 This statement need not apply if utilization is stochastic. In particular, see Chapter 14.

276

2 This statement assumes that the benefits do not spill over to other jurisdictions. If spillovers are present, then the optimal sharing size includes all benefit recipients.

3 See, for example, Adams and Royer (1977); Allen, Amacher, and Tollison (1974); Anderson, Porter, and Maurice (1979); Berglas (1976); Buchanan (1965); Färe and Grosskopf (1979); Heavey and Gunzenhauser (1978); Litvack and Oates (1970); McGuire (1972, 1974a, 1974b); Mueller (1976); Musgrave and Musgrave (1976); Polinsky (1974); Porter (1978); and Sandler and Tschirhart (1984a).

4 Mishan (1971, pp. 4–5) showed that the solutions provided by Pigou and Knight were identical. That is, Pigou considered marginal costs (of congestion) excluding a rent concept, whereas Knight used average costs including rent; but under competitive conditions these two methods converge. For a modern treatment of this problem, see Edelson (1971) and Weitzman (1974).

5 See Hillman and Swan (1979, 1983), DeVany and Saving (1977, 1980), McCormick and Adams (1983), and Sandler and Tschirhart (1984a).

6 The Berglas, Helpman, and Pines (1982) taxonomy contained only six categories. Their taxonomy also distinguished between fixed and variable utilization rates, but did not distinguish between homogeneous and heterogeneous memberships. Moreover, their "everybody in a club" and "not everybody in a club" correspond to our partitioning terminology. Another taxonomy was suggested by Sandler and Tschirhart (1980).

7 To derive these conditions, form the Lagrangean,

$$L = U^i(y^i, X, s) + \lambda F^i(y^i, X, s),$$

where λ is a Lagrangean multiplier. Partial derivatives must be taken with respect to y^i, X, s, and λ, and these partials must be set equal to zero. Eliminating λ and simplifying yield (3) and (4). Second-order conditions require the bordered Hessian of second-order partials to be positive definite.

8 This statement assumes that the numeraire's marginal cost has been set equal to one.

9 Some nonrival goods with excludable benefits (e.g., the telephone) may require a finite club size owing to resource or hookup costs needed to extend consumption services to additional people. For these goods, the marginal costs of new members account for hookup costs *and* reductions due to cost sharing. Since these marginal costs are expected to be positive over some range of membership, finite memberships are optimal. On hookup costs, see Artle and Averous (1973) and von Rabenau and Stahl (1974).

10 The model presented in the text is a slight variant of the Berglas (1976) model. If one interprets $C(\cdot)$ as reflecting congestion costs, as in the case of the McGuire (1974a) model, then s is dropped from the utility function, since congestion is captured by the budget constraint.

11 An exception is given by Pauly's (1970b, p. 56) Theorem 1. If equal sharing is enforced and all clubs are of size *s**, the core exists. An omitted member cannot bid into a club, since he or she cannot bargain for a payoff lower than the members are receiving.

Chapter 11 Clubs in general

1 Alternatively, the objective could be $W[sU(\cdot), (\hat{s} - s)\bar{U}(\cdot)]$. The Pareto-optimal conditions could also be found by maximizing an arbitrary member's utility subject to the constancy of the other members' and nonmembers' utility levels. A Benthamite social welfare function is used in the text since it simplifies the notation and yields the required results.

2 We follow standard practice by treating s as a continuous variable.

3 These conditions are both necessary and sufficient for optimality, provided that utility is nonsatiable and that the utility and the transformation functions have the assumed convexity (Chiang 1984, pp. 739–43).

4 If this is not the case, determination of an optimal membership size would entail an exercise in combinatorics, since all possible orderings and their implied optimality must be compared to find the best (see Freeman and Haveman 1977; Hillman and Swan 1983; Sandler and Tschirhart 1980).

5 The Lagrangean is

$$L = \int_1^s w(i)U(\cdot, i)di + \int_s^{\hat{s}} w(i)\bar{U}(\cdot, i)di$$
$$+ \lambda F(\cdot) + \int_1^s \beta(i)(X - v(i)),$$

where λ and the $\beta(i)$'s are Lagrangean multipliers.

6 See Sandler and Tschirhart (1984b), Berglas and Pines (1981, 1984), and Berglas (1984).

7 The Sandler and Tschirhart (1984b) paper was originally written in 1981; publication lags account for the 1984 date. Dates are important in examining when the proposed solution to the mixing issue was first given.

8 See DeSerpa (1977), Ng and Tollison (1974), and Tollison (1972). The discussion in the text is based on the DeSerpa model, since his discriminatory model is the most complete one in the literature.

9 For example, see McCormick and Adams (1983); Barzel (1974); Davis and Whinston (1967); Kamien, Schwartz, and Roberts (1973); Millward (1970); Nichols, Smolensky, and Tideman (1971); Oakland (1972); and Sandler and Cauley (1976).

10 Nichols, Smolensky, and Tideman (1971) and Feldman (1978) have demonstrated that queues can determine membership size according to the opportunity cost of time. Furthermore, the former have argued that queues are efficient allocating devices, unless alternative means are less

costly than the deadweight loss of the queue. Rationing by congestion charges differ from that by queuing because the first collects a toll, whereas the queue collects nothing (Porter, 1977).

11 See, for example, DeSerpa (1978), Oakland (1972), and Sandler (1982).

Chapter 12 Institutional forms and clubs

1 The literature on competitive provision of clubs includes Berglas (1976, 1981); Berglas and Pines (1980, 1981); Berglas, Helpman, and Pines (1982); Boadway (1980); Hillman and Swan (1983); and Sandler and Tschirhart (1980).

2 Strictly speaking, P_v should be indirectly determined by the levels of sv and X—that is, $P_v = P_v(sv, X)$—so that the participants are price-takers, as one would expect in perfect competition. Berglas and Pines (1981, pp. 148–9) indicated that this requires the firm to maximize P_v subject to the constraint already given. This procedure determines $P_v = P_v(sv, X)$. Maximizing profits for this P_v then gives the alternative solution, which is identical to that of the text. A third alternative is to represent explicitly the production function and inputs for the firm. See Berglas and Pines (1980).

3 This whole exercise is analogous to Sandler and Tschirhart's (1981) demonstration of competitive equilibrium for consumer-managed firms. Also see Scotchmer (1984).

4 See, for example, Pauly (1970b, 1967) and Sorenson, Tschirhart, and Whinston (1978a, 1978b).

5 See Sandler and Schulze (1981) for an in-depth analysis and discussion of INTELSAT.

Chapter 13 Game theory and club goods

1 On cost allocation schemes see, for example, Gately (1974), Loehman and Whinston (1976), Hamlen, Hamlen, and Tschirhart (1977, 1980), Loehman et al. (1979), Sorenson, Tschirhart, and Whinston, (1978a, 1978b), and Suzuki and Nakayama (1976).

2 The authors who have applied game theory to clubs have assumed transferable utility and have used a scalar-value characteristic function (see Luce and Raiffa 1957 for a description of transferable utility). Essentially, transferable utility refers to the ability of players to make side payments in terms of some numeraire. Pauly (1970b) defined $v(S)$ as the difference between gross benefit and gross cost functions. Both are measured in terms of a numeraire good. Total benefits are the summation of individual benefits, and total costs include resource costs, decision costs, and congestion costs. Littlechild (1975) defined $v(S)$ as the profit available from full-time operation of the club, while Sorenson, Tschirhart, and Whinston (1978b) equated consumer's surplus with the characteristic function.

3 A characteristic function game consists of a set $\hat{S}$ of $\hat{s}$ individuals and a characteristic function, $v(\cdot)$, which maps all subsets or coalitions S of $\hat{S}$ to a nonnegative real number $v(S)$, termed the coalition value.

4 Pauly (1967, p. 316) stated that maximizing average net benefit is the same as setting the marginal gross benefit equal to the marginal gross cost of adding a member. But this latter approach maximizes total net benefit for the club, which will differ from maximizing the average unless the total function is linear in s. Maximizing average net benefit also differs from maximizing the total net benefit for the *economy*.

5 This result is due to Pauly (1970b, p. 59).

6 An exception is given by Pauly's Theorem 1 (1970b, p. 56). If equal sharing is enforced and all clubs are of size s^*, the core exists. An omitted individual cannot bid into a club, since he or she cannot bargain for a payoff lower than the members are receiving.

7 Members of Ellickson's sharing groups were characterized by the utility function $U^i = y^i X$. Maximizing utility subject to a budget constraint yielded specific demand functions. By maximizing the sum of utilities subject to an economywide resource constraint, the utility vector $(U^1, U^2, U^3) = (15/8, 15/8, 15/16)$ was attained for $X = 15/8$ and $(y^1, y^2, y^3) = (1, 1, 1/2)$. Then using the demand functions, prices were found that cleared the market and that yielded the utility vector. But a second vector, $(U^1, U^2, U^3) = (2, 2, 11/16)$, was then assumed to be a possibility. This vector is not consistent with the same amount of public and private goods, and the same demand functions.

8 For a different set of numbers in Table 13.1, requiring one club can be too restrictive for Pareto optimality even when $\hat{s} \leq 6$. For example, suppose $v(S) = 3$ instead of 1.5 for $s = 2$. Then with $\hat{s} = 6$, one club of 6 members is Pareto inferior to two clubs of sizes 4 and 2. For Pareto optimality in this situation, the integer problem requires that no club be of greater size than that which maximizes average net benefits.

9 Ng (1973) has pointed out that in this case his optimality conditions are satisfied for both two clubs of 6 or three clubs of 4. This is true, but the number of clubs must be *stipulated at the outset*. His one-club formulation yields one club of 6.

10 See Luce and Raiffa (1957, pp. 163–8, and Chapter 10) for a discussion of ψ-stability.

11 These conditions are presented in Luce and Raiffa (1957, pp. 247–9) and in Shapley (1953).

Chapter 14 Uncertainty and club goods

1 Since everyone is identical and $\hat{s}$ is fixed, the objective can be either $E(U)$ or $\hat{s}E(U)$ without affecting the results. If $E(U)$ is used, however, then the constraint, $F(\cdot)$, must be changed to that of an individual.

2 Since members neither all show up nor all stay away at the same time, the

assumption of a homogeneous population should be slightly modified. The members are homogeneous in endowments and tastes, except that their visitation times are staggered.

3 For further discussion of this two-part tariff see Sandler and Tschirhart (1980, pp. 1496–7; 1984b).

4. By an interior maximum, we are also assuming $\bar{s}$ is strictly less than s.

5 In a homogeneous world where preferences are truly invariant, the problem would not arise since the design engineer has the same preferences as everyone else. In a heterogeneous world, we conjecture that some individuals would be better off, some worse off when entering at full capacity.

6 An alternative intrepretation is that the user charge is also a congestion fee that internalizes the crowding externality. To be effective, it would need to be collected at the point of entry. Such a fee would eliminate the possibility that members would be worse off since no one would enter when the fee was too high. Since this fee would be both difficult to calculate and to collect (like a variable maintenance fee, it would change with each entrant), and since we are unable to find examples of clubs that actually use such a charge, it is not considered here.

7 We know that the average percentage of the membership using the club at any given time is equal to the probability that a member will want to use the facility times the probability that he will be admitted. Since the probability that he will want to use the club is fixed at p, the probability of being admitted is directly proportional to the average percentage using the club. If θ is the amount of unused capacity at any given time, then the number of members using the facility is $\bar{s} - \theta$. Therefore, the average percentage of the membership using the facility is $E[(\bar{s} - \theta)/s]$, which is equal to $\bar{s}/s - E[\theta/s]$. Since $\bar{s}/s$ is fixed, to show that increasing club size increases the probability of being admitted, we only need to show that as s is increased $E[\theta/s]$ is decreased. The random variable n/s is normally distributed about p, with a variance that decreases as s increases. We know that $\theta/s = \text{Max} (\bar{s}/s - n/s, 0)$. We may write $n/s = p + \sigma q$, where q is $N(0, 1)$. Since q is distributed symmetrically about zero, if $|q| = z$, then conditional upon the given information, $q = z$ with probability $\frac{1}{2}$ and $q = -z$ with probability $\frac{1}{2}$. It can be shown that the expectation of θ/s, conditional upon the absolute value of q equal to z, is a monotonically increasing function of σ. The expected value of θ/s is equal to $2 \int_0^\infty E[\theta/s \mid |q| = z] f(z) dz$, where $f(\cdot)$ is the normal density function. Since $E[\theta/s \mid |q| = z]$ is a monotonically increasing function of σ, the expected value of θ/s is an increasing function of σ. Therefore, increasing club size will lower the expectation of θ/s, and thus increase the probability of being admitted to the facility.

8 For decreasing relative risk aversion, use the function $U = \ln(W + r)$ and again vary r.

9 On supply-side uncertainty, also see DeVany and Saving (1977).

Chapter 15 Intergenerational clubs

1 Carrying capacity refers to the degree of utilization beyond which an environment is no longer able to regenerate itself.
2 See Sandler (1984) on optimizing this type of model.
3 An alternative form for the depreciation function requires the average utilization in any period to surpass a threshold value before a depreciation effect is produced. Only those values of k^j that exceed this threshold and that precede the jth period or occur in the jth period are included in the jth period depreciation function. This form is relevant for environmental amenities. See Sepassi (1983).
4 The model can be reformulated to allow the life span of the good to be extendable, but not indefinitely, by maintenance; hence, the good's life span becomes a function of the maintenance decision in each period. In this case, the optimal sequence of maintenance decisions will determine the life span of the good. The resulting maintenance condition differs from the one described in the text owing to the inclusion of some discrete benefits derived from extending the good's life span.

Chapter 16 Applications and empirics

1 On the contingent valuation approach, see Brookshire et al. (1982), Schulze, d'Arge, and Brookshire (1981), Brookshire and Crocker (1981), and Desvousges, Smith, and Fisher (1983).
2 The following references serve as a good starting point for the experimental literature: Kim and Walker (1984) and Isaac, Walker, and Thomas (1984).
3 See Bergstrom and Goodman (1973), Borcherding and Deacon (1972), and Pommerehne and Frey (1976).
4 This specification is taken from Bergstrom and Goodman (1973, p. 281).
5 The hedonic approach is used by Freeman (1979); Desvousges, Smith, and Fisher (1983); Brookshire et al. (1982); and Rosen (1974).
6 See Smith, Desvousges, and McGivney (1983); Knetsch (1977); Desvousges, Smith, and Fisher (1983); and Freeman (1979).
7 See Freeman (1979, Chapter 8).
8 A price or toll equal to marginal cost of provision for a Pareto optimum results because the shared good is private. For an impure public good depicted in the models of Chapter 11, the toll per-unit equals marginal congestion cost for a Pareto optimum. The financing condition of Chapter 11 illustrates that these latter tolls equal marginal cost of provision, but will not cover total cost of provision if there are increasing returns to scale.
9 Total congestion costs are $sc(X, s)$. Therefore, marginal congestion cost is $\partial sc(X, s)/\partial s = c(X, s) + s[\partial c(X, x)/\partial s]$. The first term is the travel cost the individual driver experiences, and the second is the travel cost imposed on other drivers and must be set equal to the toll.

10 See Edelson (1977) for an in-depth discussion of INTELSAT.
11 For example, see Murdoch and Sandler (1982, 1984, 1985), Sandler (1977), and Sandler and Forbes (1980).

Chapter 17 Conclusions and directions for future research

1 This statement assumes that there are no joint products and that the underlying utility functions are quasi-linear.
2 Aggregation statements apply only in a "local" sense.
3 Goods or activities that produce a private and pure public output are sometimes called quasi-public goods.

References

Adams, R. D. and Royer, J. S., (1977), "Income and Price Effects in the Economic Theory of Clubs," *Public Finance*, 32, 141–158.

Adams, R. F. (1965), "On the Variation in the Consumption of Public Services," *Review of Economics and Statistics*, 47, 400–405.

Allen, L., Amacher, R. C., and Tollison, R. D. (1974), "The Economic Theory of Clubs: A Geometric Exposition," *Public Finance*, 29, 386–91.

Anderson, R. K., Porter, P. K., and Maurice, S. C. (1979), "The Economics of Consumer-Managed Firms," *Southern Economic Journal*, 46, 119–30.

Arrow, K. J. (1970), "The Organization of Economic Activity: Issues Pertinent to the Choice of Market versus Non-Market Allocation," in *Public Expenditures and Policy Analysis*, edited by Haveman, R. H. and Margolis, J., Markham (Chicago), 59–73.

Artle, R. and Averous, C. P. (1973), "The Telephone System as a Public Good: Static and Dynamic Aspects," *Bell Journal of Economics*, 4, 89–100.

Atkinson, A. B. and Stiglitz, J. (1980), *Lectures on Public Economics*, McGraw-Hill (New York).

Auster, R. and Silver, M. (1973), "Collective Goods and Collective Decision Mechanisms," *Public Choice*, 14, 1–17.

Axelrod, R. (1984), *The Evolution of Cooperation*, Basic Books (New York).

Bacharach, M. (1976), *Economics and the Theory of Games*, Macmillan (London).

Barzel, Y. (1974), "A Theory of Rationing by Waiting," *Journal of Law and Economics*, 17, 73–95.

Bator, F. M. (1957), "The Simple Analytics of Welfare Maximization," *American Economic Review*, 47, 22–59.

Bator, F. M. (1958), "The Anatomy of Market Failure," *Quarterly Journal of Economics*, 72, 351–79.

Baumol, W. J. (1977), "On the Proper Cost Tests for Natural Monopoly in a Multiproduct Industry," *American Economic Review*, 67, 809–22.

Baumol, W. J., Bailey, E. E., and Willig, R. D. (1977), "Weak Invisible Hand Theorems on the Sustainability of Prices in a Multiproduct Natural Monopoly," *American Economic Review*, 67, 350–65.

Baumol, W. J. and Bradford, D. F. (1972), "Detrimental Externalities and Non-Convexity of the Production Set," *Economica*, 39, 160–76.

Baumol, W. J. and Oates, W. E. (1975), *The Theory of Environmental Policy*, Prentice-Hall (New Jersey).

Becker, G. S. (1974), "A Theory of Social Interactions," *Journal of Political Economy*, 82, 1063–93.

Berglas, E. (1976), "On the Theory of Clubs," *American Economic Review*, 66, 116–21.

Berglas, E. (1981), "The Market Provision of Club Goods Once Again," *Journal of Public Economics*, 15, 389–93.

Berglas, E. (1982), "User Charges, Local Public Services, and Taxation of Land Rents," *Public Finance*, 37, 178–88.

Berglas, E. (1984), "Quantities, Qualities, and Multiple Public Services in the Tiebout Model," *Journal of Public Economics*, 25, 299–321.

Berglas, E., Helpman, E., and Pines, D. (1982), "The Economic Theory of Clubs: Some Clarifications," *Economics Letters*, 10, 343–8.

Berglas, E. and Pines, D. (1980), "Clubs as a Case of Competitive Industry with Goods of Variable Quality," *Economics Letters*, 5, 363–6.

Berglas, E. and Pines, D. (1981), "Clubs, Local Public Goods and Transportation Models: A Synthesis," *Journal of Public Economics*, 15, 141–62.

Berglas, E. and Pines, D. (1984), "Resource Constraint, Replicability and Mixed Clubs: A Reply," *Journal of Public Economics*, 23, 391–7.

Bergstrom, T. C. (1975), "The Core when Strategies are Restricted by Law," *Review of Economic Studies*, 42, 249–57.

Bergstrom, T. C. (1976), "Collective Choice and the Lindahl Allocation Method," in *Theory and Measurement of Economic Externalities*, edited by Lin, S. A. Y., Academic Press (New York), 111–31.

Bergstrom, T. C., Blume, L., and Varian, H. (1984), "On the Private Provision of Public Goods," unpublished manuscript.

Bergstrom, T. C. and Cornes, R. C. (1981), "Gorman and Musgrave are Dual—An Antipodean Theorem on Public Goods," *Economics Letters*, 7, 371–8.

Bergstrom, T. C. and Cornes, R. C. (1983), "Independence of Allocative Efficiency from Distribution in the Theory of Public Goods," *Econometrica*, 51, 1753–65.

Bergstrom, T. C. and Goodman, R. P. (1973), "Private Demands for Public Goods," *American Economic Review*, 63, 280–96.

Bergstrom, T. C., Simon, C. P., and Titus, C. J. (1983), "Counting Groves-Ledyard Equilibria via Degree Theory," *Journal of Mathematical Economics*, 12, 167–84.

Blewett, R. A. (1983), "Fiscal Externalities and Residential Growth Controls: A Theory-of-Clubs Perspective," *Public Finance Quarterly*, 11, 3–20.

Boadway, R. (1980), "A Note on the Market Provision of Club Goods," *Journal of Public Economics*, 13, 131–7.

Boardman, A. E. and Lave, L. B. (1977), "Highway Congestion and Congestion Tolls," *Journal of Urban Economics*, 4, 340–59.

Bohm, P. (1984), "Revealing Demand for an Actual Public Good," *Journal of Public Economics*, 24, 131–51.

Borcherding, T. E. and Deacon, R. T. (1972), "The Demand for the Services of Non-Federal Governments," *American Economic Review*, 62, 891–901.

Bowen, H. (1943), "The Interpretation of Voting in the Allocation of Economic Resources," *Quarterly Journal of Economics*, 58, 27–48.

Bradford, D. F. and Hildebrandt, G. C. (1977), "Observable Preferences for Public Goods," *Journal of Public Economics*, 8, 111–31.

Bresnahan, T. F. (1981), "Duopoly Models with Consistent Conjectures," *American Economic Review*, 71, 934–45.

Breton, A. (1970), "Public Goods and the Stability of Federalism," *Kyklos*, 23, 882–902.

Breton, A. and Scott, A. (1978), *The Economic Constitution of Federal States*, University of Toronto Press (Toronto).

Brookshire, D. S. and Crocker, T. D. (1981), "The Advantages of Contingent Valuation Methods for Benefit-Cost Analysis," *Public Choice*, 36, 235–52.

Brookshire, D. S. et al. (1982), "Valuing Public Goods: A Comparison of Survey and Hedonic Approaches," *American Economic Review*, 72, 165–77.

Buchanan, J. M. (1965), "An Economic Theory of Clubs," *Economica*, 32, 1–14.

Buchanan, J. M. (1975), *The Limits of Liberty*, University of Chicago (Chicago).

Buchanan, J. M. and Kafoglis, M. Z. (1963), "A Note on Public Goods Supply," *American Economic Review*, 53, 403–14.

Buchanan, J. M. and Stubblebine, W. C. (1962), "Externality," *Economica*, 29, 371–84.

Buchanan, J. M. and Tullock, G. (1962), *The Calculus of Consent*, University of Michigan (Ann Arbor).

Bush, W. C. and Mayer, L. S. (1974), "Some Implications of Anarchy for the Distribution of Property," *Journal of Economic Theory*, 8, 401–12.

Chamberlin, J. (1974), "Provision of Collective Goods as a Function of Group Size," *American Political Science Review*, 68, 707–16.

Chiang, A. (1984), *Fundamental Methods of Mathematical Economics*, McGraw-Hill (New York).

Cicchetti, C. J. and Smith V. K. (1973), "Congestion, Quality Deterioration, and Optimal Use: Wilderness Recreation in the Spanish Peaks Primitive Area," *Social Sciences Research*, 2, 15–30.

Cicchetti, C. J. and Smith, V. K. (1976a), "The Measurement of Individual Congestion Costs: An Economic Application to Wilderness Recreation," in *Theory and Measurement of Economic Externalities*, edited by Lin, S. A. Y., Academic Press (New York), 183–200.

Cicchetti, C. J. and Smith V. K. (1976b), *The Costs of Congestion: An Econometric Analysis of Wilderness*, Ballinger (Cambridge, Mass.).

Clarke, E. H. (1971), "Multipart Pricing of Public Goods," *Public Choice*, 11, 19–33.

Coase, R. (1960), "The Problem of Social Cost," *Journal of Law and Economics*, 3, 1–44.

Cornes, R. C. (1980), "External Effects: An Alternative Formulation," *European Economic Review*, 14, 307–21.

Cornes, R. C. and Homma, M. (1979), "Consumption Externalities and Stability," *Economics Letters*, 4, 301–6.

Cornes, R. C. and Sandler, T. (1983), "On Commons and Tragedies," *American Economic Review*, 73, 787–92.

Cornes, R. C. and Sandler, T. (1984a), "Easy Riders, Joint Production, and Public Goods," *Economic Journal*, 94, 580–98.

Cornes, R. C. and Sandler, T. (1984b), "The Theory of Public Goods: Non-Nash Behaviour," *Journal of Public Economics*, 23, 367–79.

Dasgupta, P. and Heal, G. (1979), *Economic Theory and Exhaustible Resources*, Nisbet/Cambridge University Press (London).

Davis, M. D. (1983), *Game Theory: A Nontechnical Introduction*, Basic Books (New York).

Davis, O. A. and Whinston, A. B. (1967), "On the Distinction between Public and Private Goods," *American Economic Review*, 57, 360–73.

Deaton, A. and Muellbauer, J. (1980), *Economics and Consumer Behavior*, Cambridge University Press (New York).

DeSerpa, A. C. (1977), "A Theory of Discriminatory Clubs," *Scottish Journal of Political Economy*, 24, 33–41.

DeSerpa, A. C. (1978), "Congestion, Pollution, and Impure Public Goods," *Public Finance*, 33, 68–83.

Desvousges, W. H., Smith, V. K., and Fisher, A. (1983), "A Comparison of Direct and Indirect Methods for Estimating Environmental Benefits," unpublished manuscript.

DeVany, A. S. and Saving, T. R. (1977), "Product Quality, Uncertainty, and Regulation: The Trucking Industry," *American Economic Review*, 67, 583–94.

DeVany, A. S. and Saving, T. R. (1980), "Competition and Highway Pricing for Stochastic Traffic," *Journal of Business*, 53, 45–60.

Diamond, P. and Mirrlees, J. (1973), "Aggregate Production with Consumption Externalities," *Quarterly Journal of Economics*, 87, 1–24.

Diewert, W. E. (1981), "The Measurement of Deadweight Loss Revisited," *Econometrica*, 49, 1225–44.

Dixit, A. K. (1973), "The Optimum Factory Town," *Bell Journal of Economics*, 4, 637–51.

Dorfman, R. (1974), "The Technical Basis for Decision Making," in *The Governance of Common Property Resources*, edited by Haefele, E. T., Johns Hopkins (Baltimore), 5–25.

Downs, A. (1957), *An Economic Theory of Democracy*, Harper and Row (New York).

Dréze, J. H. and de la Vallée Poussin, D. (1971), "A Tatonnement Process for Public Goods," *Review of Economic Studies*, 37, 133–50.

Dudley, L. and Montmarquette, C. (1981), "The Demand for Military Expenditures: An International Comparison," *Public Choice*, 37, 5–31.

Dybvig, P. H. and Spatt, C. S. (1983), "Adoption Externalities as Public Goods," *Journal of Public Economics*, 20, 231–47.

Edelson, B. I. (1977), "Global Satellite Communications," *Scientific American*, 236, 58–73.

Edelson, N. M. (1971), "Congestion Toll Under Monopoly," *American Economic Review*, 61, 873–82.

Ellickson, B. (1973), "A Generalization of the Pure Theory of Public Goods, *American Economic Review*, 63, 417–32.

Ellickson, B. (1978), "Public Goods and Joint Supply," *Journal of Public Economics*, 9, 373–82.

Ellickson, B. (1979), "Local Public Goods and the Market of Neighborhoods," in *The Economics of Neighborhoods*, edited by Segal, D., Academic Press (New York), 263–94.

Färe, R. and Grosskopf, S. (1979), "Existence of Nonprofit Clubs," unpublished manuscript.

Feldman, A. M. (1980), *Welfare Economics and Social Choice Theory*, Martinus Nijhoff (Boston).

Feldman, R. D. (1978), "Rationing Congested Goods by Preferences on Quality," *Public Finance*, 33, 225–31.

Fisher, A. C. and Krutilla, J. V. (1972), "Determination of Optimal Capacity of Resource-Based Recreational Facilities," *Natural Resources Journal*, 12, 417–44.

Fisher, A. C., Krutilla, J. V. and Cicchetti, C. J. (1972), "The Economics of Environmental Preservation: A Theoretical and Empirical Analysis," *American Economic Review*, 62, 605–19.

Fisher, A. C., Krutilla, J. V., and Cicchetti, C. J. (1974), "The Economics of Environmental Preservation: Further Discussion," *American Economic Review*, 64, 1030–9.

Foley, D. (1970a), "Lindahl's Solution and the Core of an Economy with Public Goods," *Econometrica*, 38, 66–72.

Foley, D. (1970b), "Economic Equilibrium with Costly Marketing," *Journal of Economic Theory*, 2, 276–91.

Freeman, A. M. (1979), *The Benefits of Environmental Improvement: Theory and Practice*, Johns Hopkins (Baltimore).

Freeman, A. M. and Haveman, R. H. (1977), "Congestion, Quality Deterioration, and Heterogeneous Tastes," *Journal of Public Economics*, 8, 225–32.

Friedman, J. (1983), *Oligopoly Theory*, Cambridge University Press (New York).

Frisch, R. (1933), "Monopole-Polypole-La Notion de Force dans L'Economie," *Festschrift til Harald Westergaard*. Supplement to *Nationalekonomisk Tidsskrift*, 71, 241–59, translated into English in *International Economic Papers* (1951), 1, 23–36.

Gately, D. (1974), "Sharing the Gains from Regional Cooperation: A Game-Theoretic Application to Planning Investment in Electric Power," *International Economic Review*, 15, 195–208.

Gegax, D. (1984), "The Quality of Clubs with Stochastic Supply," unpublished manuscript.

Gorman, W. M. (1953), "Community Preference Fields," *Econometrica*, 21, 63–80.

Gorman, W. M. (1980), "A Possible Procedure for Analysing Quality Differentials in the Egg Market," *Review of Economic Studies*, 47, 843–56.

Green, J. R. and Laffont, J.-J. (1979), *Incentives in Public Decision-Making*, Elsevier (New York).

Groves, T. (1982), "On Theories of Incentive Compatible Choice with Compensation," in *Advances in Economic Theory*, edited by Hildenbrand, W., Cambridge University Press (New York).

Groves, T. and Ledyard, J. (1977), "Optimal Allocation of Public Goods: A Solution to the 'Free Rider' Problem," *Econometrica*, 45, 783–809.

Guttman, J. (1978), "Understanding Collective Action: Matching Behavior," *American Economic Review Papers and Proceedings*, 68, 251–5.

Guttman, J. M. (1983), "A Non-Cournot Model of Voluntary Collective Action," unpublished Working Paper No. 8302. Centre for Agricultural Economic Research, Rehovot, Israel.

Hamburger, H. (1979). *Games as Models of Social Phenomena*, Freeman (San Francisco).

Hamlen, S. S., Hamlen, W. A., and Tschirhart, J. (1977), "The Use of Core Theory in Evaluating Joint Cost Allocation Schemes," *Accounting Review*, 52, 616–27.

Hamlen, S. S., Hamlen, W. A., and Tschirhart, J. (1980), "The Use of the Generalized Shapley Allocation in Joint Cost Allocation," *Accounting Review*, 55, 269–87.

Hardin, G. (1968), "The Tragedy of the Commons," *Science*, 162, 1243–8.

Hardin, R. (1982), *Collective Action*, Johns Hopkins (Baltimore).

Harford, J. D. (1979), "The Spatial Aspects of Local Public Goods: A Note," *Public Finance Quarterly*, 7, 122–8.

Heal, G. (1982), "The Use of Common Property Resources," in *Explorations in Natural Resource Economics*, edited by Smith, V. K. and Krutilla, J. V., Johns Hopkins (Baltimore), 72–106.

Heavey, J. F. and Gunzenhauser, M. K. (1978), "Income Effects and Club Size," *Public Finance*, 33, 84–89.

Heller, W. P. and Starrett, D. A. (1976), "On the Nature of Externalities," in *Theory and Measurement of Economic Externalities*, edited by Lin, S. A. Y., Academic Press (New York), 9–21.

Helpman, E. and Hillman, A. L. (1977), "Two Remarks on Optimal Club Size," *Economica*, 44, 293–6.

Henderson, J. M. and Quandt, R. E. (1980), *Microeconomic Theory: A Mathematical Approach*, McGraw-Hill (New York).

Hicks, J. R. (1956), *A Revision of Demand Theory*, Oxford University Press (New York).

Hildenbrand, W. and Kirman, A. (1976), *Introduction to Equilibrium Analysis*, Elsevier (New York).

Hillman, A. L. (1978), "The Theory of Clubs: A Technological Formulation," in *Essays in Public Economics: The Kiryat Anavim Papers*, edited by Sandmo, A., Heath, Lexington Books (Lexington, Mass.), 29–47.

Hillman, A. L. and Swan, P. L. (1979), "Club Participation under Uncertainty," *Economics Letters*, 4, 307–12.

Hillman, A. L. and Swan, P. L. (1983), "Participation Rules for Pareto-Optimal Clubs," *Journal of Public Economics*, 20, 55–76.

Hirsch, F. (1976), *Social Limits to Growth*, Harvard University Press (Cambridge, Mass.).

Hirshleifer, J. (1983), "From Weakest Link to Best Shot: The Voluntary Provision of Public Goods," *Public Choice*, 41, 371–86.

Hochman, H. and Rodgers, J. (1969), "Pareto Optimal Redistribution," *American Economic Review*, 59, 542–57.

Hori, M. (1975), "Revealed Preference for Public Goods," *American Economic Review*, 65, 978–91.

Hurwicz, L. (1972), "On Informationally Decentralized Systems," in *Decision and Organization. A Volume in Honor of Jacob Marschak*, edited by McGuire, C. B. and Radner, R., North-Holland (Amsterdam), 297–336.

International Monetary Fund (1983), *International Financial Statistics Yearbook* (Washington, D.C.).

Isaac, R. M., Walker, J. M., and Thomas, S. H. (1984), "Divergent Evidence on Free Riding: An Experimental Examination of Possible Explanations," *Public Choice*, 43, 113–49.

Isserman, A. M. (1976), "Interjurisdictional Spillovers, Political Fragmentation and the Level of Local Public Services: A Re-examination," *Urban Studies*, 13, 1–12.

Johansen, L. (1963), "Some Notes on the Lindahl Theory of Determination of Public Expenditures," *International Economic Review*, 4, 346–58.

Johansen, L. (1977), "The Theory of Public Goods: Misplaced Emphasis?" *Journal of Public Economics*, 7, 147–52.

Johansen, L. (1982), "On the Status of the Nash Type of Noncooperative Equilibrium Theory," *Scandinavian Journal of Economics*, 84, 421–41.

Johnson, M. B. (1964), "On the Economics of Road Congestion," *Econometrica*, 32, 137–50.

Kamien, M. I. and Schwartz, N. L. (1983), "Conjectural Variations," *Canadian Journal of Economics*, 16, 191–211.

Kamien, M. I., Schwartz, N. L., and Roberts, D. J. (1973), "Exclusion, Externalities, and Public Goods," *Journal of Public Economics*, 2, 217–30.

Kiesling, H. J. (1976), "A Model for Analyzing the Effects of Governmental Consolidation in the Presence of Public Goods," *Kyklos*, 29, 233–55.

Kim, O. and Walker, M. (1984), "The Free Rider Problem: Experimental Evidence," *Public Choice*, 43, 3–24.

Knetsch, J. L. (1977), "Displaced Facilities and Benefit Calculations," *Land Economics*, 53, 123–9.

Knight, F. H. (1924), "Some Fallacies in the Interpretation of Social Cost," *Quarterly Journal of Economics*, 38, 582–606.

Kolm, S-C. (1974), "Qualitative Returns to Scale and the Optimum Financing of Environmental Policy," in *The Management of Water Quality and the*

Environment, edited by Rothenberg, J. and Heggie, I. G., Macmillan (London), 151–71.

Koopmans, T. J. (1957), *Three Essays on the State of Economic Science*, McGraw-Hill (New York).

Laffont, J-J. (1976), "Decentralization with Externalities," *European Economic Review*, 7, 359–75.

Lancaster, K. (1971), *Consumer Demand: A New Approach*, Columbia University Press, (New York).

Leland, H. E. (1972), "The Theory of the Firm Facing Uncertain Demand," *American Economic Review*, 62, 278–91.

Lewis, W. A. (1941), "The Two-Part Tariff," *Economica*, 8, 249–70.

Littlechild, S. C. (1975), "Common Costs, Fixed Charges, Clubs and Games," *Review of Economic Studies*, 42, 162–66.

Littlechild, S. C. and Thompson, G. F. (1977), "Airport Landing and Fees: A Game-Theory Approach," *Bell Journal of Economics*, 8, 186–204.

Litvack, J. M. and Oates, W. E. (1970), "Group Size and the Output of Public Goods: Theory and Application to State-Local Finance in the United States," *Public Finance*, 25, 42–62.

Loehman, E. T. and Whinston, A. B. (1976), "A Generalized Cost Allocation Scheme," in *Theory and Measurement of Economic Externalities*, edited by Lin, S. A. Y., Academic Press (New York), 87–101.

Loehman, E. T. et al. (1979), "Cost Allocation for a Regional Wastewater Treatment System," *Water Resources Research*, 15, 193–202.

Luce, R. D. and Raiffa, H. (1957), *Games and Decisions*, John Wiley and Sons, (New York).

Mäler, K-G. (1971), "A Method for Estimating Social Benefits from Pollution Control," *Swedish Journal of Economics*, 73, 121–33.

Mäler, K-G. (1974), "Effluent Charges versus Effluent Standards," in *The Management of Water Quality and the Environment*, edited by Rothenberg, J. and Heggie, I. G., Macmillan (London), 189–212.

Malinvaud, E. (1971), "A Planning Approach to the Public Goods Problem," *Swedish Journal of Economics*, 73, 96–112.

Malinvaud, E. (1972), *Lectures on Microeconomic Theory*, Elsevier (New York).

Margolis, J. (1955), "A Comment on the Pure Theory of Public Expenditure," *Review of Economics and Statistics*, 37, 347–9.

McCormick, K. J. and Adams, R. D. (1983), "Clubs with Stochastic Demand: The Case of Fire Suppression Districts," unpublished manuscript.

McGuire, M. C. (1972), "Private Good Clubs and Public Good Clubs: Economic Models of Group Formation," *Swedish Journal of Economics*, 74, 84–99.

McGuire, M. C. (1974a), "Group Segregation and Optimal Jurisdictions," *Journal of Political Economy*, 82, 112–32.

McGuire, M. C. (1974b), "Group Size, Group Homogeneity, and the Aggregate Provision of a Pure Public Good under Cournot Behavior," *Public Choice*, 18, 107–26.

McGuire, M. C. and Aaron, H. (1969), "Efficiency and Equity in the Optimal Supply of a Public Good," *Review of Economics and Statistics*, 51, 31–9.

McGuire, M. C. and Forbes, K. (1985), "Economics of Defense in the 80's: The Southern Tier of NATO," unpublished manuscript.

McMillan, J. (1979), "The Free-Rider Problem: A Survey," *Economic Record*, 55, 95–107.

Meade, J. E. (1973), *The Theory of Economic Externalities. The Control of Environmental Pollution and Similar Social Costs*, Sijhoff (Leiden, Sweden).

Millward, R. (1970), "Exclusion Costs, External Economies, and Market Failure," *Oxford Economic Papers*, 22, 24–38.

Mishan, E. J. (1971), "The Postwar Literature on Externalities: An Interpretative Essay," *Journal of Economic Literature*, 9, 1–28.

Mohring, H. D. and Harwitz, M. (1962), *Highway Benefits: An Analytical Review*, Northwestern University Press (Evanston, Illinois).

Mueller, D. C. (1979), *Public Choice*, Cambridge University Press (New York).

Muench, T. (1972), "The Core and the Lindahl Equilibrium of an Economy with a Public Good: An Example," *Journal of Economic Theory*, 4, 241–55.

Murdoch, J. C. and Sandler, T. (1982), "A Theoretical and Empirical Analysis of NATO," *Journal of Conflict Resolution*, 26, 237–63.

Murdoch, J. C. and Sandler, T. (1984), "Complementary, Free Riding, and the Military Expenditures of NATO Allies," *Journal of Public Economics*, 25, 83–101.

Murdoch, J. C. and Sandler, T. (1985), "The Political Economy of European Neutrality," unpublished manuscript.

Musgrave, R. A. and Musgrave, P. B. (1976), *Public Finance in Theory and Practice*, McGraw-Hill (New York).

Musgrave, R. A. and Peacock, A. T. (eds.) (1958), *Classics in the Theory of Public Finance*, Macmillan and Co. (London).

Neary, J. P. and Roberts, K. W. S. (1980), "The Theory of Household Behaviour under Rationing," *European Economic Review*, 13, 25–42.

Neumann, J. von and Morgenstern, O. (1944), *The Theory of Games and Economic Behavior*, Princeton University Press (Princeton, N.J.).

Ng, Y. K. (1973), "The Economic Theory of Clubs: Optimal Tax/Subsidy," *Economica*, 41, 308–21.

Ng, Y. K. and Tollison, R. D. (1974), "A Note on Consumption Sharing and Non-Exclusion Rules," *Economica*, 41, 446–50.

Ng, Y. K. and Weisser, M. (1974), "Optimal Pricing with a Budget Constraint—The Case of the Two-part Tariff," *Review of Economic Studies*, 41, 337–45.

Nichols, D., Smolensky, E., and Tideman, T. N. (1971), "Discrimination by Waiting Time in Merit Goods," *American Economic Review*, 61, 312–23.

Niskanen, W. A. (1971), *Bureaucracy and Representative Government*, Aldine-Atherton (Chicago).

Oakland, W. H. (1972), "Congestion, Public Goods and Welfare," *Journal of Public Economics*, 1, 339–57.

Oakland, W. H. (1974), "Public Goods, Perfect Competition, and Under-production," *Journal of Political Economy*, 82, 927–39.

Oates, W. E. (1972), *Fiscal Federalism*, Harcourt, Brace and Jovanovich (New York).

Oates, W. (1983), "The Regulation of Externalities: Efficient Behavior by Sources and Victims," *Public Finance*, 38, 362–75.

Olson, M. (1965), *The Logic of Collective Action*, Harvard University Press, (Cambridge).

Olson, M. (1969), "The Principle of 'Fiscal Equivalence': The Division of Responsibilities among Different Levels of Government," *American Economic Review*, 59, 479–87.

Olson, M. and Zeckhauser, R. (1966), "An Economic Theory of Alliances," *Review of Economics and Statistics*, 48, 266–79.

Oppenheimer, J. (1979), "Collective Goods and Alliances: A Reassessment," *Journal of Conflict Resolution*, 23, 387–407.

Palfrey, T. R. and Rosenthal, H. (1984), "Participation and the Provision of Discrete Public Goods: A Strategic Analysis," *Journal of Public Economics*, 24, 171–93.

Pauly, M. V. (1967), "Clubs, Commonality, and the Core: An Integration of Game Theory and the Theory of Public Goods," *Economica*, 34, 314–24.

Pauly, M. V. (1970a), "Optimality, 'Public' Goods, and Local Governments: A General Theoretical Analysis," *Journal of Political Economy*, 78, 572–85.

Pauly, M. V., (1970b), "Cores and Clubs," *Public Choice*, 9, 53–65.

Perry, M. (1982), "Oligopoly and Consistent Conjectural Variations," *Bell Journal of Economics*, 13, 197–205.

Pigou, A. C. (1920), *The Economics of Welfare*, Macmillan and Co. (London).

Pigou, A. C. (1946), *The Economics of Welfare* (4th Edition), Macmillan (London).

Polinsky, A. M. (1974), "Collective Consumption Goods and Local Public Finance Theory: A Suggested Analytical Framework," Urban Institute Reprint, 168-1207-8, Urban Institute (Washington, D.C.).

Pommerehne, W. W. and Frey, B. S. (1976), "Two Approaches to Estimating Public Expenditures," *Public Finance Quarterly*, 4, 395–407.

Porter, R. C. (1977), "On the Optimal Size of Underpriced Facilities," *American Economic Review*, 67, 753–60.

Porter, R. C. (1978), "The Economics of Congestion: A Geometric Review," *Public Finance Quarterly*, 6, 23–52.

Posnett, J. and Sandler, T. (1986), "Joint Supply and the Finance of Charitable Activity," *Public Finance Quarterly*, 14, forthcoming.

Rabenau, B. von and Stahl, K. (1974), "Dynamic Aspects of Public Goods: A Further Analysis of the Telephone System," *Bell Journal of Economics*, 5, 651–9.

Richter, D. K. (1978), "Existence and Computation of a Tiebout General Equilibrium," *Econometrica*, 46, 779–805.

Roberts, D. J. (1974), "The Lindahl Solution for Economies with Public Goods," *Journal of Public Economics*, 3, 23–42.

Rohlfs, J. (1974), "A Theory of Interdependent Demand for a Communication Service," *Bell Journal of Economics*, 5, 16–37.

Rosen, S. (1974), "Hedonic Prices and Implicit Markets: Product Differentiation in Pure Competition," *Journal of Political Economy*, 82, 34–55.

Ruggles, N. D. (1950), "Recent Developments in the Theory of Marginal Cost Pricing," *Review of Economic Studies*, 17, 107–26.

Samuelson, P. A. (1954), "The Pure Theory of Public Expenditure," *Review of Economics and Statistics*, 36, 387–89.

Samuelson, P. A. (1955), "A Diagrammatic Exposition of a Theory of Public Expenditure," *Review of Economics and Statistics*, 37, 350–56.

Sandler, T. (1977), "Impurity of Defense: An Application to the Economics of Alliances," *Kyklos*, 30, 443–60.

Sandler, T. (1982), "A Theory of Intergenerational Clubs," *Economic Inquiry*, 20, 191–208.

Sandler, T. (1984), "Club Optimality: Further Clarifications," *Economics Letters*, 14, 61–5.

Sandler, T. and Cauley, J. (1976), "Multiregional Public Goods, Spillovers, and the New Theory of Consumption," *Public Finance*, 31, 376–95.

Sandler, T. and Cauley, J. (1977), "The Design of Supranational Structures: An Economic Perspective," *International Studies Quarterly*, 21, 251–76.

Sandler, T., Cauley, J. and Tschirhart, J. (1983), "Toward a Unified Theory of Nonmarket Institutional Structures," *Australian Economic Papers*, 22, 233–54.

Sandler, T. and Culyer, A. J. (1982), "Joint Products and Multijurisdictional Spillovers," *Quarterly Journal of Economics*, 97, 707–16.

Sandler, T. and Forbes, J. F. (1980), "Burden Sharing, Strategy, and the Design of NATO," *Economic Inquiry*, 18, 425–44.

Sandler, T. and Schulze, W. D. (1981), "The Economics of Outer Space," *Natural Resources Journal*, 21, 371–93.

Sandler, T. and Shelton, R. B. (1972), "Fiscal Federalism, Spillovers, and the Export of Taxes," *Kyklos*, 25, 736–53.

Sandler, T., Sterbenz, F. P., and Tschirhart, J. (1985), "Uncertainty and Clubs," *Economica*, 52, forthcoming.

Sandler, T. and Tschirhart, J. (1980), "The Economic Theory of Clubs: An Evaluative Survey," *Journal of Economic Literature*, 18, 1481–1521.

Sandler, T. and Tschirhart, J. (1981), "On the Number and Membership Size of Consumer Managed Firms," *Southern Economic Journal*, 47, 1086–91.

Sandler, T. and Tschirhart, J. (1984a), "Uncertainty and Clubs," unpublished manuscript.

Sandler, T. and Tschirhart, J. (1984b), "Mixed Clubs: Further Observations," *Journal of Public Economics*, 23, 381–9.

Sandmo, A. (1973), "Public Goods and the Technology of Consumption," *Review of Economic Studies*, 40, 517–28.

Sandmo, A. (1980), "Anomaly and Stability in the Theory of Externalities," *Quarterly Journal of Economics*, 94, 799–807.

Schelling, T. (1973), "Hockey Helmets, Concealed Weapons and Daylight Saving: A Study of Binary Choices with Externalities," *Journal of Conflict Resolution*, 17, 381–428.

Schmeidler, D. (1969), "The Nucleolus of a Characteristic Function Game," *SIAM Journal of Applied Mathematics*, 17, 1163–70.

Schotter, A. (1981), *The Economic Theory of Social Institutions*, Cambridge University Press (New York).

Schotter, A. and Schwödiauer, G. (1980), "Economics and the Theory of Games," *Journal of Economic Literature*, 18, 479–527.

Schulze, W. D., d'Arge, R. C., and Brookshire, D. S. (1981), "Valuing Environmental Commodities: Some Recent Experiments," *Land Economics*, 57, 151–72.

Scotchmer, S. (1984), "Profit-Maximizing Clubs," unpublished manuscript.

Sepassi, G. R. (1983), *Contribution to the Theory of Clubs*, unpublished dissertation, University of Wyoming.

Shapley, L. (1953), "Value of n-Person Games," in *Contributions to the Theory of Games*, Vol. II, edited by Kuhn, H. W. and Tucker, A. W., Princeton University Press (Princeton, N.J.), 307–17.

Shapley, L. (1971), "Cores and Convex Games," *International Journal of Game Theory*, 1, 11–26.

Shapley, L. S. and Shubik, M. (1969), "On the Core of an Economic System with Externalities," *American Economic Review*, 59, 678–84.

Sharp, C. (1966), "Congestion and Welfare: An Examination of the Case for a Congestion Tax," *Economic Journal*, 76, 806–17.

Sherman, R. (1967), "Club Subscriptions for Public Transport Passengers," *Journal of Transportation and Economic Policy*, 1, 237–42.

Shibata, H. and Winrich, J. S. (1983), "Control of Pollution when the Offended Defend Themselves," *Economica*, 50, 425–38.

Smith, V. K. (1983), "Option Value: A Conceptual Overview," *Southern Economic Journal*, 49, 654–68.

Smith, V. K., Desvousges, W. H., and McGivney, M. P. (1983), "The Opportunity Cost of Travel Time in Recreation Demand Models," *Land Economics*, 59, 259–78.

Smith, V. K. and Krutilla, J. V. (1974), "A Simulation Model for the Management of Low Density Recreation Areas," *Journal of Environmental Economics and Management*, 1, 187–201.

Sorenson, J. R., Tschirhart, J., and Whinston, A. B. (1978a), "A Theory of Pricing under Decreasing Costs," *American Economic Review*, 68, 614–24.

Sorenson, J. R., Tschirhart, J., and Whinston, A. B. (1978b), "Private Good Clubs and the Core," *Journal of Public Economics*, 10, 77–95.

Squire, L. (1973), "Some Aspects of Optimal Pricing for Telecommunications," *Bell Journal of Economics*, 4, 515–25.

Stankey, G. H. (1972), "A Strategy for the Definition and Management of Wilderness Quality," in *Natural Environments: Studies in Theoretical and*

Applied Analysis, edited by Krutilla, J. V., Johns Hopkins (Baltimore), 88–114.

Starrett, D. A. (1972), "Fundamental Non-Convexities in the Theory of Externalities," *Journal of Economic Theory*, 4, 180–99.

Starrett, D. A. (1973), "A Note on Externalities and the Core," *Econometrica*, 41, 179–83.

Stockholm International Peace Research Institute (various years), *World Armaments and Disarmament SIPRI Yearbook*, Crane, Kussak (New York).

Sugden, R. (1982), "On the Economics of Philanthropy," *Economic Journal*, 92, 341–50.

Sugden, R. (1985), "Consistent Conjectures and Voluntary Contributions to Public Goods: Why the Conventional Theory Doesn't Work," *Journal of Public Economics*, in press.

Suzuki, M. and Nakayama, M. (1976), "The Cost Assignment of Cooperative Water Resource Development: A Game-Theoretic Approach," *Management Science*, 22, 1081–6.

Taylor, M. (1976), *Anarchy and Cooperation*, Wiley (New York).

Tiebout, C. M. (1956), "A Pure Theory of Local Expenditures," *Journal of Political Economy*, 64, 416–24.

Tollison, R. D. (1972), "Consumption Sharing and Non-Exclusion Rules," *Economica*, 39, 279–91.

Tulkens, H. (1978), "Dynamic Processes for Public Goods: An Institution-Oriented Survey," *Journal of Public Economics*, 9, 163–201.

Vickrey, W. S. (1961), "Counterspeculation, Auctions and Competitive Sealed Tenders," *Journal of Finance*, 16, 1–17.

Vickrey, W. S. (1969), "Congestion Theory and Transport Investment," *American Economic Review*, 59, 251–60.

Walsh, V. C. (1970), *Introduction to Contemporary Microeconomics*, McGraw-Hill (New York).

Walters, A. A. (1961), "The Theory and Measurement of Private and Social Cost of Highway Congestion," *Econometrica*, 29, 676–99.

Weitzman, M. L. (1974), "Free Access vs. Private Ownership as Alternative Systems for Managing Common Property," *Journal of Economic Theory*, 8, 225–34.

Westhoff, F. (1977), "Existence of Equilibria in Economies with a Local Public Good," *Journal of Economic Theory*, 14, 84–112.

Williams, A. (1966), "The Optimal Provision of Public Goods in a System of Local Government," *Journal of Political Economy*, 74, 18–33.

Wiseman, J. (1957), "The Theory of Public Utility Price—An Empty Box," *Oxford Economic Papers*, 9, 56–74.

Wooders, M. H. (1985), "A Tiebout Theorem," unpublished manuscript.

Author index

Weisser, M., 255
Weitzman, M.L., 131, 277
Westhoff, F., 173
Whinston, A.B., 193, 202, 204, 206, 278, 279
Wicksell, K., 3
Williams, A., 149, 269

Willig, R., 275
Winrich, J.S., 45
Wiseman, J., 8, 162
Wooders, M.H., 173

Zeckhauser, R., 4, 259, 261, 269

Subject index

alliance theory, 259–64

binary choice, models of, 133, 137–42

capacity condition, 217–20
characteristics approach to consumer
    behavior, 116–23, 252–4
chicken, game of, 140
Clarke's demand-revealing mechanism,
    see Clarke-Groves taxes
Clarke-Groves taxes, 5, 105–9, 133,
    143–4
club goods, 7, 24–5, 45–6; competitive
    provision of, 188–90; government
    provision of, 191–2, 237–9;
    noncompetitive provision of, 190–1;
    see also uncertainty and club goods
club size, optimal, 199–203
clubs: definition of, 24–5;
    discriminatory, 184–5; exclusive,
    160, 162; fixed-utilization, 164–9,
    171–2; heterogeneous, 161, 164,
    172–3, 179–84, 206; homogeneous,
    161, 164–9, 176–9, 188–90, 206;
    inclusive, 160, 162;
    intergenerational, 163, 227–43;
    mixed, *see* clubs, heterogeneous;
    multiproduct, 274–5; optimal
    number of, 170–3, 197–206; public
    utility, 255; replicable, 183–4, 188–
    90; spatial, 275; variable-utilization,
    164, 172–3, 176–9
Coase theorem, 59–60
coefficient of resource utilization, 82

common property resources, 128–31
complements, 117–22
congestion: as a public bad, 44–5, 115,
    124–8; in clubs, 159–61, 165–9,
    177, 181, 186–7, 256
conjectures: consistent, 146, 153–5,
    270–1; nonzero, 146, 151–5; zero,
    151
convexity, 49; *see also* nonconvexity
core: club goods and, 170, 172, 197–
    203, 208–9; in private goods
    economy, 132, 134; in public goods
    economy, 133–6
crowding, *see* congestion in clubs

damage function, 80
dominant strategy, 13, 107, 133, 138–
    40, 143–4

easy riding, 22, 23, 73–5, 78, 145; index
    of, 80–2; informational, 102, 240;
    microlevel, 80; systemic, 80, 121–3
environmental standards, 48, 61
equilibrium: anarchical, 32; competitive,
    31, 48–52; consistent conjectures,
    154–5; independent adjustment, *see*
    equilibrium, Nash; Lindahl, 22–23,
    100–2, 152–3, 268; Nash, 18–22,
    69, 76–80, 142–4, 147–8, 151;
    Nash–Cournot, *see* equilibrium,
    Nash; noncooperative, *see*
    equilibrium, Nash; non-Nash, 23–4;
    stability of, 65, 76–8, 92–4;
    subscription, *see* equilibrium, Nash;

301